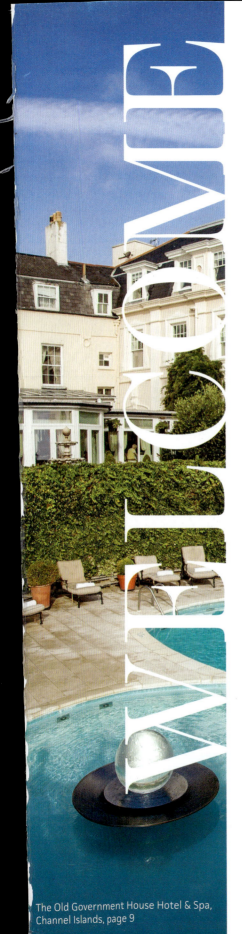

The Old Government House Hotel & Spa, Channel Islands, page 9

GW01246708

Welcome to our 2017 edition
UK, Europe & The Mediterra

The trustworthy reference fo

Whilst reading the pages of this Guide you might be interested to learn that each of the properties featured has been approved by a member of our team of Local Experts. Our Local Experts tirelessly search the globe to uncover smart, new hotels and exciting destinations for you year-on-year. You can therefore feel confident you'll have an amazing experience whichever hotel you choose.

For romance and relaxation: book one of our glamorous country house retreats, rural luxury resorts or urban escapes and dine on exceptional food, experience superb service and enjoy spa pampering. Expect special treatment such as early check-in and/or late check-out; just ask!

For sports and adventure: journey along the Seine or Danube on a luxury river cruise, tour our scenic coastal and mountainside properties, and test your skills on challenging golf courses and world-class ski slopes.

For the family: look out for our "Family friendly" feature and enjoy more informal dining options, babysitting services and kids' clubs. If the little ones are happy, everyone's happy!

For keeping on-trend: stay at an eco-friendly hotel or exclusively hire a property. Going green has never been so luxurious and hosting a party has never been so easy.

Our extensive global portfolio of properties appears on condenastjohansens.com where you can also find experience-led Special Offers, plan your itinerary and send booking enquiries directly to each property.

While visiting our site please tell us about your stay by completing one of our online feedback forms or email us at info@johansens.com. If you think a property is deserving, cast your vote for our Annual Awards for Excellence at condenastjohansens.com/awards.

Share the Condé Nast Johansens love of independent travel by giving our Gift Vouchers as a present. For more information please go to condenastjohansens.com/gift-shop or call +44 (0)800 035 1449.

Best wishes and happy travels in 2017!

Charlotte

Charlotte Evans, Group Publishing Director

The Chedi Andermatt, Switzerland,
page 140

Group Publishing Director:
Charlotte Evans

Assistant to Group Publishing Director and Account Executive: Laura Cazes

Account Director - UK & Ireland: Tim Fay

Senior Account Executive: Laura Kennedy

Junior Account Executive: Molly McLachlan

Local Experts:
Sharla Ault, Joe Cawley, Michèle Cooren-Lahaye,
Gianna Illari, Núria Llàcer Pascual, Tunde Longmore, Barbara Marcotulli,
Murat Özgüç, Olga Papadaki, Seamus Shortt, Danielle Taljaardt

Client Services Director: Fiona Patrick

Managing Editor: Laura Kerry

Copywriters:
Sasha Creed, Sarah Heron, Rachel Ingram, Jian Wei Lim,
Claire McQue, Debra O'Sullivan, Sophie Perryer, Stefanie Young

Production Director: Sarah Jenson

Marketing Manager: Adam Crabtree

Digital Marketing Manager: Julie Reid

Social Media & Digital Marketing Executive: Kelly Palmer

Designer: Lorna Morris

**Can't find Condé Nast Johansens in the shops? To order a copy, call +44 (0)800 035 1449
or go to condenastjohansens.com/gift-shop**

Copyright © 2016 Condé Nast Johansens
Condé Nast Johansens is part of The Condé Nast Publications Ltd.
ISBN 978-1-903665-80-0
Printed in England by Wyndeham Group.
Internationally distributed by Roundhouse Group.

The Condé Nast Publications Ltd.

**International Communications Director, Condé Nast International
Director of Press & PR, Condé Nast Britain:** Nicky Eaton

Marketing Director: Jean Faulkner

Financial Control Director: Penny Scott-Bayfield

Finance Director: Pam Raynor

Deputy Managing Director: Albert Read

**President, Condé Nast International
Managing Director, Condé Nast Britain:**
Nicholas Coleridge

Chairman and Chief Executive, Condé Nast International:
Jonathan Newhouse

Condé Nast Johansens, 13 Hanover Square, London W1S 1HN
Enquiries: tel: +44 (0)20 7499 9080; fax +44 (0)20 7152 3565
E-mail: info@johansens.com Web: condenastjohansens.com

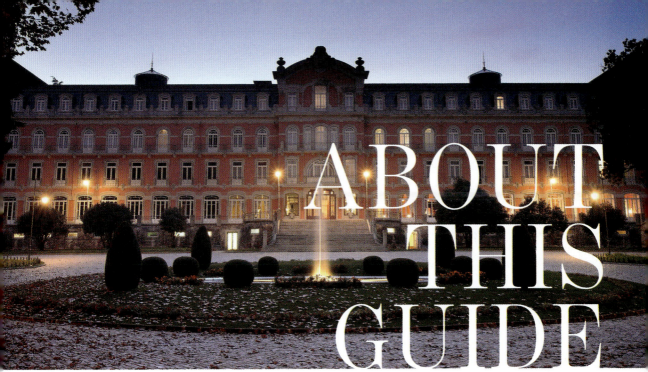

ABOUT THIS GUIDE

Choosing a property:
- Choose the country you wish to visit from the list opposite.
- Turn to the relevant page number and search alphabetically by region.
- Alternatively, turn to the map on pages 266-267 and locate a country marked by its corresponding page number.
- The index starting on page 263 provides a full list of all the properties featured within this Guide, ordered by country and then by property name.
- Once you have chosen a property, visit **condenastjohansens.com** where you may send a direct booking enquiry or call the property using the telephone number on each page. Sending a booking enquiry via **condenastjohansens.com** will guarantee great value during your stay.

When making a booking, please remember to mention you're a Condé Nast Johansens reader!

The "Price From" featured on each property's page indicates the lowest room rate available based on double occupancy per room, including tax and breakfast unless stated otherwise. You should always confirm the price and any terms and conditions directly with the property at the time of booking.

The information in this Guide is for reference only.

Top image: Vidago Palace, Portugal, page 121

2016 WINNERS OF AWARDS FOR EXCELLENCE

Image: Gran Hotel Son Net, Spain, page 130

Created to acknowledge, reward and celebrate excellence across our collection of properties, our world-renowned Awards for Excellence are a trusted mark of quality recognised by consumers and travel professionals alike.

The Condé Nast Johansens 2016 Awards were presented at The May Fair Hotel, London, on 2nd November 2015. Awards were given to properties throughout the UK, Europe and The Mediterranean that represent the finest quality and service in luxury independent travel.

An important source of information for our Awards is the feedback provided by our readers. Please continue to help us identify who really is the best in the business by nominating the property you think deserves to win one of our Awards by voting online at **condenastjohansens.com/awards**.

THE WINNERS: UK & IRELAND

BEST NEWCOMER OR BACK ON THE SCENE
Cliveden House, Berkshire, England, page 154

BEST FOR ROMANCE
Inverlochy Castle, Highlands, Scotland, page 242

BEST SERVICE
Linthwaite House, Cumbria, England, page 166

BEST VILLA OR SERVICED APARTMENT
The Milestone Hotel & Apartments, London, England, page 220

BEST FOR FAMILIES
Cheval Three Quays at the Tower of London, England, page 196

BEST VALUE
The Oakley Court, Berkshire, England, page 155

BEST HOTEL WITH SPA
Dormy House, Worcestershire, England, page 238

BEST COUNTRYSIDE HOTEL
Old Swan & Minster Mill, Oxfordshire, England, page 223

BEST URBAN HOTEL
The Marylebone, London, England, page 211

BEST FOR GREEN PRACTISES
Llangoed Hall, Powys, Wales, page 252

READERS' AWARD
Watersmeet Hotel & Restaurant, Devon, England, page 176

WINNERS: EUROPE & THE MEDITERRANEAN

BEST NEWCOMER OR BACK ON THE SCENE
Pousada Lisboa, Praça do Comércio, Lisbon & Tagus Valley, Portugal, page 113

BEST FOR ROMANCE
Gran Hotel Son Net, Mallorca, Spain, page 130

BEST SERVICE
Bahía del Duque, Tenerife, Spain, page 133

BEST VILLA OR SERVICED APARTMENT
Villa Mahal, Kalkan, Turkey, page 149

BEST FOR FAMILIES
Cornelia Diamond Golf Resort & Spa, Antalya, Turkey, page 143

BEST VALUE
Hotel Relais Villa del Golfo & Spa, Sardinia, Italy, page 57

BEST HOTEL WITH SPA
Parco dei Principi Grand Hotel & Spa, Rome & Lazio, Italy, page 49

BEST WATERSIDE HOTEL
Gran Hotel Atlantis Bahía Real, Fuerteventura, Spain, page 131

BEST COUNTRYSIDE HOTEL
Château la Chenevière, Normandy, France, page 25

BEST URBAN HOTEL
Firenze Number Nine Wellness Hotel, Florence & Tuscany, Italy, page 71

BEST FOR GREEN PRACTISES
Parkhotel Holzner, Trentino - Tyrol & Dolomites, Italy, page 67

BEST FOR MEETINGS
Palácio Estoril, Hotel, Golf & Spa, Lisbon & Tagus Valley, Portugal, page 109

READERS' AWARD
Hotel Brunelleschi, Florence & Tuscany, Italy, page 73

N.B. Winners appearing in this Guide only.

Austria

Please go to condenastjohansens.com/austria

Salzburg's beautiful Mirabell Gardens overseen by Hohensalzburg Castle

Hotel Goldgasse

A celebration of Salzburg's history and artistry

PRICE FROM:
€225

FEATURES:
Family friendly; Pet friendly; Restaurant

ACTIVITIES:
Cycling; Shopping; Sightseeing

NEARBY:
Salzburg Cathedral; Getreidegasse; Fortress Hohensalzburg;
Mozart's birthplace; Residenzplatz

GETTING THERE:
Salzburg Railway Station; Salzburg Airport

☎ +43 662 84 56 22
🌐 condenastjohansens.com/hotelgoldgasse
🏠 Goldgasse 10, 5020 Salzburg, Salzburg Province, Austria

The city that gave us Mozart and the setting for The Sound of Music is a buzzing metropolis all-year-round. From the old town's cobbled streets lined with galleries, luxury boutiques, book shops and baroque architecture to various music and art festivals and Christmas markets, Salzburg has wide-ranging appeal. Located within the historic heart of this UNESCO fairy-tale scene, Hotel Goldgasse resides at number 10 Goldgasse (Gold Alley) in one of the protected centuries-old buildings. A former coppersmith's workshop, inside is a refreshingly modern matter with pure white walls, wooden floors and splashes of bright colour that complement the huge photographs depicting the annual Salzburg Festival and city's culture. Each of the 16 uniquely fashioned bedrooms has a gigantic marble shower, king-size bed and fridge containing a welcome treat but only the two-bedroom, two-bathroom Rooftop Suite (perfect for families) has access to the roof terrace overlooking Fortress Hohensalzburg. In contrast to the clean lines and minimalism throughout the hotel, Goldgasse's regional and seasonal restaurant is traditional Austria through-and-through serving authentic dishes in miniature copper pots (a nod to the building's former life) alongside Austrian-only wines. Nice touch: The Sound of Music is pre-loaded on each guest room's infotainment system.

Channel Islands

Please go to condenastjohansens.com/channel-islands

A sheltered cove on the coast of Herm, Guernsey

The Old Government House Hotel & Spa

Guernsey's one and only five-star hotel for all the family and Fido

PRICE FROM:
£178

FEATURES:
Family friendly; Pet friendly; Pool; Restaurant; Spa

ACTIVITIES:
Sightseeing; Walking; Water sports

NEARBY:
St Peter Port High Street; St Peter Port Harbour; Candie Gardens; Guernsey Museum & Art Gallery; St James Concert and Assembly Hall

GETTING THERE:
Condor Ferries Guernsey Terminal, St Peter Port; Guernsey Airport

☎ +44 (0)1481 724921
🌐 condenastjohansens.com/theoghhotel
🏠 St Ann's Place, St Peter Port, Guernsey GY1 2NU, Channel Islands

Thoroughly British yet uniquely independent from the UK, Guernsey is an offshore escape in demand for beach lovers, intrepid walkers (check out all those cliffs and coves) and those who appreciate mild climes. As the sole five-star offering on the island, The Old Government House Hotel & Spa is as popular today as it was when it opened in 1858. And although the property retains charming Victorian character and timeless style, it delivers a wholly 21st-century experience for service, convenience and comfort. Meticulously manicured gardens with views across the English Channel and beyond surround The Old Government House, which is only five minutes from St Peter Port's harbour where various activities such as island hopping excursions can be enjoyed. Inside, the charm offensive continues. Rooms and suites are generous in size and ooze quintessential English elegance. There's a luxurious spa, gentleman's club-like bar complete with whisky tasting room and a host of dining options including a British brasserie, Mediterranean garden restaurant, curry house and an afternoon tea parlour – certainly worth saving room for. The Old Government House is also home to one of the largest and finest wine cellars on the island. The mantra here is "no request is too large, no detail no small" and this applies to every family member (children are well taken care of), even the furry ones!

The Atlantic Hotel

Spoiling service plus Jersey charm equals something special

Get yourself off the beaten track and into this beachy-chic spot tucked away in the warmest corner of the British Isles. The Atlantic Hotel and Michelin Starred Ocean Restaurant is a Channel Islands hideaway perfect for a nature lover's retreat of a weekend. Decorated in hues of blue, white and sand, The Atlantic Hotel at St Ouen's Bay echoes the dramatic natural setting that surrounds it, looking out to crystal-clear waters and a sprawling stretch of beach. Rocking a relaxed Hamptons-à-la-Jersey vibe, its façade is bedecked in white shuttered windows while inside, eye-catching modern art adorns its walls brought to life by the abundance of natural light. Kick off the heels/brogues and embrace the low-key elegance, for it's all about smart, unstuffy hospitality here. Enjoy the natural highs of surfing then relax, restore and unwind in a cosseting bedroom where the only sound is the lapping waves from the beach below and the views are breathtaking ocean vistas. It's easy to understand how The Ocean Restaurant has retained its Michelin Star since 2007 with highly qualified Restaurant Manager Martinho de Sousa and Executive Chef Mark Jordan at the helm. Only the best in fresh and local produce is served including island treats such as lobster and sole. The Atlantic is understated luxury at its best; a Med-esque spot with a British heart for guests of all ages.

PRICE FROM:
£150

FEATURES:
Family friendly; Gym; Michelin Starred restaurant; Pool; Sea views

ACTIVITIES:
Cycling; Golf; Water sports

NEARBY:
St Helier; La Mare Wine Estate; Jersey War Tunnels; Eric Young Orchid Foundation; Durrell Wildlife Conservation Trust

GETTING THERE:
Jersey Airport

+44 (0)1534 744101 ☎
condenastjohansens.com/atlantic 🌐
Le Mont de la Pulente, St Brelade, Jersey JE3 8HE, Channel 🏠
Islands

La Sablonnerie

Little Sark's little gem with a big personality

PRICE FROM:
£156 (including dinner)

FEATURES:
Restaurant

ACTIVITIES:
Fishing; Horse riding; Walking

NEARBY:
George's boat trip around the island; Bird-watching; Carriage rides; La Seigneurie Gardens; Scuba diving

GETTING THERE:
Ferry from Guernsey, Jersey, Poole, Weymouth and France; Guernsey Airport; Jersey Airport

☎ +44 (0)1481 832061
🌐 condenastjohansens.com/lasablonnerie
🏠 Little Sark, Sark, Guernsey GY10 1SD, Channel Islands

Just three miles long and a mile and a half wide, car-free, leisurely Sark is a whimsical place where horse-drawn carriages and tractor-drawn buses kick up dust from the road. It's the smallest of the four main Channel Islands and the only way to arrive here is by sea. Completely serene and naturally stunning, this is the setting for La Sablonnerie located in Little Sark, the southern, particularly remote part of the island. Hands-on owner and manager Elizabeth Perrée describes her pocket of peace as "an oasis of good living and courtesy," and with her rare passion and quirky charm, La Sablonnerie is a one-of-a-kind gem. You can't help but embrace the unhurried pace and all-encompassing cosiness that characterise this hotel whose low ceilings and 400-year-old oak beams add further personality. Elizabeth has extended and discreetly modernised the bedrooms, which over time have spread across from the original farmhouse into nearby houses and cottages. Before dining in the restaurant guests often gather in the lounge for a drink then tuck into dishes prepared from produce grown on La Sablonnerie's farm and gardens whenever possible. The locally caught lobster and oysters are a must. Proud to be: a 2014 finalist of Condé Nast Johansens Best Sustainable Hospitality & Corporate Responsibility Award and 2012 finalist for Most Romantic Hotel Award.

Croatia

Please go to condenastjohansens.com/croatia

A bird's-eye view of Kazbek's neighbourhood in UNESCO Dubrovnik, page 13

Kazbek

Discreet, private Dubrovnik villa located in the bay of Gruz

PRICE FROM:
€189

FEATURES:
Family friendly; Pool; Restaurant; Sea views

ACTIVITIES:
Shopping; Sightseeing; Water sports

NEARBY:
UNESCO Dubrovnik Old Town; ACI Yacht Marina; Elafiti Islands; Mljet National Park; Cavtat

GETTING THERE:
Dubrovnik Airport

Kazbek could be Dubrovnik's best-kept secret. This 16th-century villa set on the waterfront in the bay of Gruz has history and character in spades. A former summer residence to nobility, today it's a 12-room, one-suite boutique hotel that's been lavished with attention (and money) by its owners. They've created a laid-back-luxe hideaway in a superb location, just three kilometres from Dubrovnik's Old Town. Much of the original features remain so you can expect vaulted rooms, narrow passageways and soaring, beamed ceilings. All the furniture has been handmade locally and lashings of dark-wood panelling, overstuffed armchairs and embroidered drapes, rugs and throws adorn the private and public spaces. The sun-drenched Courtyard Terrace is a lovely spot for breakfast, while an old stone vault is the romantic setting for dinner where deftly prepared Croatian classics crowd the menu. The pool (be careful fair-skinned ones, this is a fantastic suntrap) is the perfect place to spend an afternoon but it's hard to top a trip to the nearby islands on Kazbek's speedboat moored in the marina directly opposite the hotel. However, whatever you plan to do, it's well worth talking to the concierge for some insider info on how to uncover the "real" Dubrovnik. Families and groups take note: Kazbek can be hired on an exclusive-use basis and can accommodate weddings for up to 30 guests.

☎ +385 20 362 900
🌐 condenastjohansens.com/kazbek
🏠 Lapadska Obala 25, 20000 Dubrovnik, Croatia

Villa Orsula

Smart, sharp and refreshing Dubrovnik seaside villa

A breath of fresh air to the Adriatic coast's hotel scene, Villa Orsula is everything a leading boutique retreat should be: intimate, exclusive and utterly comfortable with personal service. Its plum position beside the sea, five minutes from Dubrovnik's Old Town, also means that the city's sites are convenient to access. Villa Orsula's columned, curved Ottoman façade brilliantly contradicts the clean lines, muted colour schemes and contemporary design within. Funky elements such as surrealist artwork by Roberto Matta and Victor Vasarely's op-art dress the walls while an eclectic collection of objets d'art are purposefully dotted about. Many of the 13 bedrooms have picture windows of the seascape and small balconies, although for a special occasion book the spacious, ultra private Deluxe or Royal Suite. More dazzling views are seen from Victoria Lounge Bar whose cocktails can be served outside beside the gardens that lead down to the private beach below. Next door to Victoria Lounge Bar is the fine-dining Victoria Restaurant where health-conscious Peruvian cuisine with a Mediterranean twist is served alongside a global wine list. This is a destination in itself facing the Adriatic Sea from a pretty terrace draped in grapevines. Beauty bonus: Villa Orsula guests receive complimentary access to Hotel Excelsior's Spa & Wellness Centre located two minutes away.

PRICE FROM:
€540

FEATURES:
Beach access; Restaurant; Sea views

ACTIVITIES:
Shopping; Sightseeing; Water sports

NEARBY:
Dubrovnik's Old Town; Island of Lokrum

GETTING THERE:
Dubrovnik Airport

+385 20 300 300 ☎
condenastjohansens.com/villaorsula 🌐
Frana Supila 14, 20 000 Dubrovnik, Croatia 🏠

Hotel Heritage Martinis Marchi

Fantasy Mediterranean lifestyle becomes a reality at lush Solta Island

PRICE FROM:
€243

FEATURES:
Beach access; Pool; Restaurant; Sea views

ACTIVITIES:
Sightseeing; Walking; Water sports

NEARBY:
UNESCO Split; Solin; Kaštela; UNESCO Trogir; UNESCO Diocletian's Palace

GETTING THERE:
Split Airport

☎ +385 21 572 768
🌐 condenastjohansens.com/martinismarchi
🏠 Maslinica, Solta Island, Croatia

Unhurried, wholesome and traditional, the Dalmatian fishing town of Maslinica is home to the impossibly immaculate Hotel Heritage Martinis Marchi. Flanked by crystal blue waters and lush greenery (lemon trees galore!) Martinis Marchi is a collection of stone-walled buildings frosted with luminescent terracotta tiling. It all looks so new, as if it were built yesterday (despite its 17th-century beginnings) and inside, the rooms are equally fresh and brand-spankingly glossy. Martinis Marchi transports you back in time offering an insight into traditional Mediterranean life and staff regularly organises trips to age-old olive groves, classes in wine and olive oil production, and tours through surrounding ancient villages. There'll even be the chance to sample wild honey and try your hand at the traditional production of it too. But back at Martinis Marchi, the restaurant's exceptional seafood menu will have you waxing lyrical about its incredible freshness (try the lemon cake with wild lemon and orange from Šolta island) and sun terrace where you can enjoy the balmy evening temperatures. The fantastic marine-side location of Martinis Marchi means that boat rentals and watery excursions are a cinch to organise and events held at the marina throughout the year provide an interesting flurry of visitors to its shores. The marina also has a theatre, art gallery, numerous taverns, restaurants and cafés.

France

Please go to condenastjohansens.com/france

La Borde in full bloom, page 20

S.S. Catherine

River cruising with artistic, luxe flair along France's picturesque waterways

PRICE FROM:
£2,329 (eight-day cruise, per person, all inclusive, including transfers to/from airports)

FEATURES:
Gym; Pool; Restaurant; Spa

ACTIVITIES:
Cycling; Sightseeing; Walking

ROUTE HIGHLIGHTS:
World Heritage sites; Châteaux; Vineyards and wine tasting; Guided city tours

GETTING THERE:
Marseille Provence Airport; Lyon–Saint-Exupéry Airport

☎ +44(0)1481 753 883
🌐 condenastjohansens.com/sscatherine
⚑ France

Christened by Catherine Deneuve, the S.S. Catherine is every bit as elegant as the French icon. Opulent, plush and whimsical, the S.S. Catherine was launched in 2014 and its eight-day cruises take in all the major and lesser-known sites in and around the Burgundy and Provence regions. Inside, S.S. Catherine is a feat of modern design, inspired by the masters of Impressionism. And once on-board, it's very easy to forget this is a ship. With its glass lift, specially commissioned Murano glass chandelier in the lobby, indoor pool... it's all a wonderful trick. Guest quarters (80 Staterooms, five Suites, one Royal Suite) feature all the luxuries of a hotel such as sumptuous beds, marble bathrooms and individual climate control. Extra-spacious suites and Category 1 and 2 Staterooms have balconies. Cézanne Restaurant serves the gourmet cuisine, prepared from produce purchased on a daily basis from farmers' markets, while the colourful Van Gogh Lounge is a great spot for tea and coffee. Come the evening, it's difficult to resist the seductive powers of the Leopard Lounge bar complete with bronze leopard heads, lavish fabrics and decadent cocktails, all arranged around an emerald green swimming pool. For when the day's excursions, biking trips, walking tours and wine tasting outings have you seeking some time-out, Serenity™ River Spa and the jungle-themed pool come to the rescue.

Romantik Hôtel le Maréchal

Romance in Alsace-Lorraine's magical Colmar

Romantik Hôtel le Maréchal is an ancient, irresistibly charming hostellerie. Set in the middle of Little Venice in the French region of Colmar, it's particularly well located for weekend getaways to the winter markets. Its fascinating Franco-German history means that your stay here is an undeniably European affair where you're warmly welcomed. A beautiful 30-room town house, it's a tastefully decorated, spacious and comfortable haven, just where you want to relax after a day's sightseeing. Soak tired limbs in a bath of bubbles (while being entertained by the bathroom TV if you wish) before sauntering into A l'Echevin, Hôtel le Maréchal's restaurant. Dining on the terrace beside the canal is a particularly special setting for enjoying the tasty selection of fine local delicacies such as German snails and French calf. The menu ingeniously fuses both cultures and cuisines with skilful flair; even the wine list aligns Riesling with Côte de Provence. This is a family-friendly hotel whose knowledgeable staff can organise a whole range of excursions such as cycling, which is one of the best ways of getting around this picturesque little town.

PRICE FROM:
€115

FEATURES:
Family friendly; Lake views; Pet friendly; Restaurant

ACTIVITIES:
Cycling; Golf; Sightseeing

NEARBY:
Colmar Old Town; Ancient and traditional Alsace villages; Alsace wine route

GETTING THERE:
EuroAirport Basel Mulhouse Freiburg, Switzerland; Strasbourg Entzheim Airport

+33 3 89 41 60 32 ☎
condenastjohansens.com/marechal 🌐
4 Place Six Montagnes Noires, Petite Venise, 68000 Colmar, 🏠
Alsace~Lorraine, France

Ti al Lannec & Spa

Brittany coastal manor as pretty as its view

PRICE FROM:
€212

FEATURES:
Pool; Restaurant; Sea views; Spa

ACTIVITIES:
Golf; Sightseeing; Walking

NEARBY:
The centre of Trébeurden; Perros-Guirec; Lannion; Brittany coastline

GETTING THERE:
Brest Bretagne Airport; Lannion Airport; Dinard Airport

☎ +33 2 96 15 01 01
🌐 condenastjohansens.com/tiallannec
🏠 14 Allée de Mezo~Guen, 22560 Trébeurden, Brittany, France

Dramatic coastal setting; fabulous spa; top-notch food and wine. What's not to love about Ti al Lannec & Spa in Trébeurden on Brittany's Pink Granite Coast? On a cliff overlooking rosy, rocky coves, sandy beaches and glimmering clear water, this beautiful Edwardian country manor, run by the quite wonderful Jouanny family, really celebrates its spectacular setting. Views of the sea abound from the restaurant (stunning at sunrise, romantic at sunset), pool and leafy tiered terraces peppered with sun loungers. Stepping inside Ti al Lannec is like entering a wealthy friend's mansion lavished with English antiques, contemporary chandeliers, heavy drapes, gilt mirrors, paintings and overstuffed sofas with 33 rooms and suites varying in size, shape and décor. Some have writing tables and four posters, terraces, balconies with panoramas of the English Channel or views of the tranquil cypress groves and flower gardens. All have bags of character. (Very) Fine French cuisine is the order of the day at the à la carte restaurant, while the spa lures you in with its hammam-sauna-Jacuzzi combo after a day spent exploring the sleepy fishing villages, castles and medieval towns of the rugged Côtes-d'Armor.

La Borde

A lesson in Burgundy countryside sophistication

The most fabulous way to arrive at La Borde is by helicopter. It's also the best way to see the patchwork Burgundy countryside surrounding this exclusive 16th-century walled manor just outside the village of Leugny, Yonne. Cocooned in wide open acres of fragrant gardens, meadows and orchards, it's fairy-tale pretty with buildings festooned with fragrant climbing roses, towers, an orangery and a dovecote. Lazy days are spent around the sun-drenched pool or in the spa, while cosying up with a good book in the shaded porch adorned with period furniture and antique armchairs is hard to beat. La Borde's five rooms are pure château-chic. They're all about French country-style décor, exposed beams and waiting-to-be-stroked velvets with sink-into beds; some have fireplaces and free-standing baths. With so much space and the laid-back pace, La Borde is a place to lose yourself and nowhere more so than in the tranquil arboretum, home to 50 species of tree. To match the area's famous wines, the hotel's fresh French food is created from fruit, veg and herbs grown in the house's very own organic gardens. Châteaux, vineyards and nature parks are all waiting to be explored nearby but you might find yourself so relaxed that even an unhurried spot of sightseeing feels like too much effort.

PRICE FROM:
€325

FEATURES:
Gym; Helipad; Pool; Restaurant; Spa

ACTIVITIES:
Cycling; Golf; Tennis

NEARBY:
Vézelay; Chablis vineyards; Auxerre Abbey and Cathedral; Guédelon

GETTING THERE:
Joigny and Auxerre Railway Stations; Auxerre-Branches Airport (private charters only); Paris Airports

+33 3 86 47 69 01 ☎
condenastjohansens.com/laborde 🌐
89130 Leugny, Burgundy, France 🏠

Château d'Etoges

Beautifully renovated Champagne~Ardenne château

PRICE FROM:
€120

FEATURES:
Helipad; Pet friendly; Restaurant; Spa; Wheelchair access

ACTIVITIES:
Cycling; Sightseeing; Walking

NEARBY:
Epernay; Reims; Troyes; Champagne houses

GETTING THERE:
Paris-Charles de Gaulle (Roissy) Airport; Paris-Orly Airport

Château splendour. Gourmet French cuisine. Fine Champagne. Indulgent spa. Four fabulous reasons to spend a weekend or even a week at Château d'Etoges. This stunning 17th-century château is straight out of a fairy tale set in a rural idyll of rolling lawns and vineyards. Epernay and Rheims are minutes away where you can take cellar tours of wineries that read like a who's who of the world's finest fizz. Think Taittinger, Moët & Chandon, Dom Pérignon and Veuve Clicquot but it's not just about the bubbles here. Each tour of the area takes in some of the region's finest produce from fois gras to flamiche (local leek pie). And after this gastronomic extravaganza, recover chez Château d'Etoges and channel your inner Marie-Antoinette in a sumptuous room complete with grand canopy and views of the grounds. Alternatively, keep it simple, elegant and chic and stay in an Orangerie Room located just a moment's walk down to the restaurant. Gluttons take note: Château d'Etoges' chefs create the finest in French cuisine. Their menu is a gourmet's dream, packed with French classics and a cheese trolley to die for.

☎ +33 3 26 59 30 08
🌐 condenastjohansens.com/etoges
🏠 51270 Etoges~en~Champagne, Champagne~Ardenne, France

Château Eza

Centuries-old Côte d'Azur hilltop château infused with contemporary style

Old school chic, super-yachts, St Tropez. The French Riviera has effortless glamour by the Hermès bag-full. Add in peaceful seclusion on a luxurious scale and a heavenly sea breeze and you have the intimate, five-star Château Eza, a short hop from Nice and Monte Carlo. With only 12 rooms this is the ultimate boutique hotel de luxe, perched high on a rocky cliff overlooking the sleepy, terracotta tiled medieval village of Èze 400 metres below. The ancient stone Château Eza is all about the views. Everywhere you look there's a 180 of the Côte d'Azur and the startling blue of the Med, from the balcony of your opulent, chic room to the restaurant's terrace where you can feast on gourmet food with the stunning coastline as your backdrop. By day, enjoy lunch on the outside terrace so you can top up your tan while sampling the delights of Château Eza's fabulous French meets Mediterranean food. By night, watch the lights of the super-yachts twinkling from the secluded bay below. Special touch: a tailor-made, chauffeur-driven tour of the region with the expert help of the Château's concierge service.

PRICE FROM:
€180

FEATURES:
Restaurant; Sea views

ACTIVITIES:
Fishing; Golf; Walking

NEARBY:
Monaco; Nice; Saint-Jean Cap Ferrat; Villa Ephrussi de Rothschild; Cannes

GETTING THERE:
Nice Airport

+33 4 93 41 12 24 ☎
condenastjohansens.com/eza 🌐
Rue de la Pise, 06360 Èze Village, Côte d'Azur, France 📧

La Villa Mauresque

Intimacy and romance on the dreamy Côte d'Azur

PRICE FROM:
€225 (excluding city tax, breakfast €23)

FEATURES:
Beach access; Gym; Pool; Restaurant

ACTIVITIES:
Golf; Walking; Water sports

NEARBY:
Fréjus; Saint-Tropez; Cannes; Valescure Golf Course; Fréjus Roman theatre

GETTING THERE:
Nice Airport; Toulon-Hyères Airport; Marseille Airport

Staying at La Villa Mauresque in St Raphaël on the French Riviera leaves you with just one concern: which fabulous nearby town to visit first? St Maxime, St Tropez or Cannes? This is certainly a superb spot to ruminate the decision in style. Luxuriously boutique, this 19th-century villa soaks up plenty of sunshine in its swoon-worthy seaside location that eagle-eyed TV fans will recognise as the twice-used location for The Bachelor (UK) reality show. Romance comes guaranteed! Rooms are affectionately named in memory of great writers, poets and artists (Shakespeare, Baudelaire, Monet) and many cluster around the pool and terrace. Airy and chic interiors update the villa with a subtle Moorish feel and provide extras such as in-room coffee machines and a welcoming platter of fresh fruit. Outside, there's a hot tub overlooking the Med, plus great hiking trails and the sea itself to explore whose crystal blue waters are superior snorkelling territory. La Villa Mauresque offers its guests free use of boats and kayaks. By night, the Villa's Michelin-Starred Chef Jean-Michel Le Béon takes centre stage in Le Bougainvillier restaurant. Blissfully beach-side, it captures the heady taste of the Riviera perfectly.

☎ +33 494 83 02 42
🌐 condenastjohansens.com/mauresque
🏠 1792 route de la Corniche, 83700 Saint~Raphaël, Côte d'Azur, France

Château de l'Abbaye de Moreilles

Effortless relaxation in La Rochelle

A cheeky little number this, the Château de l'Abbaye de Moreilles. Travellers swing by as they head south to Bordeaux or the Dordogne and depart wistfully. What first appears as a modest country château with a spirited host in Madame Renard reveals itself as a bewitching rustic bolthole with a laid-back attitude. Madame and her family draw you into their home where you'll eat off-menu so it's rather like having a wonderful personal chef who conjures up regional or delicate Thai-infused flavours on a nightly basis. And the rooms and suites are beautifully designed with space and style to suit couples and families alike. A slightly off-beat room choice is the purely fantastical Richelieu Suite (a former outbuilding of the Cistercian abbey) with an immense circular bed, star-studded bathroom ceiling and private outdoor sitting area, while others beckon with Jacuzzis made for two. The children are welcome here, free to run wild in the gardens' lush green acres. But if you're travelling à deux "adult love games" discreetly placed in wardrobes are yours to discover. Take a swim in the heated outdoor pool, spend some time checking out nearby Marais Poitevin with canal trips and antique shopping or nip across the water to Île de Ré for some delicious moules and huîtres. There's something for everyone.

PRICE FROM:
€99

FEATURES:
Family friendly; Pet friendly; Pool; Restaurant; Spa

ACTIVITIES:
Cycling; Golf; Sightseeing

NEARBY:
Île de Ré; La Rochelle; Les Sables d'Olonne; Marais Poitevin Natural Park; Atlantic coast beaches

GETTING THERE:
La Rochelle Airport; Nantes Airport; Bordeaux Airport

+33 251 56 17 56 ☎
condenastjohansens.com/chateaulabbaye 🌐
85450 Moreilles, Loire Valley, France 🏠

Château la Chenevière

Pretty-as-a-picture Normandy château

PRICE FROM:
€220

FEATURES:
Helipad; Pet friendly; Pool; Restaurant; Wheelchair access

ACTIVITIES:
Cycling; Golf; Sightseeing

NEARBY:
Normandy coast; Omaha beach and the D-Day landing beaches; Port en Bessin; Golf Club; The Bayeux Tapestry

GETTING THERE:
Caen Airport; Paris-Charles de Gaulle (Roissy) Airport; Paris-Orly Airport

An 18th-century stunner, Château la Chenevière in Normandy ticks all the boxes. Grand yet welcoming, comfy yet elegant furnishings, contemporary yet full of bygone character. It's the epitome of Gallic country house charm. Following check-in (the easiest on record) you'll no doubt want to explore. Smiley staff will very sweetly equip you with a chart detailing the acres of landscaped grounds. Or there's the tennis court and heated pool beside the startlingly modern Orangery (a grand homage to the Louvre's glass pyramids when lit up) to keep you busy on-site. History hounds are in their element here with Château la Chenevière's history reading like a novel. Occupied by German soldiers and 70-80 of their horses in 1940 and then by the English Royal Army Service Corps, the walls of this impressive château contain many secrets. And the surrounding areas of Caen and Bayeux are awash with things to see and do; the Normandy American cemetery at Omaha beach being just one of them. For active types, nearby sand yachting, horse riding and golf can be arranged. But be sure to enjoy the good food accompanied by great wine in the chic surroundings at the Château's dazzling restaurant.

☎ +33 2 31 51 25 25
🌐 condenastjohansens.com/lacheneviere
🏠 Escures - Commes, 14520 Port~en~Bessin, Normandy, France

Hôtel & Spa La Belle Juliette

The epitome of Left Bank style, grace and creativity

Chic and discreet are Paris buzzwords and the boutique Hôtel & Spa La Belle Juliette provides both with aplomb. Located on the south side of the Seine, an area known for its lovers of fashion and free thinkers, this petit gem harks back to the days of sultry salons and louche lounging. The hotel's namesake, a banker's wife, was a renowned entertainer and her theatrical spirit lives on with someone often playing the hotel's baby grand piano or strumming the resident harp. A rich riot of colour, the interior of Le Clos Belle Juliette restaurant and bar mixes jewelled fuchsia and red tones with a gentleman's club grey, creating a romantic and cosseting space for taking cocktails, breakfasts and afternoon teas (think delicate porcelain and mouth-watering pastries). Boudoirs and suites are dressed in sugared almond pinks or chocolate box shades and feature elegantly simple furniture alongside opulent fabrics, whilst bathrooms are cool and crisp. Hôtel La Belle Juliette's secret weapon is its oh-so modern spa concealed in the basement, which is just the tonic to revive tired muscles after exploring the Rive Gauche café and boutique scene, and wandering the streets of the Left Bank and Saint-Germain-des-Prés with its bustling bookshops.

PRICE FROM:
€350

FEATURES:
Pool; Restaurant; Spa; Wheelchair access

ACTIVITIES:
Shopping; Sightseeing; Walking

NEARBY:
Jardin du Luxembourg; St Sulpice; Le Bon Marché department store; Saint Germain Church

GETTING THERE:
Sèvres Babylone/Vaneau Metro Stations; Montparnasse Railway Station; Paris-Orly Airport

+33 1 42 22 97 40 ☎
condenastjohansens.com/labellejuliette 🌐
92 Rue du Cherche Midi, 75006 Paris, France 🏠

Grand Pigalle Hotel

Low-key louche living in Pigalle, Paris

PRICE FROM:
€180

FEATURES:
Restaurant; Wheelchair access

ACTIVITIES:
Shopping; Sightseeing; Walking

NEARBY:
Montmartre; The Basilica of the Sacred Heart of Paris; Moulin Rouge; La Cigale

GETTING THERE:
Gare du Nord Railway Station; Paris-Charles de Gaulle (Roissy) Airport

---

☎ +33 185731200
🌐 condenastjohansens.com/grandpigalle
🏠 29 rue Victor-Massé, 75009 Paris, France

Part of the Bohemian-bourgeois revamp to Paris' 9th arrondissement, Grand Pigalle Hotel embodies the casual hedonism of this up and coming district. From the three childhood friends who brought the speakeasy-styled Experimental Cocktail Club bars to London, Paris, Ibiza and New York, this is their design-led, 37-room hotel in Pigalle. There's a den-like quality and playfulness to Dorothée Meilichzon's interior design where martini motifs line the stairs, angular mirrors complement geometric wallpapers, golden pineapple knockers hang on the doors and octagonal handles (reflecting the map of the district) open them. It all has a retro vibe - art deco meets Victoriana - and you'll even be given a traditional key to unlock your room. For a special stay, book one of the Parisian Roof rooms located on the top floor. Through their oeil-de-boeuf windows you can see the whole of Montmartre and room service allows you to enjoy the view during a spot of petit-déjeuner of freshly baked goods from the artisan boulangerie next door. Come the evening, guests and locals gather in the popular rez-de-chaussée bar for cocktails (you'll find a cocktail mini-bar in your room too) and to choose from the 200-strong, all-Italian wine menu - a reminder of the owners' connection to the sophisticated bar scene - before dining on Chef Giovanni Passerini's contemporary Mediterranean-inspired food.

Domaine des Etangs

Château splendour with a fashionable sensibility in rural Charente

A sigh-inducing sight of circular turrets pointing to the heavens and golden stone walls reflecting the sunlight, Domaine des Etangs is a remote lakeside château straight from the pages of a fairy tale. If that fairy tale happened to include subplots involving thermal Roman baths, a tennis court, outdoor pool and a fine-dining restaurant! Recently, this 11th-century château has been transformed into a luxury country escape for the public to enjoy. 2,500 acres, including forests and seven ponds, set the scene for this wholly romantic retreat of 11 rooms and suites and seven, one to five-bedroom luxury farm cottages. Local craftsmen and stonemasons brought the historic buildings back to life to maintain numerous period features (fireplaces, exposed timber, stone floors) that sit alongside contemporary finishes such as funky light fixtures, block colours, trendy vintage curios and an eclectic art collection. The kitchen garden supplies the Domaine's classic, seasonal French restaurant, which in warmer months opens out onto the grounds. You can explore these endless acres by electric car, bike, horse or from a rowing boat on the ponds.

PRICE FROM:
€500

FEATURES:
Michelin Starred restaurant; Pet friendly; Pool; Restaurant; Spa

ACTIVITIES:
Cycling; Fishing; Tennis

NEARBY:
Contemporary Art Museum, Rochechouart; National Museum of Limoges Porcelain; Golf International de la Prèze; Château and Museum of La Rochefoucauld; Lacs de Haute Charente Adventure Park

GETTING THERE:
Angoulême Railway Station; Limoges–Bellegarde Airport; Bordeaux–Mérignac Airport

+33 5 45 61 85 00 ☎
condenastjohansens.com/etangs 🌐
16310 Massignac, Poitou-Charentes, France 🏠

La Grande Maison de Bernard Magrez

A celebration of gastronomy and fine wine from two masters in Bordeaux

PRICE FROM:
€250

FEATURES:
Family friendly; Restaurant; Wheelchair access

ACTIVITIES:
Cycling; Golf; Walking

NEARBY:
Bernard Magrez Cultural Institute; Grands Crus Classés tours; Châteaux tours; Wine workshops and tastings; The Arcachon bassin

GETTING THERE:
Bordeaux Saint-Jean Railway Station; Bordeaux-Mérignac Airport

Where else but in the heart of wine capital Bordeaux for food and wine virtuosos Pierre Gagnaire and Bernard Magrez to combine their knowledge and passion? Devoted to exceptional food, extraordinary wine and artistic creativity, this palatial mansion of arched windows and wrought-iron balconies is a testament to both men's genius. The 18th-century La Grande Maison - former home of French scholar Léon Duguit - has just six guest rooms dressed in bold prints, silk wallpapers, plush carpets and four-poster beds with contrasting marble bathrooms of pure white and cream. But the main reason guests come here is to experience Mr Pierre Gagnaire's world-famous French cuisine who in 2015 was named Best Chef in the World by his peers. And to succumb to Mr Magrez's wine list of 259 Crus Classés from Bordeaux including 172 Grands Crus Classés in a wine list of 1,200 references. Served in three locations, the Napoléon III, L'Olivier and the Bibliothèque dining rooms, Pierre Gagnaire's cuisine is thoroughly modern and inspired by local products in honour of the beautiful region. Breakfasts of fresh fruit, smoked salmon, eggs to order and pastries and breads - courtesy of the on-site pastry chef and baker - may be taken on the terrace in warmer months.

☎ +33 5 35 38 16 16
🌐 condenastjohansens.com/lgmbordeaux
🏛 10 rue Labottière, 33000 Bordeaux, South West, France

Germany

Please go to condenastjohansens.com/germany

Old town Frankfurt's architectural delights

Grandhotel Hessischer Hof

City central hotel with a classic touch in the heart of Frankfurt

PRICE FROM:
€299 (excluding breakfast)

FEATURES:
Family friendly; Gym; Spa

ACTIVITIES:
Shopping; Sightseeing; Walking

NEARBY:
Messe Frankfurt; Kap Europa congress centre; Skyline Plaza shopping mall; Römerberg; Bankenviertel

GETTING THERE:
Frankfurt Central Railway Station; Frankfurt Airport

☎ +49 69 75400
🌐 condenastjohansens.com/hessischerhof
🏠 Friedrich-Ebert-Anlage 40, 60325 Frankfurt am Main, Germany

Traditional style and grace, world-class hospitality and exceptional quality are just some of the reasons why business types, families and leisure guests return time and again to Frankfurt's one and only privately run hotel, Grandhotel Hessischer Hof. Owned by the family foundation of the Landgraves and Princes of Hessen, a sense of timeless elegance is injected into every aspect of the proceedings here, in the centre of Frankfurt's action. Between the city's exhibition grounds and banking district, this five-star player is all at once a conference centre, fine-dining restaurant and medical spa retreat. And it also happens to be perfectly placed for the stores of Skyline Plaza, museums, botanical gardens and green parks of the surrounding green belt. There are 10 conference, banquet and function rooms at Grandhotel Hessischer Hof, which are so adaptable and atmospheric (panelled walls, antiques, original artwork) any formal or informal, business or social celebration can be hosted. Business lunches and special occasion dinners are best taken in Restaurant Sèvres where a private collection of priceless porcelain lines the walls and some of Frankfurt's finest French cuisine is served. Come the end of the evening, live piano music in the relaxed, smoker-friendly Jimmy's Bar sets the perfect scene to unwind after all the day's excitement.

Greece

Please go to condenastjohansens.com/greece

The blue domed churches and dusk time magic from Oia, Santorini

Image courtesy of Haris vythoulkas / Shutterstock.com

Miraggio Thermal Spa Resort

A new breed of resort hotel and thermal spa for all the family on Halkidiki's coast

PRICE FROM:
€101 (per person)

FEATURES:
Beach access; Family friendly; Restaurant; Sea views; Spa

ACTIVITIES:
Cycling; Tennis; Water sports

NEARBY:
Kassandra; Sithonia; Thessaloniki; Vergina and Pella archaeological sites; UNESCO Mount Athos

GETTING THERE:
Thessaloniki Airport

☎ +30 23744 40000
🌐 condenastjohansens.com/miraggio
🏠 Kanistro, Paliouri, Halkidiki 63085, Greece

Taking full advantage of Halkidiki's south-west coastal splendour from the Kassandra peninsula, Miraggio Thermal Spa Resort faces awesome Aegean vistas from a luminescent green pine forest. According to Greek mythology, the natural hot springs that criss-cross this land are the result of a buried Titan trying to escape from beneath Kassandra's surface. There's certainly something otherworldly about this spectacular corner of northern Greece (Aristotle's city of birth, Stagira, is a drive away). And the newly opened Miraggio provides a very 21st-century perspective of a dream world. This consists of the two-storey Myrthia Thermal Spa incorporating the natural thermal pools, five restaurants - buffet, Italian, seafood and local dishes - four bars, three pools, a children's pool, an 81-berth marina, 300 guest rooms and suites, and incredible childcare facilities for four-month-year-olds to 17-year-olds. Kids' Planet is a particularly impressive childrens' club with varied scheduled activities. When you've managed to tear yourself away from your sleek, designer guest room, junior suite or private pool suite that look out to the finest sea views, there are various watery adventures on the glassy ocean to take part in. These include chartering a yacht from Miraggio's marina and scuba diving, while land lovers can opt for some mountain biking, beach volleyball or a spot of tennis.

De.light Boutique Hotel

Sun, sea and mythology on the west coast of Mykonos

When the views are this overwhelming and the hospitality this intuitive, it's difficult to prise yourself away from the deeply comforting spot. But as spellbinding as De.light Boutique Hotel is, its location just 10 minutes from Mykonos Town, set above the quiet Agios Loannis Bay (aka the Shirley Valentine beach) facing the sacred island of Delos (birthplace of Artemis Goddess of Hunt and Apollo God of Light), means there's plenty of reasons to vacate the cooling pool or your private Jacuzzi. Romancing, relaxing and reconnecting comes easy at De.light where enduring pampering and mouth-watering gastronomy are always on the agenda. Breakfast is a generous Mediterranean spread. Lunch is a Greek/international affair. And dinner is served by candlelight under the stars beside the pool and gourmet Authentic restaurant. For all the hours in between, a 24-hour concierge team takes care of anything you wish, whether that's booking day excursions, renting yachts or arranging massages at the hotel's spa room. But all this becomes immaterial when you're kicking back in your suite, taking in the crystalline blue vista from your terrace, patio or balcony. Most suites have their own Jacuzzi, which is just one of their luxurious and designer features that somehow manage to be all-at-once traditionally Greek and cutting-edge.

PRICE FROM:
€240

FEATURES:
Pool; Restaurant; Sea views; Spa

ACTIVITIES:
Shopping; Sightseeing; Water sports

NEARBY:
Agios Ioannis traditional fisherman's port; Mykonos Town; Delos archaeological site

GETTING THERE:
Mykonos Cruise Port; Mykonos Airport

+30 22890 78038 ☎
condenastjohansens.com/delightmykonos 🌐
Agios Ioannis, 84600 Mykonos, Greece 🏠

Tharroe of Mykonos

Traditional Mykonos marries contemporary flair

PRICE FROM:
€180

FEATURES:
Pet friendly; Pool; Restaurant; Sea views

ACTIVITIES:
Horse riding; Shopping; Sightseeing

NEARBY:
Mykonos Town; Ornos Bay; Fabrika Square; Ornos beaches; Little Venice

GETTING THERE:
Mykonos Airport

Pitch up at boutique hotel Tharroe of Mykonos to escape or get the party started. Oozing laid-back, arty sophistication, the Tharroe is the perfect base to explore Mykonos that's reinvented itself as a Greek chic boho hangout for those in-the-know. Celeb-watch at Paradise or Psarou beaches or simply enjoy spectacular poolside views back at the hotel. Tharroe of Mykonos sits atop a small hill gazing over the Aegean and captures traditional Mykonian romance with a contemporary edge. Rooms and suites are light and airy, mixing fresh, colourful fabrics with classic furniture. Some raise the modern stakes even higher with mid-century design touches and Jacuzzi baths; most feature patios or balconies and views directly from the bed. The hotel is also a testament to good old fashioned Greek hospitality. Whether they're serving delicious Mediterranean dishes in the Barbarossa restaurant, booking you a spin in a convertible, organising a yoga session or mixing a mean cocktail on the pool terrace, the Tharroe team cannot help enough. Check out the wine tastings, tête-à-tête dinners and book an alfresco massage. A trip to Mykonos Town is worth it for the shopping, famous windmills and nightlife, then return to Tharroe in time for breakfast and those glorious sunrise vistas. Calling all dog lovers: Tharroe of Mykonos is the only hotel on the island that can accommodate large dogs.

☎ +30 22890 27370
🌐 condenastjohansens.com/tharroe
🏠 Mykonos Town, Angelica, 84600 Mykonos, Greece

Astra Suites

Vertiginous, sultry Santorini suites

The divinity of Astra Suites, Imerovigli, is no Greek myth. For starters it's located on Santorini, arguably the prettiest Greek island of them all. Then there's the bells and whistles: relaxing spa treatments, a steam room, Jacuzzi, heated infinity pool, poolside bar, 24-hour concierge service, free WiFi, crazy-comfy beds, above-and-beyond service and the most romantic atmosphere. All this and there's a heartbeat-skipping view of the caldera and Aegean at every turn. Whether staying in a cosy studio or luxury suite, the flawlessly blue Santorini skyline and sea is your stunning view. Everything here impassions love. George the manager and his staff welcome you to this heavenly retreat where Champagne flows, rose petals are sprinkled, chocolates offer temptation and a Jacuzzi bubbles in anticipation. And if all that wasn't enough, culinary delights from Astra's chef deliver Greek and Mediterranean flavour in the bucket-load alongside the finest wines Greece has to offer. It doesn't matter where you choose to dine - in the restaurant or on your own balcony - you're guaranteed the best seat in the house at sunset.

PRICE FROM:
€210

FEATURES:
Pool; Restaurant; Sea views; Spa

ACTIVITIES:
Horse riding; Sightseeing; Water sports

NEARBY:
Fira; Oia; Caldera; Beaches; Akrotiri excavation site

GETTING THERE:
Santorini Port; Santorini Airport

+30 22860 23641 ☎
condenastjohansens.com/astrasuites 🌐
Imerovigli, 84700 Santorini, Greece 🏠

The Lesante Luxury Hotel & Spa

A haven for die-hard romantics and nature lovers in the seaside resort of Tsilivi

PRICE FROM:
€120

FEATURES:
Family friendly; Pool; Restaurant; Sea views; Spa

ACTIVITIES:
Cycling; Fishing; Water sports

NEARBY:
Zakynthos Town; Tsilivi beach; Bohali village; The famous Shipwreck beach; Sea Blue Caves

GETTING THERE:
Zakynthos Airport

The Lesante Luxury Hotel & Spa hits the mark for a stylish beach escape. Situated on the Greek island of Zakynthos' north-east coast – all white-sand bays, rocky coves and clear, calm water – it's a lesson in contemporary cool with trendy décor, fashionable furniture and pops of mint green and fuchsia. The minimalist rooms are predominantly white with huge beds, marble bathrooms and high-tech gadgetry at every turn. The Grand Suites live up to their name with huge terraces complete with hot tubs, daybeds and Ionian Sea vistas. Landscaped gardens sweep through the resort, at the centre of which are curvaceous, palm-studded lagoon-like pools where you'll find both adults and children having the best of times. Whatever you do, don't miss a zingy fruit cocktail at the Nectar pool bar and a visit to The Lesante's spa. It's the biggest on the island so allow plenty of time to delight in the pool, Jacuzzi, hammam, sauna, mood shower and treatments. Top and tail your days at the Ambrosia restaurant where indulgent American breakfasts and Mediterranean dinners are the order of the day. And at lunchtime, it's all about the poolside Neptune restaurant, which is also great for seafood under the stars. Packing tip: think pared-back luxe by day, glam at night. There's a jewellery shop on-site if you need a touch more bling.

☎ +30 2 69 50 41 330
🌐 condenastjohansens.com/lesante
🏠 Tsilivi, 29100 Zakynthos, Greece

Hungary

Please go to condenastjohansens.com/hungary

The Széchenyi Chain Bridge linking Buda and Pest across the River Danube

S.S. Maria Theresa

Regal and glamourous river cruises along the River Danube

PRICE FROM:
£2,329 (eight-day cruise, per person, all inclusive, including airport transfers)

FEATURES:
Gym; Restaurant; Spa

ACTIVITIES:
Cycling; Sightseeing; Walking

NEARBY:
World Heritage Sites; Vineyards and wine tasting; Castles; Markets

GETTING THERE:
Budapest Ferenc Liszt International Airport; Munich Airport, Germany

Not so much a cruise ship as a floating palace, S.S. Maria Theresa ambles majestically along the River Danube during its eight-day trips. Named after the 18th-century Austrian empress (ruler for 40 years and mother of Marie Antoinette), the ship reflects Maria Theresa's penchant for opulence. Decorative coronets hand-painted with 22-carat gold leaf, silk-clad walls, custom furniture and vast portraits produce an element of baroque drama. This lavish design is also evident in The Royal Suite, Suites and Staterooms with handcrafted beds, luxurious marble bathrooms and French or open-air balconies that allow you to drink in the fresh air from sunrise to sunset. And the spoiling indulgence continues with the wide range of culinary choices on-board. On the Bavarian deck, the charming Viennese Café serves traditional Austrian sweet treats, while gourmet excess abounds in the grand baroque restaurant whose local delicacies such as Bavarian cheeses and Sachertorte are must-tries. To help keep your waistline in check, shore excursions include various walking tours and bike rides of towns and villages on your journeys through Germany, Austria and Hungary. Bonus amenities on-board: the Serenity River Spa™, intimate cinema and tranquil pool.

☎ +44(0)1481 753 883
🌐 condenastjohansens.com/ssmariatheresa
🏠 Hungary

Ireland

Please go to condenastjohansens.com/ireland

Whiling away the hours on Lough Corrib at Ashford Castle, page 43

Castlemartyr Resort

Utterly arresting resort with the "wow" factor near East Cork

PRICE FROM:
€165

FEATURES:
Family friendly; Gym; Pool; Restaurant; Spa

ACTIVITIES:
Fishing; Golf; Horse riding

NEARBY:
Kinsale; The Titanic Trail, Cobh; Old Jameson Distillery; Fota Wildlife Park

GETTING THERE:
N25; M8; Cork International Airport

☎ +353 21 4219000
🌐 condenastjohansens.com/castlemartyr
🏠 Castlemartyr, County Cork, Ireland

Hundreds of acres of emerald green land, a gently meandering river, rich woodland and 800-year-old castle ruins complete the cinematic scene of Castlemartyr Resort near East Cork. Suffice to say, there's nothing average about this country manor house-cum-premier resort steeped in history dating back to the 17th century. Famous owners of Castlemartyr include Sir Walter Raleigh and Richard Boyle, the first Earl of Cork, and today, it's every bit the aristocratic playground drenched in luxury and elegance complemented by an outstanding level of service. Lavished with opulence and impeccable style, guest rooms and suites are spacious, filled with antiques, elegant fabrics and modern touches (electronic touch panels operate the lights and drapes). A contemporary theme also runs through Castlemartyr Resort's style of cooking served in three venues: the fine-dining Bell Tower; lounge-style Knights Bar; and the golf club's casual Club House. Franchini's is the newest addition offering an Italian option with pizza, pasta and risotto. A spa like no other, Castlemartyr Resort's spacious and naturally-lit idyll presents a holistic approach to complete well-being with ESPA treatments and therapies. Outside, there are countless activities such as the 18-hole golf course par 72, cycling routes, archery, laser clay pigeon shooting, horse riding and carriage rides.

The Westbury

Understated elegance at the epicentre of cosmopolitan Dublin

The iconic Westbury in Dublin is loved by the locals as much as its far-flung visitors. This is in no small part due to its superb position on the bustling Grafton Street, equidistant between Trinity College and St Stephen's Green (in the city's premier retail and cultural quarter). Plus, its perfect blend of five-star, traditional hospitality and modern convenience, buzzing atmosphere and natural bonhomie. This all combines to make The Westbury perfect for all manner of events and business meetings. And if the guest rooms were designed to soothe and calm, they've certainly succeeded, with neutral tones, crisp Lissadell linens and the softest Blanc d'Ivoire throws. Among The Westbury's eateries there is but one theme: quality achieved from fresh, expertly sourced Irish produce. This is certainly the case in Balfes Bar & Brasserie, which offers an informal dining experience. Dishes prepared in its open kitchen feature Parisian and New York influences and can be served on the heated outdoor terrace. Afternoon tea on The Gallery is the place to see and be seen with a view onto Grafton Street below before adjourning for cocktail hour at The Sidecar, aptly named after the classic and stylish 1920s' cocktail. If you have one too many cocktails, there's your in-room Nespresso machine for a caffeine boost!

PRICE FROM:
€200

FEATURES:
Family friendly; Restaurant; Wheelchair access

ACTIVITIES:
Shopping; Sightseeing; Walking

NEARBY:
Trinity College; The Abbey Theatre; Grafton Street luxury shopping; The National Gallery of Ireland

GETTING THERE:
Connolly Railway Station; Heuston Railway Station; Dublin Airport

+353 1 679 1122 ☎
condenastjohansens.com/westburydublin 🌐
Grafton Street, Dublin 2, County Dublin, Ireland 🏠

Ashford Castle

Spectacular timepiece of County Mayo history and majesty

PRICE FROM:
€305

FEATURES:
Family friendly; Helipad; Lake views; Restaurant; Spa

ACTIVITIES:
Fishing; Golf; Horse riding

NEARBY:
Galway city; Connemara National Park; Westport; Céide Fields

GETTING THERE:
N84; Galway Railway Station; Ireland West Airport Knock

Beside the peaceful Lough Corrib, the impressive Ashford Castle near Cong is the image of fairy-tale fantasies. Spanning hundreds of acres of leafy estate, this is one of Ireland's greatest castle hotels brimming with history, character and a guest list crammed with famous names (King George V, Oscar Wilde, Omar Sharif, Brad Pitt). On the border of County Galway and Mayo, the first recorded brick on this site was laid in 1228, and from the mid-1800s until 1921 it was the prolific Guinness family's country retreat. Since becoming a hotel in 1939, Ashford developed into the pre-eminent countryside playground it is today. Days are filled with falconry, golf, horse riding, clay-pigeon shooting, cruises on Lough Corrib and fishing with an Orvis-endorsed guide. Plus, pampering at the new Victorian conservatory-style spa with ozone-filtrated pool, five treatment rooms and gym. Ashford Castle is also a mecca for food lovers. Chef Philippe Farineau's exceptional cuisine showcases seasonal, organic produce in a variety of ways: the formal dining five-course table d'hôte evening menu in the George V Dining Room (adorned with 11 Waterford crystal chandeliers); the Irish themed, casual bistro-style à la carte menu at Cullen's at the Dungeon; and the international menu influenced by owner Mrs Tollman at (the seasonally open) Cullen's at the Cottage. Proud to be: part of the Red Carnation Hotels Collection.

☎ +353 94 95 46003
🌐 condenastjohansens.com/ashfordcastle
🏠 Cong, County Mayo, Ireland

Italy

Please go to condenastjohansens.com/italy

The poolside scene at Monaci delle Terre Nere, page 66

Mezzatorre Resort & Spa

Keeping guard of life's indulgent pleasures on Ischia's coast

PRICE FROM:
€300

FEATURES:
Family friendly; Pool; Restaurant; Sea views; Spa

ACTIVITIES:
Sightseeing; Tennis; Water sports

NEARBY:
Capri; Naples; Negombo Thermal Gardens; Giardini La Mortella botanical gardens; Ischia villages

GETTING THERE:
Molo Beverello Port; Naples Airport

☎ +39 081 986111
🌐 condenastjohansens.com/mezzatorre
🏠 Via Mezzatorre 23, 80075 Ischia (NA), Campania, Italy

Centuries ago the tower of Mezzatorre was built as a look-out on the dramatic, rocky coastline of Ischia. Fast-forward to the 21st century and it's now home to one of Italy's most strikingly beautiful boutique hotels popular with royalty and celebs alike. Standing in seven acres of pine forest, Mezzatorre Resort & Spa's tower has been meticulously restored and perches on the edge of a promontory overlooking the Bay of Naples, Mount Epomeo and Vesuvius. Outside, you can still see the battlements of this ancient fort. Inside, it's a grand, sophisticated affair. Whitewashed walls are the backdrop for opulent décor from the chic bar and sea-viewing suites to the Chandelier restaurant named after the elegant silver candelabra that creates the romantic dining room's only light. Food here is refined Mediterranean on a gastronomic scale. And down below is the spa; a modern, immaculate space that draws upon the natural thermal waters of the island in its wide-ranging treatments and therapeutic programmes. Grouped around Mezzatorre's tower, several buildings designed to blend seamlessly into the pinewood forest host more rooms, suites and Sciue-Sciue restaurant with palm-frond roof. This is where informal and delicious Campania foodie delights are served overlooking the breathtaking views of the Mediterranean as well as the pool on the pretty terrace below.

Hotel Waldorf - Premier Resort

Where fun-seekers and style mavens converge on Italy's Adriatic Coast

Since the early 1900s Milan's jet set has retreated to beachy Milano Marittima for its fresh sea air and pine forest beauty. Today, this scenic piece of the Adriatic Coast remains a favourite with Italy's discerning fashionistas. Its proximity to Bologna, Florence, Ravenna and Venice makes it one well-connected seaside charmer too. Hotel Waldorf is one of three Premier Resort hotels in the vicinity and strikes a modern confection of curved glass and chrome. This is the swanky hotel of choice providing design-led rooms, suites and penthouses overlooking the beach with glamour oozing from every inch of the interior. The luxury suites are especially glitzy and live up to their names of Silver, Gold, Platinum and Diamond; the Diamond Suite has a rooftop pool and jaw-dropping view of the coastline. As one of the three Premier Resort hotels, Hotel Waldorf guests may dine at and enjoy the facilities of its sister hotels (Hotel Premier & Suites and Le Palme Hotel). These include a conference centre, children's club, wellness centre, beach club and evening entertainment. However, there are plenty of reasons to remain at the Waldorf such as Aurora Restaurant's impressive buffet breakfasts, La Settima Restaurant's gourmet Italian fare and Stars Bridge Restaurant's grilled dishes and market-fresh fish come the evening. There's also the relaxing pool area (with elegant swim-up lounge bar).

PRICE FROM:
€190 (city tax excluded)

FEATURES:
Beach access; Pool; Restaurant; Sea views

ACTIVITIES:
Golf; Tennis; Water sports

NEARBY:
Milano Marittima town centre; Bologna; Rimini; San Marino Republic; Ravenna

GETTING THERE:
A14/E45; Rimini Airport; Bologna Airport

+39 0544 991632 ☎
condenastjohansens.com/waldorfravenna 🌐
Via VII Traversa Mare 17, 48015 Milano Marittima, Cervia, 🏠
Ravenna, Italy

Casa Montani - Luxury Town House

Chic town house B&B in the heart of Rome

PRICE FROM:
€180

ACTIVITIES:
Shopping; Sightseeing; Walking

NEARBY:
Spanish Steps; Vatican City; Trevi Fountain; Navona Square; Pantheon

GETTING THERE:
Port of Civitavecchia; Rome Fiumicino Airport; Rome Ciampino Airport

☎ +39 06 3260 0421
🌐 condenastjohansens.com/casamontani
🏠 Piazzale Flaminio 9, 00196 Rome, Lazio, Italy

Just like the ancient entrance to the city (Porta del Popolo) that Casa Montani overlooks, this urban oasis is a gateway to Rome. Within seconds you're at Piazza del Popolo, Villa Borghese and Via Babuino. In just five minutes you're fighting for a photo opportunity at the Spanish Steps. A further five and you'll be faced with the mighty Pantheon and wondrous Vatican City. This is what's so fantastic about Casa Montani: so many of Rome's treasures are on your doorstep. You'll feel like a local socialite going about your business from your exclusive city cubbyhole complete with staff who'll bring continental breakfast to your room each morning. Owner Giuseppe Montani has put everything into his family business (the Montanis have owned the third floor of this towering flamingo-pink building since 1916) to create an upscale town house vacation spot. The man himself is often on hand, plus co-owner Charlotte Bontemps, to offer local, inside info on where to eat, shop and visit. They know this city inside/out and their unquestionable taste and penchant for superior quality is evident by the swanky custom-made furnishings and finest Italian/French fabrics in each room and suite. The city may be outside your window but there's nothing but peace and quiet inside. Sound-proofed windows guarantee an undisturbed night's sleep.

Hotel dei Borgognoni

Sophisticated sleek hideaway a few steps from Rome's popular sites

You know you're in Rome when the hotel welcomes small dogs amongst their guests (mention your pooch upon booking and they'll be provided with their very own bed). Hotel dei Borgognoni provides an exceptional location for your "Roman Holiday" just a three-minute saunter from the Spanish Steps and Trevi Fountain, close to Villa Borghese and the Pantheon. It's perfectly placed to observe that wonderful Italian tradition: the passeggiata (when residents take a gentle evening stroll through the centro storico). However, your wallet won't thank you for the proximity to Rome's famous shopping streets! Despite being at the centre of it all, Hotel dei Borgognoni benefits from the coveted commodity of a garage, and is surprisingly secluded. The enclosed terrace garden of this 19th-century mansion house is a pin-drop quiet spot to soak up the sun after a hectic day. Choose a room with a private terrace to enjoy this utter serenity and spoil yourself even further with a massage in your room or within an equally private area in the hotel. Bedrooms are pleasantly bright and inviting with splashes of red velvet and dark wood that characterise the sleek décor of Hotel dei Borgognoni. Before heading out for the evening, speak to the friendly staff who will assist with restaurant recommendations and directions to the city's hottest nightlife.

PRICE FROM:
€225

FEATURES:
Pet friendly

ACTIVITIES:
Shopping; Sightseeing; Walking

NEARBY:
Trevi Fountain; Spanish Steps; Navona Square; Campo dè Fiori

GETTING THERE:
Rome Ciampino Airport; Rome Fiumicino Airport

+39 06 6994 1505 ☎
condenastjohansens.com/borgognoni ⊕
Via del Bufalo 126 (Piazza di Spagna), 00187 Rome, Lazio, 🏠
Italy

Parco dei Principi Grand Hotel & Spa

A bejewelled, brazen and bold hedonistic slice of Rome

PRICE FROM:
€275

FEATURES:
Family friendly; Gym; Pool; Restaurant; Spa

ACTIVITIES:
Golf; Shopping; Sightseeing

NEARBY:
Galleria Borghese Canova Museum; Via Veneto; Spanish Steps; Vatican City; Trevi Fountain

GETTING THERE:
Termini Railway Station; Rome Fiumicino Airport; Rome Ciampino Airport

☎ +39 06 85442500
🌐 condenastjohansens.com/parcodeiprincipi
🏠 Via G Frescobaldi 5, 00198 Rome, Lazio, Italy

Cool off in the Eternal City of historic romance at Rome's Parco dei Principi Grand Hotel & Spa. This oasis of calm next to the Villa Borghese gardens is a white-glove service stunner with an outdoor summer pool. Designed by architect Giò Ponti, Parco dei Principi was built in 1964 and has recently been subject to a facelift. Taking inspiration from 17th-century style mavens, rooms are sumptuous and swagged with rich wood panelling, classic furnishings and a liberal sprinkling of artwork and antiques. Minimalist it is not. At the behest of each and every guest, cocktails can be shaken to specific tastes; chaise longues or a chi-chi gazebo can be acquired for extra privacy. The staff await your command! This anything-is-possible attitude is also present at Prince Spa where wellness and soul rejuvenation is the ultimate goal. Serious thought has gone into the materials that create its elegant spaces, which include a boxing ring and natural stone, untreated wooden Finnish sauna with jewelled mosaics. It's rock-star OTT opulence at every turn. How about kicking back in the bubbling Jacuzzi with Swarovski-starred ceiling above, followed by an ice-cream cocktail and dinner at the well-renowned restaurant, Pauline Borghese? It's a done deal. And best of all, you can be in the centre of Rome in a heartbeat - just hop on the complimentary bus to downtown Veneto Street.

Villa Spalletti Trivelli

The quintessential Roman urban villa

Live like nobility at Villa Spalletti Trivelli, an early 20th-century Neoclassical palazzo, former home to the aristocratic Spalletti-Trivelli family. Occupying a prime position in the heart of Rome, steps from Piazza del Quirinale, minutes from the Coliseum and Trevi Fountain, the Villa is perfectly located for exploring the city. Inside, opulent interiors are fashioned with art, antiques and tapestries. Marble fireplaces, tall ceilings and wooden floors appear throughout the grand reception rooms while the cosy wood-panelled library is a little slice of Roman history; listed by the Italian Heritage Ministry. A wellness centre with gym, Turkish bath and hammam completes the relaxed-luxe vibe. And a stunning new Rooftop Garden features comfortable shaded sofas and sun loungers. The rooftop bar and Jacuzzis offer additional tranquil areas and benefit from breathtaking views of the Eternal City. First-floor bedrooms overlook the Villa's private gardens (THE dining spot du jour in the summer) or those of the Quirinale. But for longer stays and family getaways, the two Garden Suites and two apartments located next door are perfect. Days at Villa Spalletti Trivelli begin with breakfast of just-made breads and pastries, buffalo mozzarella and prosciutto, while lunches and dinners feature a selection of home-made dishes accompanied by wines and olive oil from the owners' Umbrian vineyard.

PRICE FROM:
€470

FEATURES:
Family friendly; Gym; Restaurant; Spa

ACTIVITIES:
Shopping; Sightseeing; Walking

NEARBY:
Trevi Fountain; Spanish Steps; The Coliseum; Roman Forum; Navona Square

GETTING THERE:
Termini Railway Station; Rome Fiumicino Airport; Rome Ciampino Airport

+39 06 48907934 ☎
condenastjohansens.com/villaspallettitrivelli 🌐
Via Piacenza 4, 00184 Rome, Lazio, Italy 🏠

Hotel Vis à Vis

Family-run Italian Riviera bolthole for gastronomes

PRICE FROM:
€210

FEATURES:
Pet friendly; Pool; Restaurant; Sea views; Spa

ACTIVITIES:
Golf; Horse riding; Walking

NEARBY:
Chiavari; Cinque Terre; Bay of Silence; Fairytale Bay; Portofino

GETTING THERE:
Genoa Cristoforo Colombo Airport; Pisa Airport; Milan Malpensa Airport

☎ +39 0185 42661
🌐 condenastjohansens.com/visavis
🏠 Via della Chiusa 28, 16039 Sestri Levante (GE), Liguria, Italy

Top-notch food and wine, stunning scenery, ludicrously beautiful beaches. What's not to love about the Italian Riviera? And while Portofino and Cinque Terre are the top tourist hotspots, Sestri Levante, nestled between the two, is the place to go if you crave peace with your Prosecco. Perched on the top of a hill, looking down to the pretty former fishing village below (reached by a lift carved into the rocks) and Bay of Silence, Hotel Vis à Vis is pure Riviera magic. Jaw-dropping vistas abound from every terrace, while all of the 46 rooms come with a balcony or private garden; Junior Suites are divine with panoramas of the Gulf of Tigullio. Dining at Vis à Vis is pretty special too. The Olimpo restaurant is one of the area's finest, dishing up first-rate, ultra-fresh Italian dishes against the rugged Ligurian coastline (floor-to-ceiling windows ensure you don't miss a thing). And the fourth-floor Ponte Giunone is where the style-set "do" lunch. However, in the heart of all the coastal action below in the Bay of Silence is the hotel's beach-front restaurant, Portobello, serving sublime seafood dishes. When you're not cruising the Riviera, lazy days can be spent by the olive-tree fringed pool or in the super-luxe beauty centre before sundowners on the top-floor Ponte Zeus sky bar with, you've guessed it, more of those fabulous views. Magnifico!

Agriturismo L'Unicorno

Food, wine, romance and phenomenal panoramas in lush Lombardy

As rich in history as the land surrounding it, Agriturismo L'Unicorno in western Lombardy embodies refined rural living with irrepressible Italian charm. Since 1654 this Roman-style villa has been the centre of a working farm whose acres of vineyards and land still produce red and rosé wines, grappa, preserves and extra virgin olive oil. Now owned by husband and wife team, Corrado and Gabriella, their passion for good food and fine wine is the foundation of this sumptuous 10-bedroomed bolthole close to Lake Garda, Verona, Venice and Milan. It's an idyllic vision of vineyards and cypress trees on the outside and a romantic portrait of vaulted, frescoed ceilings, antique furniture and stone carvings inside. Each bedroom tells a story of a historic local event such as the Mille Miglia room (inspired by the famous open-road endurance races from 1927 to 1957) and hopelessly romantic Guiliette e Romeo (balcony included). Agriturismo L'Unicorno's restaurant makes the most of its home-grown produce and wines to deliver daily-changing dishes characteristic of the region while Caffè Novecento serves espressos guaranteed to knock your socks off (this is seriously strong stuff). But if you've come to sample the local vino, the 16th-century wine cellar stocks vintages of Lombardy's groppello grape, best savoured with a selection of local cheeses and meats.

PRICE FROM:
€195

FEATURES:
Helipad; Pet friendly; Pool; Restaurant; Wheelchair access

ACTIVITIES:
Golf; Sightseeing; Water sports

NEARBY:
Lake Garda; The Verona Arena; Lake Como; Milan; Venice

GETTING THERE:
Milan Orio al Serio International Airport; Verona-Villafranca "Valerio Catullo" Airport; Milan Linate "Enrico Forlanini" Airport

+39 030 674339 ☎
condenastjohansens.com/unicorno 🌐
Via Quarena 17, Località Macesina, 25081 Bedizzole, Brescia, 🏠
Lombardy, Italy

QC Terme Bagni di Bormio

Invigorating, mountain-fresh Lombardy grande dame

PRICE FROM:
€120 (per person)

FEATURES:
Gym; Pet friendly; Pool; Restaurant; Spa

ACTIVITIES:
Cycling; Golf; Skiing

NEARBY:
Livigno; Stelvio Pass; St Moritz, Switzerland; Bagni Vecchi's hot spring thermal baths; Stelvio National Park

GETTING THERE:
Milan Orio Airport; Milan Linate Airport; Milan Malpensa Airport

---

☎ +39 0342 910131
🌐 condenastjohansens.com/bagnidibormio
🏠 Località Bagni Nuovi, 23038 Valdidentro (Sondrio), Lombardy, Italy

At "the boot's" thigh-high point where Italy meets Switzerland and Austria, there's Bormio. A tourist hotspot for several reasons: its natural thermal springs; high mountain passes including the legendary Stelvio Pass; and year-round skiing. Visitors have been coming en masse since 1st-century BC seeking the therapeutic benefits of its waters. Waters that QC Terme Bagni di Bormio has tapped into to offer an outstanding indoor/outdoor Alpine spa at its Grand Hotel Bagni Nuovi. Standing from on high in Stelvio National Park, this is a sought-after wellness holiday destination whose hotel looks down to the Valley of Bormio and beyond to an eye-popping mountain vista. Bespoke spa treatments and massages take full advantage of the stunning surroundings to include time spent in the outdoors. One of which is forest bathing, a Japanese therapy that features a walk into Bagni di Bormio Park (located within Stelvio National Park) aiming to "clean" the mind, body and soul. The hotel itself - open since 1836 - is a celebration of Belle Époque design with the impressively theatrical Ristorante Salone dei Balli, an extensive garden and Light Café (where you can dine in your bathrobe), plus The Spa & Wellness Centre. Subdivided into four sections the Centre spans the sunny Giardini di Venere, the underground Grotta di Nettuno, revitalising Bagni di Giove and tranquil Bagni di Ercole.

Hotel Bellerive

Warm and inviting Italian hospitality at Lake Garda

Dashing in white beside the marina of Salò, Hotel Bellerive beams across the hypnotically calm blue waters of Lake Garda dotted with bobbing sail boats. Inside, sophistication and tradition welcome you to an unadulterated Mediterranean experience. Rooms, suites and oh-so exclusive apartments in the Villa are fresh as a daisy, relaxed and inspired by the seasonal colours of Lake Garda. Days begin with a kick-start courtesy of a Bellerive breakfast that's a frenzy of baked goods featuring fresh sweet and savoury pastries. Taken on the terrace basked in morning sunlight, the blistering lake views are your backdrop, then, just when you think life couldn't get much better, come the evening there's the allure of Restaurant 100KM. So-called because it sources ingredients from within a 100km radius, its ingredient-led concept produces an elegant menu alongside fresh bread and pasta, which are freshly prepared each day. Hotel Bellerive's prime waterfront location means that sailing on Lake Garda and courses on the nautical pastime can be arranged before you can say "ahoy". But golfers will want to take advantage of the special guest rates at the local course. Take note food fans: don't go home without sampling the traditional flavours of the Mediterranean with the "Taste of Gardalake Experience."

PRICE FROM:
€190

FEATURES:
Family friendly; Lake views; Pet friendly; Pool; Restaurant

ACTIVITIES:
Shopping; Tennis; Walking

NEARBY:
Verona; Mantova; Enogastronomic tours; Arena di Verona Opera; Golf

GETTING THERE:
Brescia Airport; Verona Airport; Bergamo Airport

+39 0365 520 410 ☎
condenastjohansens.com/bellerive 🌐
Via Pietro da Salò 11, 25087 Salò (BS), Lake Garda, Lombardy, 🏠
Italy

Hotel de la Ville & La Villa

Monza's most enchanting family-run luxury hotel with exclusive villa

---

PRICE FROM:
€134

FEATURES:
Gym; Restaurant; Wheelchair access

ACTIVITIES:
Cycling; Golf; Tennis

NEARBY:
Milan; Monza race circuit; Monza royal palace and park; Lake Como

GETTING THERE:
Bergamo Airport; Milan Linate Airport; Milan Malpensa Airport

Splendid is the adjective best used to describe Hotel de la Ville & La Villa in Monza, just 15km from Milan. This family-run luxury hotel and private villa has stood opposite Monza's Royal Palace (la Villa Reale) since 1800. Its spacious terrace faces the Neoclassical palace and its park, whilst the interior is a majesty of its own: polished wooden floorboards, oak panelling, Persian rugs, 18th-century Chinese porcelain and a myriad of exquisite antiques. The inviting bedrooms are adorned with plush fabrics, crisp linen-clad beds and marble bathrooms, and all have the technological comforts you could wish for. Unwinding with apéritifs and cocktails is encouraged in the intimate American Bar (a trip to the hotel's sauna beforehand will help set the relaxed mood) followed by dinner at Derby Grill, Hotel de la Ville's award-winning restaurant. Executive Chef Fabio Silva's mouth-watering menu has collected an impressive number of accolades. The close proximity of Hotel de la Ville to Monza's Formula 1 circuit is of course a big draw, and its short walk to Monza's historical city centre is a huge bonus. Milan is also tantalisingly close. Most impressive of all though, is the exceptional service at Hotel de la Ville. All manner of whims are taken care of thanks to the friendly and attentive staff. This is a hotel with character and lashings of charm.

☎ +39 039 39421
🌐 condenastjohansens.com/hoteldelaville
🏠 Viale Regina Margherita di Savoia 15, 20900 Monza (MB), Lombardy, Italy

Relais San Maurizio

Utter tranquillity in the Piemonte hills

This completely secluded sanctuary in the Piemonte hills is the ultimate wellness and medical spa housed within the meditative confines of a former 17th-century Cistercian monastery. Tapping into the natural bounty of the hilly, fertile Langhe Valley, Relais San Maurizio is the perfect antidote to a hectic lifestyle combining modern medical knowledge with the healing powers of nature. These include mineral-rich salt caves, thalassotherapy, wine therapy, pre-ageing and anti-ageing treatments all aiming to soothe the senses and harmonise the mind, body and soul. The Relais is nestled in Santo Stefano Belbo's vine-covered countryside and has 29 exclusive rooms and suites, each uniquely decorated and located in various buildings. Choose a room in the converted stable or a former monk's cell. Each oozes charm, history, all-encompassing quiet, elegant simplicity and look out to incredible views. Trekking, biking and golfing are the favoured activities in these hills but let's not forget that this is Langhe Valley, an area world-renowned for its food and wine. The Relais' Guido da Costigliole restaurant earned its Michelin Star by combining the abundance of local flavours with those from Provence. And now there's Truffle Bistrot open for lunch and dinner with a menu dictated by flavour and home-grown produce showcasing local specialities.

PRICE FROM:
€295

FEATURES:
Family friendly; Gym; Michelin Starred restaurant; Pet friendly; Spa

ACTIVITIES:
Cycling; Sightseeing; Walking

NEARBY:
Alba; Asti; Langhe wine cellars of Barolo and Barbaresco; White truffle fair; Truffle hunting and wine making experiences; Royal residence in Turin

GETTING THERE:
Turin Airport; Genoa Cristoforo Colombo Airport; Milan Malpensa Airport

+39 0141 841900 ☎
condenastjohansens.com/relaissanmaurizio 🌐
Località San Maurizio 39, 12058 Santo Stefano Belbo (CN), 🏠
Langhe Wine District, Piemonte, Italy

CONDÉ NAST
johansens
Luxury Hotels · Spas · Venues
AWARD WINNER 2016

Hotel Relais Villa del Golfo & Spa

Stylish Sardinian seaside charmer

PRICE FROM:
€290

FEATURES:
Gym; Pool; Restaurant; Sea views; Spa

ACTIVITIES:
Golf; Sightseeing; Water sports

NEARBY:
San Pantaleo; Baia Sardinia; Porto Cervo; Emerald Coast
beaches; Marine park

GETTING THERE:
Olbia Airport; Alghero Airport

☎ +39 0789 892091
🌐 condenastjohansens.com/hotelvilladelgolfo
🏠 Via Monti Corru, Loc La Conia, 07020 Cannigione,
Olbia-Tempio, Sardinia, Italy

Sofas on balconies, magnificent vistas and someone on hand to cater to your every whim. This is Hotel Relais Villa del Golfo & Spa on Sardinia's dazzling shore of Cannigione where kicking back has never been so luxurious, so spoiling and bewitching. But if sofa-surfing in the sun has you itching for some adventure, Hotel Relais Villa del Golfo's private yacht is readily available for exploring the Maddalena archipelago, Corsica and the Emerald Coast's impossibly beautiful beaches. But before you take to the water or head out on a tour by foot, horse or jeep and maybe enjoy a cooking and/or wine-tasting course, days begin with an incredible breakfast of home-made, freshly baked bread and cakes, just-picked fruit and veg, Italian cold meats and cheeses. Happy Hours follow on later at the bar in addition to fine gastro fare at Miraluna prepared from fresh ingredients sourced from the hotel estate. An alternative option is Le Colti located at the nearby farm, which serves traditional dishes of home-made pasta and bread, and meat and vegetables reared and grown on-site. No visit is complete without a swim in the sea via the hotel's beach deck and a trip to Harmony Spa, which guarantees to take stresses away. Once in your jelly-like state of relaxation, there's nothing for it but to flop into your luxury suite facing the stunning bay (most rooms have sea views and a private garden).

Hotel Abi d'Oru

Timeless Sardinian seaside favourite

Follow the super-yachts to Sardinia's Emerald Coast for beach-side glamour, the Italian way. Where the cognoscenti come to party and devoted sun worshippers spend their summers, the secluded Golfo di Marinella is a private slice of this coastal glory. Hotel Abi d'Oru was the first hotel to welcome visitors to this beauty spot in 1963 and an ageless Italian finesse pervades every corner. Facing its very own pristine stretch of private beach, every guest room, junior suite and suite has a view of the watery scene before it. A short stroll through the hotel's Mediterranean garden takes you to the beach but there's tennis, football, volleyball, aquagym lessons, daily Pilates classes, the nearby Pevero Golf Club and water sports galore as alternatives to basking in the Sardinian sun. There are also various dining options. Hotel Abi d'Oru has four restaurants offering a tasty mix of Sardinian specialities and international flavours from the elegant Fenicotteri to the beach-side Marinella, while cocktails accompanied by live music are shaken and stirred in the lobby. Worth noting: weddings can be hosted at Hotel Abi d'Oru on the beach, by the pool or in the photo-pretty garden.

PRICE FROM:
€200

FEATURES:
Beach access; Family friendly; Pool; Sea views; Wheelchair access

ACTIVITIES:
Golf; Tennis; Water sports

NEARBY:
Porto Rotondo; Olbia; Porto Cervo; San Pantaleo; Golfo Aranci

GETTING THERE:
Olbia Port; Olbia Costa Smeralda Airport

+39 789 309019 ☎
condenastjohansens.com/hotelabidoru 🌐
Località Golfo di Marinella, Porto Rotondo, 07026 Olbia, 🏠
Sardinia, Italy

Costa dei Fiori Hotel

Traditional south Sardinian hideaway for sun, sea and a soupçon of romance

PRICE FROM:
€140

FEATURES:
Family friendly; Pool; Sea views

ACTIVITIES:
Cycling; Golf; Tennis

NEARBY:
Cagliari; Pula; Nora archaeological area; Chia; Zuddas Caves

GETTING THERE:
SS195; Port of Cagliari; Cagliari Elmas Airport

☎ +39 070 924 5333
🌐 condenastjohansens.com/costadeifiori
🏠 SS195 km 33, 09010 Santa Margherita di Pula, Sardinia, Italy

Beaches to rival the finest in the Caribbean and parkland filled with age-old pine trees set the dream scene of south-west Sardinia, home to the serene Costa dei Fiori Hotel. This is a sanctuary for the soul and escape from the stresses of everyday life where you have the freedom to relax, romance and explore to your heart's content. Costa dei Fiori Hotel's traditional Sardinian charm attracts honeymooners, families and couples, plus location scouts and companies seeking the quintessential pretty Italian setting for a photo shoot or convention. In fact, Costa dei Fiori is a great base for exploring the most beautiful beaches Sardinia has to offer such as the award-winning Chia (via shuttle) and Tuerredda. So where better for an exclusive event for 20 to 30 guests and the picture-perfect wedding? Excursions by boat, trips to a 27-hole pitch and putt golf course as well as car, scooter and mountain bike hire can all be organised. However, tearing yourself away from the sea-facing, sea-water infinity pool will prove challenging. Thank goodess for the irresistible restaurant to lure your away. Its refined, locally-inspired dishes and wide-ranging wine and Champagne list emphasise Italy's reputation as a gastronomic power. Don't forget: to quote "Condé Nast Johansens" upon booking a superior room or suite to enjoy complimentary VIP service and an apéritif on arrival.

Lanthia Resort

Wild and wonderful Sardinia meets elegant design and hospitality

Sardinia's mountainous east coast province of Ogliastra is a scene-stealer of natural rich forest, fearsome granite rock and deepest blue sea. Off the tourist radar until recent years (still relatively unknown by many), the raw beauty of this undulating landscape is untouched and undamaged. And its coastal town of Santa Maria Navarrese remains an authentic Sardinian village where locals go about their day-to-day business unaffected by any lingering tourists. Protected by forests on one side and hugged by the Tyrrhenian Sea on the other (the beach is just 40 metres away), Lanthia Resort in Santa Maria Navarrese keeps matters elegantly simple with the purpose of allowing the surrounding natural wonderland to do all the talking. Materials from the island such as granite were used to build Lanthia Resort in the 1960s and following a recent revamp it's become a celebration of Sardinia and its artistic influence (ceramics, original artwork and hand-woven linens abound). Named after a Sardinian town, each of the 28 rooms and suites is indicative of the place they represent and tells a story with their fabrics, paintings and colours. Lanthia Resort restaurant's aim is to stimulate the senses with its creative spin on traditional local dishes prepared from Sardinian produce as the scents of juniper, fresh salty air and embracing forest fill the air.

PRICE FROM:
€182

FEATURES:
Beach access; Pool; Restaurant; Sea views

ACTIVITIES:
Horse riding; Walking; Water sports

NEARBY:
Cala Goloritzé; Cala Luna; Cala Mariolu; Arbatax; Gennargentu

GETTING THERE:
The port of Olbia; Cagliari Airport; Olbia Airport

+39 0782 615103 ☎
condenastjohansens.com/lanthiaresort 🌐
Via Lungomare, 08040 Santa Maria Navarrese, Ogliastra, 🏠
Sardinia, Italy

Hotel Signum

Secret Sicilian hideaway for the rich and famous

PRICE FROM:
€150

FEATURES:
Helipad; Michelin Starred restaurant; Pool; Sea views; Spa

ACTIVITIES:
Walking

NEARBY:
Vulcano; Lipari; Salina vineyards; Panarea; Stromboli and
Monte Fosse trekking

GETTING THERE:
Catania Fontanarossa Airport; Palermo Airport

Tucked away in the lush green landscapes of the island of Salina hides Hotel Signum; a charming boutique hotel at the edge of the sea. Hotel Signum was born when an ancient country hamlet was renovated to allow the public to experience the beauty and serenity that this naturally picturesque town offers. Inhabited since the Bronze Age, Salina is a breathtaking and beautiful volcanic island, dotted with vineyards and flowering capers. And from the hotel's chic antique-filled rooms you can look out over the crystal blue sea upon the silhouettes of Stromboli and Panarea while taking in the scent of jasmine and citrus in the passing breeze. That's if you're not breathing in the enticing aromas of the Michelin Starred restaurant's seasonal, elegantly simple cuisine courtesy of chef parton Martina Caruso and sampling wines collected from every part of Italy and Europe. In-keeping with the traditional essence of the hotel, the spa offers the finest natural therapy techniques and has steam baths (inspired by the very first thermal baths built over 3,500 years ago) alongside numerous other harmonising treatments. Hotel Signum is truly a haven of rest and relaxation for revitalising your mind, body and soul. Top recommendation for: a honeymoon. Top day out: a boat trip (boats are available for private hire) to the nearby islands of Stromboli, Panarea, Lipari, Vulcano, Filicudi and Alicudi.

☎ +39 090 9844222
🌐 condenastjohansens.com/signum
🏠 Via Scalo 15, 98050 Salina~Malfa, Aeolian Islands, Sicily, Italy

Masseria della Volpe

Sicily at its pastoral, enchanting best

Citrus groves, olive orchards and rows of carob trees set the dreamscape for Masseria della Volpe: a rural hideaway for the soul in the south east of Sicily. What makes this bucolic bolthole extra special is the combination of local character, premium resort facilities and ecological sustainability. For instance, the Masseria's electricity is powered by solar panels, the building materials were locally sourced and many kitchen ingredients, such as olive oil, are grown on-site. This was a 19th-century farm after all. Inside, the rooms and suites are pared back and inviting. Handmade Sicilian tiles and exposed local stone walls bring a warmth to the modernity, while avant-garde works of art bring colour and an element of fun. All rooms either have gardens, terraces or balconies overlooking the valley and across to the sea. But it's the three-bedroom Royal Family Suites with both rooftop and ground-floor terraces that have everyone wow-ing. The private three-bedroom apartment is a favourite with small groups. However, La Masseria della Volpe is incredibly romantic and discreet, enhanced by its peaceful isolation. Visiting couples love the intimate spa, heated outdoor pool area, sports facilities (tennis court, biking, diving, nearby golf) and the seasonal, authentic Mediterranean dishes, wines and champagnes at Ristorante Codarossa.

PRICE FROM:
€130

FEATURES:
Pool; Restaurant; Spa; Wheelchair access

ACTIVITIES:
Cycling; Tennis

NEARBY:
Noto; Greek Theatre of Syracuse; Ortygia; Palazzolo Acreide; Scicli; Modica

GETTING THERE:
Catania–Fontanarossa Airport; Comiso Airport

+39 0931 856055 ☎
condenastjohansens.com/masseriadellavolpe 🌐
Contrada Casale s/n, 96017 Noto (SR), Sicily, Italy 🏠

Masseria Susafa

A taste of centuries-old pastoral pleasures in rural Sicily

PRICE FROM:
€95

FEATURES:
Pool; Restaurant

ACTIVITIES:
Horse riding; Walking

NEARBY:
Madonie Regional Natural Park; Palermo; Cefalu; Valley of the Temples; Mosaics of Piazza Armerina

GETTING THERE:
A19; Falcone–Borsellino Airport; Catania–Fontanarossa Airport

A part of Sicily's bucolic landscape for centuries, Masseria Susafa is as integral to the land as the rolling green hills that envelop it. The pace of life is set to a gentle rhythm in this south-west corner of the island and Masseria's low rise, ancient stone buildings tell a story of bygone agricultural living. The Saeli-Rizzuto family has taken care of this farmhouse and surrounding acres for five generations and there's a relaxed, homely vibe about the place. This chilled atmosphere is accompanied by a low-key, chic décor, which adds to the welcoming ambience perfect for a quiet break away from the hustle and bustle of everyday life. In fact, the entire property can be exclusively hired for a truly relaxed, private getaway and for parties, family celebrations and weddings. Capacious indoor spaces and sumptuous green lawns with panoramic views of the cultivated land are the idyllic settings. And elegant, local fare is served under the arched stone walls of the former granary. Masseria's team are a well-oiled machine of efficiency and great taste so all you need to do is kick back and let them take care of you. Perhaps relax by the pool, explore the estate's olive grove and/or take part in a cooking class.

☎ +39 338 960 8713
🌐 condenastjohansens.com/masseriasusafa
🏠 Contrada Susafa, Polizzi Generosa 90028, Palermo, Sicily, Italy

The Ashbee Hotel

Where Sicilian scenery marries Arts and Crafts grace in Taormina

The Ashbee Hotel is a taste of England on the Sicilian coast. Constructed by famed Arts and Crafts architect Charles Robert Ashbee in 1907, Charles didn't just build his good friend Colonel Shaw-Hellier (director of the British Royal Military School of Music) a breathtaking villa but a 20th-century work of art. Looking down to the Ionian Sea and across to Mount Etna and Calabria beyond, this is the heart of Taormina just 100 metres from its famous Greek amphitheatre and pedestrianised streets of designer boutiques, cosy trattorias and palazzos. Inside, there are 25 guest rooms and suites dressed in tasteful baroque wallpaper alongside sleek orchid-coloured furniture. Ultra-deluxe, ultra-spacious suites provide the wow factor from the homely Family Suite with private entrance and garden - which can sleep up to six - to the sensorial Spa Suite complete with hydrotherapy steam bath and cavernous quadruple-jetted shower. And then there's the air of romance that reaches every corner of The Ashbee and charming town of Taormina, which has seduced many literary greats over the decades (D H Lawrence, Tennessee Williams and Truman Capote all lived here). So where better for a wedding party catered for by the Mediterranean St George Restaurant whose terrace allows you to soak up that spectacular view while The Terrace Bar pours the cocktails, fine wines and champers.

PRICE FROM:
€350

FEATURES:
Family friendly; Pool; Restaurant; Sea views

ACTIVITIES:
Sightseeing; Walking; Water sports

NEARBY:
Ancient theatre of Taormina; Taormina Film Fest; Isola Bella nature reserve and beach; Catania; Mount Etna

GETTING THERE:
Catania Airport

+39 0942 23537 ☎
condenastjohansens.com/ashbee 🌐
Viale San Pancrazio n 46, 98039 Taormina, Messina, Sicily, 🏠
Italy

Villa Ducale Boutique Hotel

Pure romance, panoramic vistas and foodie feasts on Sicily's north-eastern coast

Owners Andrea and Rosaria Quartucci were born to run this charming hillside hideaway overlooking the undulating Sicilian coast. Attentive, knowledgeable and passionate hosts, it's obvious they love this place and it's easy to see why. Built as a luxury home, Villa Ducale Boutique Hotel has the kind of views you never forget: over terracotta rooftops to Mount Etna and down to Taormina Bay and the deep blue Mediterranean. Stone steps encircle the entire Villa with pretty, colourful flowers lining the way. And inside, the 17 double rooms and suites come in all different shapes and sizes. The design team from Studio Area have done a great job of modernising the traditional Sicilian style combining vibrant colours, patterns and fabrics with a contemporary edge. From dawn till dusk, the terrace is the main hub of the Villa looking out to the panoramic views of the coast. This is where you'll feast on delicious breakfasts of pastries and fresh fruit, mouth-watering lunches of pastas, salads and sandwiches, sunset cocktails and made-to-order candlelit suppers of traditional Sicilian, gluten-free cuisine cooked exactly to your taste. Nothing is too much trouble for Chef Santina and her brigade. The Villa's free, regular shuttle service will take you to the fascinating town centre whose celebrated ruins and ancient (still in use) Greek theatre draw a crowd year-round.

☎ +39 0942 28153
🌐 condenastjohansens.com/villaducale
🏠 Via Leonardo da Vinci 60, 98039 Taormina (ME), Sicily, Italy

Monaci delle Terre Nere

A possessing Sicilian sanctuary with eco-cred

More than a boutique hotel, Monaci delle Terre Nere is a realised dream for owner Guido Coffa. And his love affair with this 200-year-old villa and surrounding acres with vineyard (originally attended by monks of the Saint Anna order) is evident in every detail. From the vestiges of its past, the carefully chosen sculptures and colourful paintings to its passionate principles of organic living, the five years in the making has been well-worth it. Set on the rich, volcanic slopes below slumbering Mount Etna, this is possibly one of Sicily's best-kept secrets. Inside, décor is fresh and artistic with rustic elements (wooden beams, exposed black rock walls) reminding you of Monaci delle Terre Nere's former life. But this is a very 21st-century bolthole and proudly one of three eco-bio certified hotels in Sicily. Giant Sicilian cherries and flowering zucchinis go directly from tree to table with pots of golden Zafferana honey, fresher-than-fresh juice and fluffy focaccia served up for breakfast; taken in the old wine press during winter months. Hands-on Guido is a gracious host, able to organise cooking classes, wine and oil tasting evenings or SUV trips to Etna's peak and nearby lost-in-time villages. But there's plenty to keep you occupied here with the infinity pool, massages, cinema under the stars and alfresco yoga. Top tip: reserve Suite Amabile for the views from its bathtub over Etna's crater!

PRICE FROM:
€220

FEATURES:
Family friendly; Pool; Restaurant; Sea views

ACTIVITIES:
Cycling; Horse riding; Walking

NEARBY:
Taormina; Baroque cities; Mount Etna excursions; Aeolian Islands; Catania

GETTING THERE:
Fleri Bus Station; Catania Fontanarossa Airport

+39 095 708 36 38 ☎
condenastjohansens.com/monaci 🌐
Via Monaci, 95019 Zafferana Etnea, Catania, Sicily, Italy 🏠

Parkhotel Holzner

Wholesome family fun in the Italian Alps

PRICE FROM:
€188 (including public transport passes for the region)

FEATURES:
Family friendly; Pool; Restaurant; Spa

ACTIVITIES:
Golf; Skiing; Walking

NEARBY:
Bolzano; Historic Rittner Railway; Earth Pyramids; Ötzi, The Iceman Archeaology Museum

GETTING THERE:
Bolzano Airport; Verona Airport; Innsbruck Airport, Austria; Munich Airport, Germany

☎ +39 0471 345 231
🌐 condenastjohansens.com/parkhotelholzner
🏠 39054 Oberbozen Ritten/Soprabolzano Renon, Südtirol/Alto Adige, Trentino - Alto Adige / Dolomites, Italy

In 1908 it was cutting edge; today it's packed with character. Welcome to Parkhotel Holzner, a family-run business and slice of art-nouveau history on the Renon Plateau, 1,200 metres high up in the Italian Dolomites. The scenery is pure mountain drama, and the view from the monorail as you approach the front door from the town of Bolzano is jaw-dropping. The drama continues inside the hotel, where original features (Thonet chairs, turn-of-the-20th-century furniture, glistening chandeliers) effortlessly sit beside modern luxuries. These include gorgeous bathrooms, marshmallow-like beds with the softest duvets and a super spa (the Alpine herbs massage is divine). This is a great family-friendly hotel with a fun-packed children's programme of activities and designated dining room for the little ones. The kitchen presents light Mediterranean cuisine matched by an impressive drinks list with an emphasis on South Tyrol wines. But a visit to Parkhotel Holzner is all about being outdoors. Aside from the mountain backdrop, which you can marvel at while lounging by the sunny pool or sipping Gewürztraminer on the terrace, there's the surrounding parkland to explore. Plus, depending on when you visit, hiking routes, cycling and skiing. When you find time, hop on the monorail to medieval Bolzano lined with arcaded streets, castles, museums and Christmas markets.

Hotel Gardena Grödnerhof

Classic Tyrolean mountain escape, serene spa and romantic restaurant

A slice of sublime mountain magic, Hotel Gardena Grödnerhof nestles amongst the spectacular pale peaks of the Dolomites. This turreted South Tyrolean lodge is a supersized sanctuary with a focus on regeneration where snow fans can get their fix of winter sports with ski lifts a blessed 200 metres away. (The in-house ski service will kit you out to conquer the myriad of slopes.) Spring brings hiking and biking opportunities with guided mountain excursions and guided mountain bike tours as bonus add-ons. But if all this Alpine air doesn't refresh you then the spa wellness centre will. This soothing sanctum of self-indulgence has various steam baths and saunas - Turkish bath and Finnish sauna included - and is accompanied by a first-class beauty farm offering numerous massages such as Ayurvedic and aromatic baths (the hay bath is a must). All are guaranteed to send you into an utter jelly-like state. Simply reading the extensive treatment list will relax you! Newly refurbished rooms and suites now offer heavenly levels of comfort; even the smallest rooms at Gardena Grödnerhof are generous in size. And each one has a balcony overlooking the gardens or Ortisei's pretty town centre. Dine on top quality regional fare at the hotel's gourmet restaurant, Anna Stuben, and strike up a conversation with the expert sommelier to enjoy a glass of fine wine chosen by his very wise hand.

PRICE FROM:
€314

FEATURES:
Family friendly; Gym; Michelin Starred restaurant; Pool; Spa

ACTIVITIES:
Golf; Skiing; Walking

NEARBY:
Bolzano; Sella Ronda ski route and ski carousel at Dolomiti Superski; Cable gondola to Alpe di Siusi; Mountain hiking trails; Visits to local wineries

GETTING THERE:
Verona Airport; Venice Airport; Innsbruck Airport, Austria

+39 0471 796 315 ☎
condenastjohansens.com/gardena 🌐
Str Vidalong 3, 39046 Ortisei, Trentino - Alto Adige / 🏠
Dolomites, Italy

Castel Porrona Relais

Five-star standards with a medieval spirit in the Tuscan hills

PRICE FROM:
€390

FEATURES:
Family friendly; Pool; Restaurant; Spa

ACTIVITIES:
Cycling; Sightseeing; Walking

NEARBY:
Montalcino; Siena; Saturnia hot springs; Punta Ala; Pienza; San Gimignano

GETTING THERE:
Grosseto Airport; Florence Airport; Rome Fiumicino Airport

This is no ordinary hotel. Castel Porrona Relais is a medieval borgo (village) dating back to the 12th century, restored with decadent abandon. The renovation of these ancient buildings, including the five-suite turreted castle (available for exclusive use), was a labour of love for the owner and it shows. The village itself is home to 22 residents and its location within Montecucco wine country is a prime spot for enjoying the Tuscan dream scene of rolling hills, vineyards, olive groves and cypress trees. These views can be seen from the large outdoor pool and many of Castel Porrona Relais' lavish guest rooms, suites and apartments. Local materials and quality fabrics set a palatial picture. Some have four posters, original wooden beams and double spa tubs, while the apartments with kitchen areas, are great for families. With Siena and San Gimignano nearby, and opportunities for horse riding, mountain biking and wine tasting, there's plenty to do. And for a day on the water, the Italian coastline of Porto Ercole and Punta Ala can be explored by private yacht. Just ask a member of the concierge team to help organise. If all this wasn't enough, Castel's Agua Spa features a Moroccan-inspired hammam, pools and wine therapy bath. Plus, there's authentic Tuscan cuisine - in addition to freshly baked pastries - served at Il Chiostro for lunch and dinner.

☎ +39 0564 993 206
🌐 condenastjohansens.com/castelporrona
🏠 Via della Fiera, Porrona, 58044 Cinigiano (Grosseto), Tuscany, Italy

Hotel Villa Fiesole

Where Tuscan panoramas and romantic dramas sweep you off your feet

Looking down to the terracotta rooves and iconic edifices of Florence, Hotel Villa Fiesole hides away high in the cypress and pine-dotted Tuscan hills. An 18th-century private villa-turned-smart boutique hotel in 1995, Fiesole has been the Tuscan retreat of choice for dignitaries for hundreds of years. And it's easy to see why. Moments from the buzz of Florence in the ancient town of Fiesole, the views from here are captivating. The panoramic terrace, which is home to the divine restaurant, La Terrazza, serves up the best views and exceptional Tuscan/Mediterranean fare. This picturesque spot is a popular setting for formal and informal events, cocktail receptions and weddings in addition to the pretty garden, where guests often relax with a glass of local Tuscan wine. More of these special views are seen from the windows, terraces and patios of the 15 elegant, individually appointed Deluxe and Prestige bedrooms (some overlook the garden). These superior rooms are located in the Villa's adjacent greenhouse. For when you want to be in the city rather than looking at it, a regular public bus service from the Villa will take you there. But before you head out, consult the friendly, attentive staff for tips on the best sightseeing spots, restaurants and shopping - they know it all. Be sure to fit in a visit to the Chianti region to acquaint yourself with the local wines.

PRICE FROM:
€150

FEATURES:
Family friendly; Pet friendly; Pool; Restaurant; Wheelchair access

ACTIVITIES:
Golf; Sightseeing; Walking

NEARBY:
Fiesole; Florence; Lucca; Chianti; Versilia coast

GETTING THERE:
Firenze Santa Maria Novella Railway Station; Florence Airport, Peretola; Pisa International Airport

+39 055 597252 ☎
condenastjohansens.com/villafiesole 🌐
Via Beato Angelico 35, 50014 Fiesole, Florence, Tuscany, Italy 🏠

CONDÉ NAST
johansens
Luxury Hotels · Spas · Venues
AWARD WINNER 2016

Firenze Number Nine Wellness Hotel

The jet set's hotel of choice in the pulsing heart of Florence

PRICE FROM:
€149

FEATURES:
Family friendly; Gym; Restaurant; Spa; Wheelchair access

ACTIVITIES:
Cycling; Shopping; Sightseeing

NEARBY:
San Lorenzo Church with Medici Chapels; Il Duomo di Firenze (Florence Cathedral); Santa Maria Novella Church; Accademia and Uffizi Galleries; Ponte Vecchio

GETTING THERE:
Florence Santa Maria Novella Railway Station; Florence Airport, Peretola; Pisa Airport

☎ +39 055 293777
🌐 condenastjohansens.com/firenzenumbernine
🏠 Via dei Conti 9, 50123 Florence, Tuscany, Italy

Firenze Number Nine is a chameleon of a hotel. To some it's a romantic retreat, for others it's an ideal base for business, while the body-beautiful flock here for its fitness centre and new Ayurvedic day spa. A restored 17th-century palazzo, Firenze Number Nine's central location means all of the city's Renaissance glory is at your fingertips such as the Medici Chapels, Duomo and Ponte Vecchio. However, the hubbub outside remains outside and Firenze Number Nine maintains an incredibly peaceful vibe, tucked away in its quiet cobblestoned lane. A strong emphasis on well-being emerges from the ARYA - Beauty & Comfort Zone whose Ayurvedic rituals, facials, massages, yoga and Pilates classes ensure visitors leave in a Zen-like state; its fitness centre is cutting-edge. Exceptionally spacious for a city hotel, guest rooms and suites are enhanced by the light and airy décor that's fresh with a touch of funk. Each one is different but all deliver upscale comfort with hypoallergenic materials, top-class beds and displays of art by local artists that create a museum-like quality. But there's no stuffiness here, as highlighted by Le Muse Restaurant & Lounge Bar. Recently opened, Number Nine's restaurant is a social focal point where people gather for breakfasts, light lunches, meetings, cocktails and elegant Italian dinners.

Golden Tower Hotel & Spa

Time out in timeless Florentine architecture

For total rejuvenation head for the new kid in town: Golden Tower Hotel & Spa. In the heart of Florence, no expense has been spared at this glitzy glamourpuss in a city where space comes at a premium. Golden Tower is a boutique hotel with an exceptional wellness centre offering escape from the city life that buzzes just outside its doors. Located minutes from the famous high-end Via Tornabuoni shopping district and many of Florence's popular tourist sites and restaurants, this urban hideaway delivers the best of both worlds: city centre convenience and peaceful seclusion. It also effortlessly combines history (Golden Tower's building and furnishings are a Renaissance masterpiece) with the modern technological world. Comprising a Beauty Centre and Spa Lounge, the wellness centre is a haven of luxury and tranquillity where a wide variety of massage treatments perfect for both city breaks and longer stays await you. Equipped with a Turkish bath, tropical showers and a Jacuzzi you'll feel pampered above and beyond the typical spa experience. Take to the Tower for a particularly special stay where sparkling marble and techy gadgets go hand-in-hand. Their bathrooms of grey marble exude sumptuousness as you soak away any remnant of tension before an apéritif or tipple at the bar followed by a delicious dinner of dreamy Italian dishes.

PRICE FROM:
€250

FEATURES:
Family friendly; Restaurant; Spa; Wheelchair access

ACTIVITIES:
Shopping; Sightseeing; Walking

NEARBY:
Accademia and Uffizi Galleries; Ponte Vecchio; Il Duomo di Firenze (Florence Cathedral)

GETTING THERE:
Florence Airport, Peretola; Pisa Airport

+39 055 287 860 ☎
condenastjohansens.com/goldentowerhotel 🌐
Piazza Strozzi 11/R, 50123 Florence, Tuscany, Italy 🏠

Hotel Brunelleschi

A fusion of historic Florentine architecture and contemporary opulence

PRICE FROM:
€289

FEATURES:
Family friendly; Gym; Restaurant; Wheelchair access

ACTIVITIES:
Shopping; Sightseeing

NEARBY:
Uffizi Gallery; Bargello Museum; Ponte Vecchio; Academy of Fine Arts; Il Duomo di Firenze (Florence Cathedral)

GETTING THERE:
Florence Airport, Peretola; Pisa Airport; Bologna Airport

☎ +39 055 27370
🌐 condenastjohansens.com/hotelbrunelleschi
🏠 Piazza Santa Elisabetta 3, 50122 Florence, Tuscany, Italy

Hotel Brunelleschi's biggest attraction is its unbeatable location. A stone's throw from Florence's spectacular cathedral, its terracotta-toned dome engineered by Filippo Brunelleschi is so close, you'll think you can touch it. Many of the rooms and suites afford bedside views of the Duomo; one has a rooftop terrace with Jacuzzi and skyline panorama. But all give you a heart-stirring glimpse of the historic city's buzzing life and breathtaking architecture. Poised in a peaceful piazza moments from the Uffizi Gallery, Piazza della Signoria and many other of Florence's Renaissance glories - not to mention the shopping stradas - Hotel Brunelleschi is secluded yet wonderfully central. This is a hotel of congruous contradictions. Housed within a 6th-century circular Byzantine tower and a medieval church (the hotel has a private museum that includes a Roman caldarium), the interior is a juxtaposition of contemporary design. Modern furnishings grace parquet flooring and marble bathrooms adjoin discreetly decadent boudoirs. The silver basins and sleek four-poster beds are particularly fine. Every audio-visual amenity is available, free high-speed WiFi is accessible in the guest rooms and common areas, and speedy service is dispensed 24/7. Then there's Restaurant Santa Elisabetta and the Osteria della Pagliazza serving up Italian food with soul that's so good it's a sin to miss.

Monsignor Della Casa Country Resort & Spa

The heart of Tuscan adventure, romance and family fun

It's hard to pin down what makes Monsignor Della Casa Country Resort & Spa quite so special. There's so many highlights it's difficult to know where to start. Perhaps the location: Monsignor Della Casa is set in acres of undulating Tuscan countryside, just a short drive from the charms of Florence. Then there's the hotel itself, a beautifully restored Tuscan hamlet alongside wonderfully welcoming apartments and private villas that instantly feel like your pastoral home-from-home. Endless activities such as tennis, trekking, biking, volleyball and swimming have you working up an appetite while serious gourmands can join a local truffle tour to then enjoy their discoveries by candlelight shaved over some fresh pasta on the elegant terrace. The stock of local and national wines, freshly pressed olive oil and selection of regional cheeses are also well worth a try. If craving some peace and relaxation, Monsignor Della Casa is an expert in slowing down the pace. Try a cooking class or head to the spa housed in an old stone farmhouse bathed in light from the huge windows. Here, you can relax with facials and body treatments that use local grapes and olive oil before planning your next Tuscan adventure on this beautiful estate.

PRICE FROM:
€179

FEATURES:
Family friendly; Pool; Restaurant; Spa; Wheelchair access

ACTIVITIES:
Golf; Shopping; Sightseeing

NEARBY:
Florence; White truffle hunting; Mugello car and motorbike circuit; Chianti wine tasting; Designer fashion outlet

GETTING THERE:
Florence Airport, Peretola; Bologna Airport; Pisa Airport

+39 055 840 821 ☎
condenastjohansens.com/monsignor 🌐
Via di Mucciano 16, 50032 Borgo San Lorenzo, Florence, 🏠
Tuscany, Italy

Hotel Byron

Liberty-style luxe and Michelin-Star fodder on the Tuscan coast

PRICE FROM:
€290

FEATURES:
Family friendly; Michelin Starred restaurant; Pool; Sea views

ACTIVITIES:
Golf; Walking; Water sports

NEARBY:
Cinque Terre; Pisa; Puccini Opera Festival; Tour of Carrara marble caves

GETTING THERE:
Pisa Airport; Florence Airport, Peretola

Dolce vita. The phrase that could have been coined for Hotel Byron. Built over 100 years ago as a party pad for one of Italy's leading socialites (back then, you were no-one if you didn't have a villa in Forte dei Marmi), today, the glamour is still here but without the showy glitz. This is old school elegance meets Italian charm and Forte dei Marmi is as equally loved for its woodlands and serenity as it is for its fabulous shopping, haute couture boutiques and gourmet restaurants. Hotel Byron is a stately villa, built with style and comfort in equal measure and if you're looking for a hotel with star quality, this is for you. Moments from the Tyrrhenian Sea and beach, and with the Apuan Alps as a backdrop, it's a peaceful, beautiful retreat just a short walk from Forte dei Marmi. Rooms are high ceilinged, chic and simple, and the hotel's restaurant, La Magnolia, is one of the best in town. Chef Cristoforo Trapani holds a Michelin Star for his traditional, regional cooking that uses the finest local produce to create traditional specialities with creative flair. Easily reached from either Florence or Pisa, Hotel Byron is a hidden treasure on this stunning stretch of the Italian coast.

☎ +39 0584 787 052
🌐 condenastjohansens.com/byron
🏠 Viale A Morin 46, 55042 Forte dei Marmi (LU), Tuscany, Italy

Vitigliano Tuscan Relais & Spa

Out of this world Tuscan paradise

A realised dream, beauty spot, wellness retreat and boutique hideaway, Vitigliano Tuscan Relais & Spa is really special. Perched on a hilltop with phenomenal 360-degree views of the Tuscan landscape, this former Roman hamlet and aristocratic residence is situated mid-way between Florence and Siena. Surrounded by acres of private land encompassing vineyards, olive groves, holme-oak forests, cypress alleys and pine trees, this magical place was a seven-year project in the making for owner Marion Hattemer. Repurposed materials fill every corner of the six - one and two-bedroomed - suites, which can accommodate just 14 guests at one time. This means big family holidays and vacationing friends often take over the entire estate when a conference, well-being retreat filled with yoga, time in the Wellness House and Bath House aren't taking place. But whether you're here to romance, recharge or explore, you'll always remember Vitigliano's gourmet food and fine wine. Produce is local, light and born from passion, and it's always prepared from sustainably grown ingredients packed with antioxidants. Neighbour and viticulturist Tommaso Cavalli (son of fashion designer Roberto) has created a limited edition of wines just for Marion who encourages her guests to help themselves.

PRICE FROM:
€350

FEATURES:
Family friendly; Gym; Pool; Restaurant

ACTIVITIES:
Cycling; Golf; Sightseeing

NEARBY:
Greve; Panzano; Florence; Ugolino Golf Club; Siena

GETTING THERE:
Florence Santa Maria Novella Railway Station; Florence Airport, Peretola; Pisa Airport

+39 333 77 41 692 ☎
condenastjohansens.com/vitigliano 🌐
Localita Vitigliano di Sotto, Via Case Sparse 64, I-50022 🏠
Greve in Chianti (FI), Tuscany, Italy

Villa le Barone

A taster of 16th-century aristocratic life in the Tuscan hills

PRICE FROM:
€190

FEATURES:
Family friendly; Gym; Pool; Restaurant

ACTIVITIES:
Sightseeing; Tennis; Walking

NEARBY:
Florence; Siena; Cooking classes; Pieve di San Leolino's festivals, concerts and markets; Greve in Chianti

GETTING THERE:
Florence Airport, Peretola; Pisa Airport

☎ +39 055 852621
🌐 condenastjohansens.com/villalebarone
🏠 Via San Leolino 19, 50022 Panzano in Chianti (FI), Tuscany, Italy

Villa le Barone does grand: after all, it is the former summer house of Florentine nobility situated amid vineyards and cypress groves in rolling Chianti countryside. It does gourmet: just as you would hope, excellent wines and skilful Tuscan cooking classes (learning to make pasta was never more fun!) are on the agenda. It does Italian hospitality: the staff are so passionate and full of gusto. This handsome Renaissance manor house is big on character with endless nooks and crannies inside and out; a maze of rooms and staircases, and beautiful, fragrant rose and lavender gardens made for intimate afternoons. Add in the home-from-home vibe, fresh-cut flowers, log fires on chilly evenings and an honesty bar, and le Barone has laid-back escape written all over it. Each of the Villa's 28 rooms is brimming with paintings, antiques and country-chic fabrics. Some are located in the main house, others in ivy-clad cottages. Some are big. Some are small. All add up to irresistible charm. Wine-tasting tours in Chianti cellars, golf, markets and various cultural sites are all within easy reach and there's an on-site tennis court, plus various cycling and hiking routes. Florence and Siena are just a short drive away (ask a member of staff about scheduled concerts), however, one of the best journeys you'll make will be from your room to the pool and the candlelit terrace for dinner.

Hotel Torre di Cala Piccola

Peace, romance and dream scenes from the cliffs of Monte Argentario

While not technically an island, Monte Argentario's peninsula off the coast of Tuscany benefits from all the privileges an island affords: 360-degree views, fresh ocean breezes and a circumference of coastline. Positioned directly on its rocky edge, at the furthermost point from the mainland, Hotel Torre di Cala Piccola is perched above the magnificence of the Med, five minutes from Porto Santo Stefano facing Giglio Island. A stay here feels like you're privy to a little-known secret that entitles you to enjoy this oasis of serenity and, most importantly, its privacy. This sense of isolation has attracted many illustrious guests to Hotel Torre di Cala Piccola over the years including Elizabeth Taylor and Richard Burton in their love-struck 1960s' prime. And the personalised service makes you feel every inch the movie star. Rooms and suites are low-key, contemporary dens. Outside, the jaw-dropping ocean vistas surround you at every turn, from the infinity pool to the dramatic rocky Caletta suntrap, beneath which is a red coral cliff. La Torre d'Argento restaurant serves creative Tuscan dishes (veggie and gluten-free options are available) to visitors and guests each evening and uses seasonal, local ingredients. Naturally, seafood is the highlight of the show. Must visit: before/after dinner head to Caffè La Torre - located in a 16th-century tower - and enjoy a cocktail, tea, coffee or glass of wine.

PRICE FROM:
€299 (limousine airport transfers available)

FEATURES:
Beach access; Pool; Restaurant; Sea views; Wheelchair access

ACTIVITIES:
Golf; Walking; Water sports

NEARBY:
Porto Santo Stefano; Porto Ercole; Orbetello; Capalbio; Parco Regionale della Maremma

GETTING THERE:
Orbetello Railway Station; Civitavecchia Port; Leonardo da Vinci–Fiumicino Airport

+39 0564 825111 ☎
condenastjohansens.com/torredicalapiccola 🌐
Via della Cala, 58019 Cala Piccola, Porto Santo Stefano, 🏠
Monte Argentario (GR), Tuscany, Italy

Villa Curina Resort

Romantic Tuscan villa in the rolling hills of Siena

PRICE FROM:
€160

FEATURES:
Pool; Restaurant

ACTIVITIES:
Cycling; Horse riding; Tennis

NEARBY:
Siena; Perugia; Chianti wine routes; Gastronomic tours

GETTING THERE:
Florence Airport, Peretola; Perugia Airport; Pisa Airport

Villa Curina Resort isn't your typical "resort." It's a re-imagined 16th-century hamlet. Located between Tuscany and Umbria, all the prerequisites of a resort are here: tip top accommodation, smart restaurant, pool and outdoor pursuits. However, this is a family-run business where everything expresses a genteel, rural Italian quality and style. Rooms and suites are achingly romantic with quaint nooks and crannies, odd shaped spaces, wooden beams and antiquities. There are fewer more romantic spots oozing charm and natural beauty, and Il Convito di Curina restaurant makes the most of this unmatched setting with a panoramic terrace overlooking the rolling Tuscan hills with Siena on the horizon (the sunset vistas from here are something out of a fairy tale). The menu's unique dishes are prepared by Chef Federico alongside an awesome selection of wine stored in the Villa's impressive wine cellar. Guests may visit the cellar where there are approximately 400 labels from the finest Sienese and Italian winemakers. There's no denying the owner's passion who is a professional A.I.S. sommelier as well as a Chevalier de l'Ordre des Couteaux de Champagne since 2013. Be prepared: you're in store for one helluva wine tour of the highest level!

☎ +39 0577 355630
🌐 condenastjohansens.com/villacurinaresort
🏠 Strada Provinciale 62, No 24, Località Curina, 53019 Castelnuovo Berardenga (Siena), Tuscany, Italy

Borgo Lucignanello Bandini

Well-heeled Tuscan living in Lucignano d'Asso

Borgo Lucignanello is Tuscan heaven. Reached by winding roads, passed tiny villages and majestic cypress trees, the miniature hamlet of Lucignano d'Asso is home to Borgo Lucignanello Bandini, a handful of beautiful retreats. The Piccolomini family has owned this enclave for over 600 years and you can feel the love that's been poured into every inch. It has everything you could want for the perfect Tuscan escape from an idyllic infinity pool looking out over the Tuscan plains to rustic yet elegant interiors oozing a cosy, welcoming atmosphere. Choosing where to rest your head isn't easy. Among your choices is the romantic honeymoon favourite Casa Maria, complete with rose-decked pergola and Casale Sarageto, a stunning 18th-century farmhouse with its own pool, garden and pizza oven. One thing's for sure, during a stay at Borgo Lucignanello Bandini you certainly won't go hungry. There's a different market for every day of the week in the nearby villages with local producers tempting you with everything from white truffles to the greenest and freshest olive oil you'll ever taste. While the foodies are salivating, oenophiles are swooning over the internationally renowned Brunello Montalcino wine. Before you know it, you'll be living like a resident Italian and looking like one too; there's a Prada outlet just a short drive away.

PRICE FROM:
€129

FEATURES:
Family friendly; Helipad; Pet friendly; Pool

ACTIVITIES:
Cycling; Horse riding; Walking

NEARBY:
Pienza; Montalcino and its Brunello wineries; Siena; Truffle hunting in the Crete Senesi; Hot-air ballooning

GETTING THERE:
Perugia Airport; Florence Airport, Peretola; Pisa Airport

+39 0577 803 068 ☎
condenastjohansens.com/lucignanello 🌐
Località Lucignano d'Asso, 53020 San Giovanni d'Asso, Siena, 🏠
Tuscany, Italy

Hotel Plaza e de Russie

Simple elegance on the Tuscan Riviera

PRICE FROM:
€175

FEATURES:
Family friendly; Michelin Starred restaurant; Pet friendly; Sea views; Wheelchair access

ACTIVITIES:
Golf; Horse riding; Water sports

NEARBY:
Lucca; Montecarlo and its wineries; Puccini Opera Festival; Tour of Carrara marble cave; Cinque Terre

GETTING THERE:
Pisa Airport; Florence Airport, Peretola; Genoa Cristoforo Colombo Airport

The Tuscan Riviera is a soothing scene of yellowstone canopies, wrought-iron verandas and colourfully patterned tiles. It's one of Italy's most popular tourist destinations and the charming Hotel Plaza e de Russie sits directly in one of its art deco-styled plazas where life happens at a relaxed pace and the sunshine feels like a warm embrace. You'll find yourself naturally easing into the carefree lifestyle and craving the Mediterranean flavours of La Terrazza, Plaza e de Russie's fine-dining restaurant. Presiding high on the top floor, mouth-watering meals are devoured to a backdrop of phenomenal ocean views. Here, you'll be served a continental breakfast of fresh pastries, yoghurt and fruit each morning, setting you up for a leisurely saunter to the fine sandy shoreline of Viareggio's stunning stretch of beach. A forest of fragrant pine trees lines the walk home back to the comfort of your room where well-deserved R&R involving a long-lingering bubble bath or a snooze before a pre-dinner cocktail in the American Bar will have you rejuvenated for another gastronomic feast. Top tip: reserve a room with balcony for the finest sea views.

☎ +39 0584 44449
🌐 condenastjohansens.com/russie
🏠 Piazza d'Azeglio 1, 55049 Viareggio, Tuscany, Italy

Borgo Pignano

21st-century principles marry traditional Tuscan charm

An elegant 750-acre rural escape in the heart of Tuscany, Borgo Pignano is a short drive from Volterra, San Gimignano, Florence and Siena comprising a hamlet dating back to Etruscan times and an 18th-century villa. All of this magnificence is privately owned and provides warm hospitality in a tranquil, natural environment with far-reaching views over to the coastline. Inside the main villa are spacious public rooms including the library, billiards room, ballroom and lounge as well as the 14 elegant en-suite rooms and suites. Some of the guest rooms have original frescoes, while all are furnished with exquisite antiques, original artwork, Italian linens and chandeliers. Additional luxurious accommodation is available at La Canonica, a beautifully renovated ancient priest's house spanning two private apartments with shared drawing room and medieval kitchen. Secluded maisonettes, country cottages and a large lakeside farmhouse with kitchen and lounge facilities are perfect for families. For a fine-dining experience, head to Villa Pignano's à la carte restaurant, which uses the freshest ingredients harvested from the estate's organic vegetable gardens. Meals may be taken on the terrace overlooking the town of Volterra or at the casual alfresco restaurant with wood-fired pizza oven. Each morning, breakfast is served in the shade of the courtyard amidst the scented lemon trees.

PRICE FROM:
€220 (open 18th March to 4th November)

FEATURES:
Family friendly; Gym; Pet friendly; Pool; Restaurant

ACTIVITIES:
Cycling; Horse riding; Walking

NEARBY:
Volterra; San Gimignano; Casole d'Elsa; Siena; Florence

GETTING THERE:
Pisa Airport; Florence Airport, Peretola

+39 0588 35032 ☎
condenastjohansens.com/borgopignano 🌐
Località Pignano 6, 56048 Volterra (PI), Near Siena, Tuscany, Italy

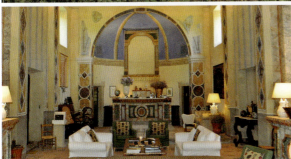

Borgo di Carpiano

Unplug, unwind and surrender to the pleasures of life at Umbria's unhurried pace

Just as owners Riccardo and Marilisa Parisi fell in love with this enchanting paradise, each one of their guests is hopelessly besotted from the moment they step upon its cobbled terrain. For this ancient Umbrian hamlet is a living, breathing example of rural Italy drenched in history and cultural significance. Close to the medieval town of Gubbio, with Apennine mountains backdrop, Borgo di Carpiano's buildings date back to the 10th century. Once home to the noble Rovaldo Baldassini, this age-old castle, church and various buildings are linked by narrow pathways with stone steps caressed by foliage covered by archways flanked by hidden nooks and crannies. Umbria's olive trees and forested hills seen beyond Borgo di Carpiano's infinity salt-water pool are where the ingredients for Borgo's home-made pasta, breads, cakes and truffle-infused dishes come from. The gourmet cuisine – served alongside an extensive wine list including local Sagrantino di Montefalco – is rich in flavour thanks to these regional delights, which also include produce grown within the Borgo's organic garden. Dining here is one of life's great pleasures! And Riccardo and Marilisa's after-dinner chats (plus, chocolates and liqueurs!) add to the whole experience. Don't miss a shiatsu session in the garden's gazebo immersed in nature and mention Condé Nast Johansens when booking to receive VIP treatment.

☎ +39 075 920337
🌐 condenastjohansens.com/borgodicarpiano
🏠 Località Scritto, 06024 Gubbio, Umbria, Italy

Castello di Petroia

Magical Umbrian medieval castle

It doesn't get more fairy tale than this: a honey-stone castle perched on an Umbrian hillside. Once the setting for the Montefeltro clan's juicy tales (think Henry VIII's court with an Italian twist) Castello di Petroia is now home to a rustic-chic bolthole. So peaceful and snug with just 11 rooms amidst three ancient tower-hugging buildings, it's easy to imagine you're reigning supreme. Capturing an authentic castle mood, interiors are infused with warm woods, rich damasks and floaty four posters. Windows let in breathtaking views (autumn colours and misty mornings are captivating) and the scent of trees. Sleek modern touches stay politely discreet until you need them, though the spacious all-singing, all-dancing bathrooms of the Junior and Deluxe Suites feature whirlpool baths tucked beneath beamed or vaulted ceilings. Kingly breakfasts of baked goodies with home-made fig jam set you up for the day. Come the evening, a table for two in Accumandugi Hall with candlelight bouncing off the walls works the Castello's magic all over again. Nothing but farm-fresh produce, including meat from the estate's land, serves as the young chef's inspiration. Gubbio, Assisi and Orvieto are all easy drives away, however, with this kind of spellbinding scenery featuring walking trails and a pool surrounded by olive tree prettiness, it's tempting to stay on-site and drink it all in.

PRICE FROM:
€130

FEATURES:
Family friendly; Pet friendly; Pool; Restaurant

ACTIVITIES:
Cycling; Walking

NEARBY:
Gubbio; Perugia; Assisi; Siena; Umbria Jazz Festival

GETTING THERE:
Perugia Airport; Ancona Airport; Rome Fiumicino Airport

+39 075 92 02 87 ☎
condenastjohansens.com/castellodipetroia 🌐
Località Scritto di Gubbio, Petroia, 06024 Gubbio (PG), 🏠
Umbria, Italy

Castello di Postignano

A fantastical medieval village in Umbria's green hills

PRICE FROM:
€160

FEATURES:
Family friendly; Pet friendly; Pool; Restaurant

ACTIVITIES:
Cycling; Walking; Water sports

NEARBY:
Spoleto; Norcia; Bevagna; Trevi; Spello

GETTING THERE:
Spoleto/Foligno Railway Stations; Perugia Airport

☎ +39 0743788911
🌐 condenastjohansens.com/castellodipostignano
🏠 Postignano, 06030 Sellano, Umbria, Italy

Looking out from on high across to Umbria's Nerina Valley is the captivating medieval village of Castello di Postignano. Dating back to the 9th century, this terracotta-tiled timepiece is a triangular network of narrow cobbled streets and sun-kissed terraces. Offering 14, one and two-bedroom suites with kitchenettes (great for families) and a bygone atmosphere, Castello di Postignano has been brought back to life. Many original frescoes and period features remain intact and old pictures, paintings and sculptures of the borgo are displayed in the museum room. The perfect mix of charm, culture and comfort, this former battleground for neighbouring village dominance is now a peaceful enclave set apart from the outside world. While away the hours in the wellness area and pool or kick back in the wine bar and sample Umbrian wines, cheeses, cured meats, truffles and olive oil. The panoramic terrace of the Caffetteria is where you'll take breakfast, whilst La Casa Rosa is Castello di Postignano's romantic trattoria presenting regional recipes with an exciting twist from seasonal, local produce. Cognac, cigars and a chocolate bar complete the indulgence in the billiards room. Top tip: visit La Bottega for its excellent Umbrian handicrafts and check out the village's spring to autumn events programme. VIP treatment is granted to all Condé Nast Johansens guests.

Il Baio Relais & Natural SPA

The ultimate rural Umbrian hideaway

Run to the Umbrian hills and reconnect with nature at Il Baio Relais & Natural SPA in stunning Spoleto. In an age where time-out is a precious commodity, Il Baio allows you to do just that. You're under no pressure to detox or botox here but simply to relax and soak up the laid-back atmosphere. The original farm and stable buildings that comprise the relais and spa have been transformed with classic, clean lines and muted colours. And by night they ooze a mellow rusticity with warming light reaching into cosy corners. For those in need of a little me-time, there's the Wellness Center & Natural SPA: a soporifc den offering personalised health programmes, a Kniepp circuit, hydromassage, chromotherapy, music therapy and Turkish bath. Outside these cosseting walls a whole host of back-to-nature therapy is available courtesy of Umbria's glorious countryside. Glossy conker-brown thoroughbreds or "Il Baios" are available for cantering in the surrounding paddocks, while loungers beside the outdoor pools encourage afternoon naps and sunbathing. Come mealtimes, Il Baio's restaurant dishes up fine Italian fare prepared from top-notch, regional ingredients including extra olive oil and fruit produced/grown by the farm next door, alongside Montefalco Sagrantino Rosso and Secco DOCG labels from nearby vineyards.

PRICE FROM:
€150

FEATURES:
Family friendly; Helipad; Pet friendly; Pool; Restaurant

ACTIVITIES:
Cycling; Horse riding; Walking

NEARBY:
Spoleto; Assisi; Perugia; Todi; Trasimeno Lake

GETTING THERE:
Spoleto Railway Station; Perugia Airport; Rome Airports

+39 0743 252103 ☎
condenastjohansens.com/ilbaio 🌐
Località Camporoppolo, 06049 Spoleto (PG), Umbria, Italy 🏠

Romantik Hotel Tenuta di Canonica

Rural Umbrian charisma with a kooky kick

PRICE FROM:
€170

FEATURES:
Family friendly; Lake views; Pet friendly; Pool; Restaurant

ACTIVITIES:
Fishing; Golf; Horse riding

NEARBY:
Todi; Orvieto; Assisi; Spoleto; Civita di Bagnoregio (aka the dying town)

GETTING THERE:
Perugia Airport; Rome Airport

☎ +39 075 8947545
🌐 condenastjohansens.com/tenutadicanonica
🏠 Località Canonica 75, 06059 Todi (PG), Umbria, Italy

Sitting on the edge of the Umbrian medieval town of Todi is Romantik Hotel Tenuta di Canonica. Its ancient stone structure with watch tower may date back to the Roman era (original parts of the impressive Roman tower bring a real sense of authenticity) but the beautifully furnished suites are a mass of modern homely comfort oozing character. In this relaxed atmosphere you're surrounded by acres of unspoilt Umbrian forest, fields and lines of olive and fruit trees. Walk around the lush gardens (look out for the elves on the tree branches), check out the old well in the hall (it still works) and chat with Mozart the multilingual parrot. Although this hotel appeals to travellers in search of tranquillity, there's no denying that its quirks make it an unforgettable experience. A stay here is more home-away-from-home than hotel. Ask a member of the knowledgeable reception staff about Le Marmore Falls, an excursion through the spectacular scenery, or there's always the option to remain closer to home with a swim in the outdoor pool. Returning ravenous from a day trip, a spread of simple but delicious dishes by candlelight are yours to devour. The food is exceptional and 100% organic, with a mindfulness to health and well-being without compromising on flavour or local tradition.

Romantic Hotel & Spa Jolanda Sport

Wood-tastic hideaway with spa in the Monterosa ski resort

Located in the three valley Monterosa ski district, Romantik Hotel & Spa Jolanda Sport is THE destination for travellers who enjoy mountainous activities. It's the biggest ski resort in Europe. But when the waves of laziness wash over you, there's also plenty of opportunity to be indulgent. Bedecked in the warmth of natural wood and traditional embroideries, this inviting and friendly (great value for money too) hotel offers both summer and winter options. And with Jolanda Sport on the doorstep of the gondola, you can wave goodbye to carrying equipment around and focus on enjoying yourself. Whether it's the thrills of the downhills, the challenges of the summit or the opportunity to admire the breathtaking Monte Rosa vista, there's something for everyone. Featuring two saunas, four relaxation areas, four treatment rooms, a Jacuzzi, pool and aromatising bath, Jolanda Sport's ever-expanding spa (future plans include an outdoor pool) await your weary return. As does your room or suite where wood and refined textiles combine for an Alpine welcome that's both stylish and comfortable; the bathrooms are particularly roomy. The motto here is, "fresh air, healthy food," which means the cuisine of the lively restaurant is home-made and locally sourced, served with the region's finest wines. Those with a sweet tooth should leave some room: the desserts are sensational!

PRICE FROM:
€110 (per person, half board)

FEATURES:
Gym; Pool; Restaurant; Spa

ACTIVITIES:
Fishing; Golf; Skiing

NEARBY:
Aosta; Turin; Regina Margherita Alpine refuge; Heli-skiing; Climbing and tracking

GETTING THERE:
Turin Airport; Aosta Airport

+39 0125 366 140 ☎
condenastjohansens.com/jolandasport 🌐
Località Edelboden 31, 11020 Gressoney~La~Trinité, Valle d'Aosta, Italy 🏠

Ca Maria Adele

Discreet designer hideaway in Venice

PRICE FROM:
€363

FEATURES:
Pet friendly; Sea views

ACTIVITIES:
Shopping; Sightseeing; Walking

NEARBY:
Gondola rides; Punta dalla Dogana Museum; St Mark's Square;
Peggy Guggenheim Museum; Magazzini del Sale

GETTING THERE:
Treviso Airport; Venice Marco Polo Airport

☎ +39 041 52 03 078
🌐 condenastjohansens.com/camariaadele
🏠 Dorsoduro 111, 30123 Venice, Veneto, Italy

Ca Maria Adele, Venice, is an indulgent mix of two worlds. Lying within the walls of a 16th-century Venetian palazzo and hidden amongst the waterways of the city, it's a private bolthole of contrasts demonstrating old grandeur on the exterior with a modern, sleek and luxurious interior. It's lavish, quirky, intimate, romantic and utterly lovely. For an arrival that befits the Adele, hop on a vintage speedboat (à la Bond) direct from Marco Polo Airport to the hotel lobby where a cool glass of Prosecco awaits, along with the relaxed breakfast policy: whenever, wherever and however! This is a grown-up getaway to make the honeymooners hallelujah; where 12 rooms are dressed-up-to-the-nines in swathes of velvety soft fabrics that hang floor-to-ceiling. Fur lines the walls as dazzling oversized Murano glass chandeliers hang from the ceiling to shine upon exotic teak wood furnishings. (Book the Noir Room whose black theme sets a highly dramatic scene.) Ca Maria Adele is 21st-century palazzo perfection and a hedonistic feast for all the senses where you'll find a Moroccan-styled terrace with couples whispering sweet-nothings at twilight and a beautifully laid-out honesty bar for a nightcap under the stars. Interesting titbit: all the staff at Ca Maria Adele are male - welcoming and caring, they also happen to be very attractive!

Ca' Sagredo Hotel

Venetian noble elegance on the world-famous Grand Canal

The sheer beauty of Ca' Sagredo Hotel is weep-with-joy wondrous. As you pull up alongside the Grand Canal, you'll need to pinch yourself, and again when you step inside. This 15th-century palazzo has been declared a National Monument and it's certainly a monument to decadence! It oozes romance while the opulently frescoed ballroom and lounge echoes with epic events of the past when Count Sagredo lived in this den of iniquity. Just gliding up the imposing marble staircase (whilst resisting a tap on a cherub's peachy cheek) feels positively regal. Ca' Sagredo's views of the canal traffic and Rialto Market opposite are storybook scenes of old. And all rooms are a seriously sexy sight to behold with classic Venetian styling. The suite dedicated to art (the aptly named Arts Suite) is an ode to 18th-century artists such as Abbondio Stazio and Carpoforo Mazzetti. Art lovers be warned: there are so many treasures here, it's easy to forget the outside world. But there's always the hotel's panoramic waterside L'Alcova restaurant with terrace over the Grand Canal to remind you, serving dishes that are a celebration of Italy on a plate courtesy of new Executive Chef Damiano Bassano.

PRICE FROM:
€450

FEATURES:
Family friendly; Gym; Restaurant; Wheelchair access

ACTIVITIES:
Shooting; Shopping; Sightseeing

NEARBY:
Ca' d'Oro; Grand Canal; Rialto Market; Rialto Bridge; St Mark's Square

GETTING THERE:
Venezia Santa Lucia Railway Station; Venice Cruise and Ferry Terminal; Venice Marco Polo Airport

+39 041 2413111 ☎
condenastjohansens.com/casagredo 🌐
Campo Santa Sofia 4198/99, 30121 Venice, Veneto, Italy 🏠

Palazzo Selvadego

A taste of 13th-century Venice with a 21st-century twist

PRICE FROM:
€160

FEATURES:
Sea views; Wheelchair access

ACTIVITIES:
Shopping; Sightseeing; Walking

NEARBY:
St Mark's Square; Rialto Bridge; Accademia; Peggy Gugenheim Museum; Theatre La Fenice

GETTING THERE:
Venezia Santa Lucia Railway Station; Venice Cruise and Ferry Terminal; Venice Marco Polo Airport

---

☎ + 39 041 5200211
🌐 condenastjohansens.com/palazzoselvadego
🏠 San Marco 1124/B, 30124 Venice, Veneto, Italy

Slip through the hidden entrance of Palazzo Selvadego, Venice, behind St Mark's Square and leave the teeming hordes and lagoon behind. Seemingly a world apart once inside, all of the city's iconic sites are a mere whisper away. Arrive by water taxi, check-in at the Palazzo's sister property Hotel Monaco around the corner and you're in prime position for uncovering Venice's greatest attractions: the Basilica San Marco; the Bridge of Sighs; La Fenice... Intimate and charming are the best words to describe the late 13th-century Palazzo Selvadego. Its handsome Venetian gothic façade has beautiful Byzantine windows like watchful eyes concealing the cool marble, exposed beams and parquet floors of the interior. Rooms are spacious, have access to free WiFi and look out to glimpses of the city's jumble of rooftops and a distant window box. If you have breakfast reservations head on over to Hotel Monaco where the canal-side views are simply amazing; from its terrace you can watch this unique city come to life. Ask Palazzo Selvadego's concierge desk for restaurant recommendations - they can direct you through the winding watery-lined streets of Venice with their eyes closed - and details of a private tour of Venice's favourite ridotto (gaming hall), circa 1648, at San Moisè Palace.

Color Hotel style & design

Lake Garda's most colourful designer resort hotel

When the climate is mild year-round it does something to a place. Everything feels heightened and everyone is more pleasant. Lake Garda is the evidence for this and in its south-east corner, Color Hotel style & design is irrefutable confirmation. Set back from the water, Color Hotel is slightly off the tourist track, five minutes from Bardolino, the poster-boy for the archetypal Italian lakeside town, below a swathe of green mountains filled with ancient churches and sun-dappled piazzas. Color Hotel's intention is to harmonise guests' emotional and physical states by way of chrometherapy and clever design. Those on romantic breaks should reserve a red (red = passion) room or suite. Those in search of tranquillity should opt for one dressed in blue (blue = calm). Outside, the garden is a sea of green (green = relaxation) and there's more blue thanks to the four pools (the Sun Bay Pool is heated from September to June). Chances are, if you can't see the water, you'll hear it. And it's no coincidence that La Veranda restaurant is a colourful explosion of fresh, creative and simply delicious cuisine. The slaveringly good local dishes and wine can also be enjoyed at Citronella or on the terrace. Must do: a special wine-tasting session at La Cantina.

PRICE FROM:
€125

FEATURES:
Family friendly; Lake views; Pool; Restaurant; Wheelchair access

ACTIVITIES:
Cycling; Golf; Water sports

NEARBY:
Bardolino centre; Venice; Lake Garda; Opera; Juliet's balcony

GETTING THERE:
Verona Airport; Brescia Airport; Bergamo Airport

+39 045 621 0857 ☎
condenastjohansens.com/colorhotel 🌐
Via Santa Cristina 5, 37011 Bardolino (VR), Veneto, Italy 🏠

Malta

Please go to condenastjohansens.com/malta

Rooftop vistas of Grand Harbour from Ursulino Valletta, page 94

Ursulino Valletta

Cool, artistic B&B behind ancient baroque walls in Valletta's historic city

As the European Capital of Culture for 2018 and a UNESCO World Heritage Site since 1980, Malta's capital has a lot to shout about. It's also seen a major redevelopment in recent years by "starchitect" Renzo Piano of Pompidou Centre fame. There's a great deal to see and do - gardens, theatres, museums, churches, palazzos, shops, restaurants, bars and cafés - in the capital, so it's vital to locate yourself in the best spot to enjoy it all: Ursulino Valletta overlooking the ancient Grand Harbour. This discreet B&B is a wonderful discovery with just seven rooms and suites. Each is a tribute to clever contemporary design that intelligently uses the limited space and shapes of this age-old town house; beautiful tiling, block colours and eclectic artwork come together effortlessly. You'll be feeling like a local as you come and go to your stylish city pad whether staying for a short getaway or longer break. If you are planning to stay in Valletta for an extended time, book Ursulino's three-storey penthouse suite, which has the capacity to sleep four. It has a lounge, dining area, fully-equipped kitchenette and private roof terrace. The services of a private chef can be arranged - just ask Ursulino's concierge. Enquire about boat charters while you're at it or a massage on the panoramic roof terrace.

PRICE FROM:
€140

FEATURES:
Sea views

ACTIVITIES:
Shopping; Sightseeing; Walking

NEARBY:
Grand Harbour; Grand Master's Palace; St John's Co-Cathedral; National Museum of Acrhaeology; Parliament Building

GETTING THERE:
Malta International Airport

+356 2122 8024 ☎
condenastjohansens.com/ursulinovalletta 🌐
82A St Ursula Street, Valletta VLT 1234, Malta 🏠

Montenegro

Please go to condenastjohansens.com/montenegro

Marina magnificence at Porto Montenegro, page 96

Porto Montenegro

Year-round glamorous marina village on Montenegro's north-west coast

Popular with socialites, yachties and professionals escaping their daily routine, the pleasure playground of Porto Montenegro is a glitzy residential village-cum-five-star resort. Everything's here from boutiques, nightclubs, restaurants and bars to a sports club, yacht club, luxury residences and world-class hotel. For those seeking apartment-style freedom and comfort the one to three-bedroom Residences (housed within six residential/rental units) are ideal. Their beautiful Montenegrin architecture, contemporary trappings and local character have you feeling at home within an instant. Each one stands at the water's edge and faces beautiful sea or mountain views from private balconies. Residences within the Ksenija unit are the most sought-after for their prime position close to the finely manicured communal spaces, restaurants, cafés and shops. Plus, there are those incredible vistas of Tivat Riviera. However, Porto Montenegro isn't short of magnificent scenery. The marina, flanked by mountains, is a sight to behold and is often the epicentre of regattas, special events and sailing lessons run by The Porto Montenegro Yacht Club (PMYC) that also has a 64-metre infinity pool, tennis courts, gym and a yoga studio. Additional facilities such as a spa, gourmet restaurant, café and bar are also available at Porto Montenegro's 86-room Regent Hotel.

PRICE FROM:
€180 (room only, excluding €1 tax per person per day)

FEATURES:
Gym; Pool; Restaurant; Sea views; Spa

ACTIVITIES:
Walking; Water sports

NEARBY:
Kotor old town; Perast; Sveti Stefan; Budva old town

GETTING THERE:
Tivat Airport; Dubrovnik Airport, Croatia; Podgorica Airport

+382 32 661 037 ☎
condenastjohansens.com/portomontenegro 🌐
Adriatic Marinas D.O.O., Obala bb, 85320 Tivat, Bay of Kotor, 🏠
Montenegro

Morocco

Please go to condenastjohansens.com/morocco

Shady courtyard relief at El Fenn, page 100

Paradis Plage Surf, Yoga & Spa Resort

Morocco's one and only surf, yoga and spa resort

The first of its kind in Morocco, Paradis Plage Surf, Yoga & Spa Resort delivers exactly what its name promises: a surfer's paradise, yoga lover's retreat and spa enthusiast's sanctuary. The Atlantic Coast setting, just north of Agadir, couldn't be more tranquil and the resort's relaxed luxury, chic boho style and home comforts (choose from junior suites to a three-bedroom villa) enhance the unpretentious vibe. Paradis Plage is moments from the surfer haven of Taghazout village, which means it's in prime position for enjoying the long right hand point breaks. And The Surf House provides all your surfing needs - paddle boarding too - from the latest kit to personal training with one of Morocco's finest surfers, Tarik Wahbi. A beach-side bar and outdoor cinema screen are also located here. Balancing, stretching and focusing of the yoga variety take place at the Paradise Yoga Shala on the beach where from sunrise to sunset daily classes take place. Private lessons and specialised courses can be arranged with resident yogi Karim Fadali or a visiting master. Then there's Paradise Spa & Wellness, a truly Moroccan experience using local products (argan oil, Taliouine saffron, ghassoul) and hammam therapies. Philosophy, The 27 and The Ocean restaurants also celebrate Morocco's riches with local organic produce and fresh fish. Don't miss: beach-side meals at Chiringuito.

PRICE FROM:
€105

FEATURES:
Beach access; Family friendly; Pool; Sea views; Spa

ACTIVITIES:
Golf; Water sports

NEARBY:
Taghazout; Souk El Had; The waterfalls of Immouzer Ida Outanane; Mirleft; Imessouane

GETTING THERE:
Agadir–Al Massira Airport

+212 528200382 ☎
condenastjohansens.com/paradisplage 🌐
Km 26 route d'Essaouira, Imi Ouaddar, Agadir, Agadir-Ida Ou
Tanane Province, Morocco

L'Amandier

Where serenity meets adventure in the High Atlas Mountains

PRICE FROM:
€270

FEATURES:
Family friendly; Pool; Restaurant

ACTIVITIES:
Horse riding; Tennis; Walking

NEARBY:
Marrakech; Atlas Mountains; Asni; Terres D'Amanar Accro Park;
Toubkal mountain peak

GETTING THERE:
Marrakech Railway Station; Marrakech Menara Airport

☎ +44 (0) 207 754 5563
🌐 condenastjohansens.com/lamandier
🏠 L'Amandier Plateau, Ouirgane Valley, Near Marrakech,
Morocco

It seems that where brothers Anwar and Riaz Harland-Khan go, others follow. Namely, Ouirgane Valley in the High Atlas Mountains, just an hour south of Marrakech. A special location they came upon in 2002, this is now a bourgeoning tourist destination for its proximity to Marrakech, red earth landscape, pine forests and dramatic Atlas peaks (also home to Sir Richard Branson's Moroccan retreat). The brothers chose this spectacular spot for their six-room, luxury boutique hotel and villa collection, L'Amandier. Where scrubland once ran wild, beautifully manicured gardens now bloom. Previously barren earth is now dotted with cubist, designer structures. This sensitive man-made wonder is immediately surrounded by olive and citrus groves, which further enhance the incredible scene. Inside, interior guru Michael Kopinski's modern Moroccan design draws upon local inspiration by fusing European and Moroccan design. Traditional, authentic craftsmanship and materials are exhibited in the zellige tile work and bejemat flooring. Open fireplaces add a homely touch. Each of these elements is found in the lounge/bar, which opens out to the terrace, infinity pool and Atlas Mountains beyond. This is where guests gather for cocktails, teas and local delicacies to gain energy for the next day's activities such as trekking, cycling and horse riding over this fascinating, unique terrain.

El Fenn

Marrakech at its most colourful, artistic and indulgent

Inner courtyards, jewel colours, intricate lanterns, antique wooden carvings... El Fenn is a Moroccan gem in a peaceful pocket of Marrakech. A traditional riad reborn by Vanessa Branson (art enthusiast, eco-warrior and Richard's sister) and Howell James (PR guru and political advisor), this 29-room sanctum is a blend of Moorish architecture and innovative artistry. Every corner is ablaze with vibrant oranges, pinks and reds with airy courtyards lined by trees and hallways dressed in Fred Pollock prints and Guy Tillim portraits. El Fenn is truly the king of kick-back cool. Each guest room and suite has individual luxuries: a hot pink tadelakt bathroom, private terrace, hand-stitched camel leather floor and 23-carat gold leafing. You'll be so distracted by the details, you won't even notice the absence of phones and TVs. Days are spent discovering the city, lazing by the pool or taking a cookery class in El Fenn's kitchen. But it's the personal service that will have you returning. Breakfast can be served anywhere, food can be ordered any time and afternoon tea is at 3.30pm. Weather permitting, Moroccan and European meals can be taken on The Rooftop Terrace with far-reaching views of the Atlas Mountains. Or there's El Fenn's shop/bar/restaurant where not only can you eat and drink but listen to DJs and pianists on the weekend, as well as peruse the clothes, accessories and homeware on sale.

PRICE FROM:
€200

FEATURES:
Pool; Restaurant; Spa

ACTIVITIES:
Horse riding; Sightseeing; Walking

NEARBY:
Djemaa El Fna square; Bab El Ksour gate; Guéliz; Ben Youssef Medersa Koranic college; The Jewish quarter

GETTING THERE:
Marrakech Railway Station; Marrakech Menara Airport

+212 524 44 1210 ☎
condenastjohansens.com/elfenn 🌐
Derb Moullay Abdullah Ben Hezzian, Bab el Ksour, Medina, ✉
Marrakech, Morocco

Portugal

Please go to condenastjohansens.com/portugal

Tivoli Lisboa's poolside sanctuary, page 115

Bela Vista Hotel & Spa

A kaleidoscopic vision of colour and shapes in Portugal's Algarve

Bright, bold, fun and clever, Bela Vista Hotel & Spa is a funky little number set apart from the Algarve's golf buggy brigade. Beside Portimão's golden-sand Praia da Rocha, this estate has been owned by the same family since the 19th century and run as a hotel since the 1930s. From the "smoothie of the day" to fresh cookies at turndown, it's cute little touches (always presented with an avant-garde spirit) such as these that you remember long after your stay. Interiors are eclectic and somewhat eccentric; brilliantly flamboyant with clashing primary colours and patterns that somehow all come together to work in refreshing harmony. Check out the Character Rooms and Junior Suites whose explosions of colour and designer mash-ups include intricate mosaic bathrooms, stained-glass windows and quirky nods to Portuguese heritage such as the Azulejos (rustic ceramic tiles). A spectacle of aquamarine and serene greens, Bela Vista's L'Occitane Spa extends the hospitality hug with a menu of luscious treatments. But there's always hanging out by the beach-viewing pool or on the sweeping beach (reached by private walkway) to keep you in a permanent state of Zen. Worth a special mention: the Bela Vista staff. Whether serving breakfast, coffees or dinner in the fabulous Vista Restaurante, they are always super-attentive.

PRICE FROM:
€200

FEATURES:
Beach access; Pool; Restaurant; Sea views; Spa

ACTIVITIES:
Fishing; Golf; Water sports

NEARBY:
Shopping in Portimão; Vilamoura Golf Course; Royal Course at Vale de Lobo; Silves; Algarve international race track

GETTING THERE:
Faro Airport; Lisbon Airport

+351 282 460 280 ☎
condenastjohansens.com/hotelbelavista 🌐
Avenida Tomás Cabreira, Praia da Rocha, 8500-802 Portimão, ✉
Algarve, Portugal

Monte Rei Golf & Country Club

Golfy pleasures, class and sophistication in the Algarve

PRICE FROM:
€204

FEATURES:
Family friendly; Gym; Pool; Restaurant

ACTIVITIES:
Golf; Tennis; Walking

NEARBY:
Tavira; Vila Real de Santo António; River Guadiana; Ayamonte, Spain; Seville, Spain

GETTING THERE:
Faro Airport; Seville Airport, Spain

☎ +351 281 950 950
🌐 condenastjohansens.com/monterei
🏠 Sitio do Pocinho, Sesmarias, 8901-907 Vila Nova de Cacela, Algarve, Portugal

There are few places in Portugal's eastern Algarve quite as impressive as Monte Rei Golf & Country Club. A stunning resort, its fantastic Jack Nicklaus Signature golf course offers rack rates and lessons to any level of player. However, there's much more to Monte Rei than golf with many outdoor pursuits on the doorstep. At the heart of the villa complex (known as Miradouro Village), there's Veranda where you'll find the Veranda Restaurant, a bar, gym, tennis courts, pools and spa facilities. The Kid's Villa (an unsupervised playroom) is also just steps away. And a short distance from Miradouro Village is Monte Rei's Clubhouse (housing Vistas Restaurant and Grill Restaurant), Golf Academy and golf course. After a long day on the challenging stadium green, the fine-dining Vistas Restaurant provides a taste of gourmet heaven thanks to Executive Chef Albano Lourenço, former Chef of the Michelin-Starred Arcadas Da Capela. His dishes showcase all that's exceptional about Mediterranean cuisine. Each one, two and three-bedroom classically-styled villa, which has access to a communal pool at Veranda, is complete with a fully-equipped kitchen and spacious bathroom. Offering a little more space are detached three and four-bedroom villas featuring their own private gardens and pools. Each villa benefits from a daily cleaning service and turndown, and has a flatscreen TV, DVD player and free WiFi.

Tivoli Marina Vilamoura

The Algarve at its glitzy, swanky best

As well as being home to some of the world's most beautiful beaches, the Algarve is a magnet for golfers, spa lovers and foodies. And this is most certainly the case at the resort town of Vilamoura known for its nightlife and bars, a short drive west of Faro. Overlooking the yacht-rich marina, Tivoli Marina Vilamoura is right in the heart of town delivering glamour by the bucket-load. A lesson in contemporary cool with minimalist décor, retro-chic furniture and pops of colour, all the 383 rooms have a sink-into bed, rain shower and high-tech touches aplenty. Activities of the lively variety include water sports, football, tennis and golf (a fully staffed Golf Desk helps with bookings at the 31 nearby courses). Lazier options include lounging by the shapely pool, on the beach (powder-soft sand) or at the sublime Angsana Spa by Banyan Tree. All the while, the children (aged two - 10) are occupied with excursions and activities organised by T/Kids. The siren call of Pepper's Steakhouse draws carnivores from across Vilamoura while the fresh Portuguese fare at Chili Restaurant and the new, relaxed Oregano Restaurant vie for your stomach's attention. When you want to up the glamour ante even higher, head to Side Bar for cocktails overlooking the marina or the hot - summer-only - nightspot, Purobeach Vilamoura, set beside the sea with restaurant, bar and massage area on the beach.

PRICE FROM:
€150

FEATURES:
Family friendly; Pool; Restaurant; Sea views; Spa

ACTIVITIES:
Fishing; Golf; Water sports

NEARBY:
Falésia beach; Loulé market; Faro shopping; Historic Silves; Almancil

GETTING THERE:
Faro Airport

+351 218 507 708 ☎
condenastjohansens.com/tivolimarina 🌐
Marina de Vilamoura, 8125-901 Vilamoura, Algarve, Portugal 🏨

Casa Hintze Ribeiro

Smart, designer base for exploring all the Azores has to offer

PRICE FROM:
€120

FEATURES:
Family friendly; Gym; Pool

ACTIVITIES:
Shopping; Sightseeing; Walking

NEARBY:
Lagoa das Sete Cidades; Furnas; Terra Nostra Botanical Garden;
Lagoa do Fogo; Caldeira Velha waterfall

GETTING THERE:
João Paulo II Airport

The largest of the nine Azores islands, São Miguel embodies all the beauty and adventure of these mid-Atlantic outcrops. Culturally rich, full of natural treasures and artistic heritage, there's so much to see on and around this volcanic isle. And there's nowhere more central to discover it all than Casa Hintze Ribeiro. In the heart of Ponta Delgada's capital, this boutique gem is surrounded by restaurants, shops and historic sites. It was named after Ernesto Hintze Ribeiro - born on this street in 1849 - the man responsible for the politico-administrative autonomy the Azores enjoys today. The building itself is a converted warehouse with direct access to a high-end shopping gallery. Casa Hintze Ribeiro's public spaces, 22 suites and studios cleverly combine functionality and contemporary style due to internationally awarded interior designer Nini Andrade Silva. Nini's use of blues, beige and greens reflect the sea, land and forests of São Miguel to create a thoroughly modern, chic and welcoming vibe. This is evident from the breakfast room where cosy sofas tempt you to kick back, to each of the apartments. All apartments have kitchenettes. Some have living rooms with sofa beds (the biggest can sleep two adults and two children). Some have terraces where you can admire the city views below and Atlantic beyond. More of these panoramas are seen from the pool on the second-floor terrace.

☎ +351 296 302 160
🌐 condenastjohansens.com/casahintzeribeiro
🏠 Rua Hintze Ribeiro 62, 9500-049 Ponta Delgada, São Miguel
Island, Azores, Portugal

Terra Nostra Garden Hotel

An untapped natural wonder in Portugal's Azores

Emerging as a destination du jour, the mid-Atlantic's secret is now out: the Azores Islands. Formed where three tectonic plates collide, these nine volcanic isles are a beguiling landscape of spiny ridges covered by bright green farmland, huge craters of turquoise water and enormous rock formations under the ocean. On the archipelago's largest island of São Miguel, the thermal spring epicentre of Furnas Valley (a dormant volcanic crater) is where Terra Nostra Garden Hotel is located. Providing upscale comfort and all the trappings of a top-class hotel, this art-deco charmer is packed with architectural vestiges from its origins as a 1930s' retreat including geometric iron balconies all around the curved golden façade. Inside, each soothing suite is dressed with botanical prints and dark furnishings, while Terra Nostra Restaurant serves up traditional dishes of cozido das Furnas stew, slow cooked underground by volcanic steam. Spa treatments are available in the Wellness Place and a heated indoor pool, reading room and games room are also all on-site. But the most popular attraction of them all, and in fact, on the entire island, is the adjacent Terra Nostra Botanical Garden. A 200-year-old park (guests have free access) with geothermal lake and pool, this is an ecological wonderland of flora and fauna alongside serpentine paths and hidden mystical grottos.

PRICE FROM:
€125

FEATURES:
Family friendly; Pool; Restaurant; Spa; Wheelchair access

ACTIVITIES:
Cycling; Horse riding; Walking

NEARBY:
Terra Nostra Botanical Garden; Tea plantations of Porto Formoso and Gorreana; Lagoa das Furnas (Furnas Lake); Caldeiras das Furnas (Furnas hot springs); Ribeira Quente beach

GETTING THERE:
João Paulo II Airport

+351 296 549 090 ☎
condenastjohansens.com/terranostra 🌐
Rua Padre José Jacinto Botelho 5, 9675-061 Furnas, São Miguel Island, Azores, Portugal

The Albatroz Hotel

Former seaside royal retreat now boutique retreat for all in Cascais

PRICE FROM:
€150

FEATURES:
Beach access; Family friendly; Pool; Restaurant; Sea views

ACTIVITIES:
Golf; Sightseeing; Water sports

NEARBY:
Cascais town centre; Estoril; Sintra; Lisbon

GETTING THERE:
Cascais Railway Station; Lisbon Airport

☎ +351 21 484 73 80
🌐 condenastjohansens.com/albatroz
🏠 Rua Frederico Arouca 100, 2750-353 Cascais, Lisbon & Tagus Valley, Portugal

Like a vessel on the sea, The Albatroz Hotel beside the bay of Cascais rises majestically from a promontory overlooking the azure blue water. Just 30 minutes from Lisbon, the family-run Albatroz is coastal living at its glamorous best. Elegant and relaxed, guests typically return time and again and often strike up longstanding relationships with the owners and staff. The tan-limbed set head for the sun terrace with its 180-degree views of the sea while water babies hone their swimming techniques in the sea-facing pool, admiring the view as they glide. When thirst kicks in, there's the sea-front bar serving fruity cocktails and local gourmet snacks, and The Albatroz restaurant to satisfy the gourmand. Carefully designed to maximise the stunning vista, the dining room is a Mediterranean-inspired affair dominated by fabulously fresh fish and seafood with a Portuguese twist. After dinner, nothing beats watching the twinkling lights of the Estoril coast over a glass of local Port. If feeling a little curious about the local scene, a saunter into Cascais (just a two-minute stroll away) might be more the ticket. At the end of a day, comfort awaits in your room, which is guaranteed to differ from your neighbour next door; all 44 have been thoughtfully and individually decorated. And their views, well, let's just say they're full of watery wonder.

Farol Hotel

Unique hotel, unique location, unique Cascais find

The preferred Portuguese coastal town of the smart and savvy, Cascais is a cosmopolitan, affluent suburb beside the Atlantic Ocean just half an hour west of Lisbon. Where Portugal's 19th and 20th-century royal family once holidayed, both Portuguese and international visitors now flock, attracted to its yacht scene and outdoor lifestyle with jogging and running paths, water sports, golf, quaint sandy beaches, historic centre's cobblestoned streets and Atlantic views. Staggering panoramas are just one of Farol Hotel's outstanding facets from its elevated position on the rocky Cascais cliffs. It's also a design masterpiece transformed from 19th-century mansion house to slick, extremely cool hotel. Thanks to the creative talents of local and world-renowned fashion designers, the predominantly black and white interior makes the displays of modern art pop and views from the picture windows sing. There are 33 rooms and suites in total including the spectacular Penthouse located a short drive away equipped with a gym, spa, private chef and 24-hour butler service. Back at the hotel, the two restaurants and two bar areas serve Mediterranean fusion cuisine, sushi and cocktails while lounge tunes set a chilled vibe. There's also outdoor space for drinking and socialising, a massage service, opportunities to take part in yoga lessons, plus designated areas for corporate events and fairy-tale weddings.

PRICE FROM:
€300

FEATURES:
Pet friendly; Pool; Restaurant; Sea views

ACTIVITIES:
Cycling; Golf; Sightseeing

NEARBY:
Paula Rego Museum; Marechal Carmona Park; Guincho beach; Cascais Marina; Cascais historic city centre

GETTING THERE:
Cascais Railway Station; Lisbon Airport

+351 21 482 34 90 ☎
condenastjohansens.com/farolhotel 🌐
Avenida Rei Humberto II de Italia 7, 2750-800 Cascais, Lisbon 🏠
& Tagus Valley, Portugal

Palácio Estoril, Hotel, Golf & Spa

Estoril's glamourpuss whose recent facelift has worked wonders

PRICE FROM:
€320

FEATURES:
Family friendly; Pool; Restaurant; Sea views; Spa

ACTIVITIES:
Cycling; Golf; Water sports

NEARBY:
Cascais; Sintra; Lisbon; Obidos; Guincho beach and restaurants

GETTING THERE:
Lisbon Airport

☎ +351 21 464 80 00
🌐 condenastjohansens.com/estoril
🏠 Rua Particular, 2769-504 Estoril, Lisbon & Tagus Valley, Portugal

Behind the grand white façade of this fabulous 1930s' palace are romantic stories of royalty in exile, espionage and none other than James Bond himself. During World War II, European heads of state flocked to neutral Portugal and the elegant Palácio Estoril was their HQ. Just 20 minutes from Lisbon, these days Palácio Estoril, Hotel, Golf & Spa combines its old world charm with 21st-century touches including a Banyan Tree spa. Rooms and suites are classically styled, supremely comfortable and many have views of the stunning Estoril coast located a minute away. Golfers love it here too. Spoiled for choice, the internationally renowned Estoril Golf, one of the oldest and smartest in Portugal, is right on the doorstep and there are six more within putting distance. But if you simply wish to relax and soak up the sun, head to Palácio Estoril's alluring pool next to the Bougainvillea Terrace restaurant, which also overlooks the verdant garden. The Four Seasons Grill gives a sophisticated, modern take on traditional Portuguese and international cuisines and should you feel like exploring the local scene it's lined with top quality bars and cafés representing every corner of the globe. It's easy to see why Estoril is known as the Coast of Kings. Worth noting: this is a fantastic, impressive choice for weddings and functions.

Heritage Avenida Liberdade Hotel

Lisbon palace-turned-refined 21st-century town house accommodation

You'll find this boutique gem in the heart of Lisbon, the buzzing capital packed with great restaurants and museums. Heritage Avenida Liberdade Hotel is the perfect base from which to explore this historic hotspot. Step inside through the antique wooden door and you'll find a smart, modern town house hidden behind the elegant 18th-century façade. Painstakingly restored with modern touches, this is a smart and contemporary, yet distinctly Portuguese idyll located directly on the famous Avenida da Liberdade dotted with sculptures. The hotel couldn't be more central. In fact, there's so much to do and see from here, it's wise to sit down with a member of staff for some insider knowledge to help you choose between all the city's museums, shops and tourist sites. But come the evening and you'll not want to leave the comfortable confines (and surprisingly good value) of Heritage Avenida Liberdade Hotel whose antique wooden tea station and attentive, discreet staff are on hand to brew up the perfect cup. Or you might prefer to prop up against the bar before exploring the fantastic range of Lisbon's restaurants right on your doorstep.

PRICE FROM:
€148

FEATURES:
Pool; Wheelchair access

ACTIVITIES:
Golf; Shopping; Sightseeing

NEARBY:
Avenida da Liberdade; Restauradores Square and tram to Bairro Alto; Alfama

GETTING THERE:
Lisbon Airport

+351 213 404 040 ☎
condenastjohansens.com/avliberdade 🌐
Avenida da Liberdade 28, 1250-145 Lisbon, Lisbon & Tagus 🏠
Valley, Portugal

Hotel Britania

Fabulous art-deco blast from the past in the heart of Lisbon

PRICE FROM:
€131

ACTIVITIES:
Shopping; Sightseeing; Walking

NEARBY:
Avenida da Liberdade; Restauradores Square and tram to Bairro Alto; Alfama

GETTING THERE:
Lisbon Airport

☎ +351 21 31 55 016
🌐 condenastjohansens.com/britania
🏠 Rua Rodrigues Sampaio 17, 1150-278 Lisbon, Lisbon & Tagus Valley, Portugal

Tucked away on a quiet Lisbon street, yet moments from the buzz of Avenida da Liberdade, is the art-deco brilliance of Hotel Britania. It's a museum piece and the only art-deco hotel left standing in the city. Lovingly and carefully restored to all its 1940s' glory, the marble sparkles in the lobby and the elegant, warm tones of the spacious bedrooms hark back to yesteryear. There are 32 rooms and one junior suite in total, spread across six floors; each one a nest of quietude (thank you double glazing). Hotel Britania is traditional, old fashioned and conservative in all the most charming of ways. Service is discreet and excellent. By day, Hotel Britania's location is hard to beat with Avenida da Liberdade - the city's main boulevard featuring world-class shopping and art galleries - and funicular railways waiting to whisk you to Lisbon's prettiest gardens and town squares on your doorstep. By night, Hotel Britania really comes into its own with guests gathering at the bar and lounge for a cocktail or two before heading out to Lisbon's hotspots. If you're unsure where to dine or explore, you can always call upon the tour and travel desk, concierge and multi-lingual staff to help you make the most of your time in this great city.

Hotel PortoBay Liberdade

The new kid on Lisbon's block with smart style and classic grace

Modern and classic. Historic and high-spec. Relaxed and refined. Hotel PortoBay Liberdade is a wonderful mix of contradictions. But above all else, it's a slick urban space on Lisbon's desirable Avenida da Liberdade. From the outside, this city central sanctuary hides behind a classic Portuguese façade amidst dazzling designer store fronts. Inside, the décor is as stylish as the avenue itself. Rooms and suites are fashioned in clean lines and soothing rustic hues. Most have a veranda bringing that wonderful natural light on in and each one has a fantastically comfortable bed (300-thread count Egyptian cotton sheets). Mirrored TVs come as standard too. It's also very techy in the gym, meeting rooms and spa. The Spa at PortoBay Liberdade not only has a heated indoor pool with jets, a steam room and sauna but an accompanying fitness centre fitted with Technogy equipment. But the heartbeat of the hotel is Deck7 rooftop bar and lounge. It's the vistas of the city from its comfy sofas and bubbling Jacuzzi that will have you lounging here for hours before dining at Bistrô4 - yet another highlight. Bistrô4's haute French fare prepared from market produce is attracting foodies' attention in addition to the choice of 300 beverages at Aviator6 that's fast becoming the stylish space to see and be seen in.

PRICE FROM:
€157

FEATURES:
Gym; Pool; Restaurant; Spa; Wheelchair access

ACTIVITIES:
Shopping; Sightseeing; Walking

NEARBY:
Alfama; Belém; Cascais

GETTING THERE:
Lisbon Airport

+351 210 051 700 ☎
condenastjohansens.com/portobayliberdade 🌐
Rua Rosa Araújo 8, 1250-195 Lisbon, Lisbon & Tagus Valley, Portugal

Pousada de Lisboa, Praça do Comércio

A breath of fresh air in Lisbon's historic, central square

PRICE FROM:
€235

FEATURES:
Gym; Restaurant; Spa; Wheelchair access

ACTIVITIES:
Shopping; Sightseeing

NEARBY:
Sintra; Old districts of Lisbon; Cascais; Estoril

GETTING THERE:
Lisbon Airport

Inhabiting one of the palatial Pombaline buildings in Lisbon's Praça do Comércio (Commerce Square), Pousada de Lisboa is a great example of 18th-century Portuguese architecture. After the city's devastating 1755 earthquake, the Marquês de Pombal initiated the restoration of the city, including this building. And just recently, this magnificent timepiece has been transformed into a knockout high-end hotel ideal for a special city break of days filled with shopping and culture. The position in central Lisbon, opposite the River Tagus, couldn't be better but perhaps one of its most impressive assets is the salon now reinstated to its former glory with burnished wood floor, delicate stucco ceiling and low hanging chandelier. However, a modern touch is never far away with contemporary art on the walls, fashionable colour schemes and art-deco-inspired furniture beside Moorish elements. Rooms and suites have retained their lofty ceilings and relief plasterwork; some view directly across to the river while others look down to the hustle and bustle of Lisbon's streets. Vestiges of the Pousada's past are also present in the Portuguese restaurant where vaulted ceilings and colourful orbs of hand-blown glass add glamour to the gastronomic proceedings.

☎ +351 218 442 001
🌐 condenastjohansens.com/pousadalisboa
🏠 Praça do Comércio 31-34, 1100-148 Lisbon, Lisbon & Tagus Valley, Portugal

Santiago de Alfama Hotel

Reincarnated 15th-century palace in Lisbon's Alfama

The finest city hotels have the finest locations. This is certainly the case for Santiago de Alfama Hotel betwixt Lisbon's medieval São Jorge Castle and Miradouro de Santa Luzia viewpoint. Sitting pretty in the city's ancient Alfama district, this 19-room urban retreat is surrounded by charming, narrow cobbled streets and bustling street markets, with a wealth of theatres and museums on its doorstep. A former royal palace, Santiago de Alfama now comprises six suites and 13 bedrooms set around an inner courtyard. Shiny hardwood flooring, plump beds, elegant neutral colour schemes and traditional wood-panelled ceilings keep matters fresh and stylish. The pure white bathrooms with glossy metro tiles are pristine and clinical in the most designer-cool way. For a special occasion, opt for the fourth-floor Santiago Suite with triple aspect views over to the River Tagus and book the private terrace for a special four-course meal accompanied by a bottle of Champers. A cheeky visit to The Beauty Bar will have you feeling a million dollars. Breakfasts of smoked salmon bagels with scrambled eggs and sweet syrupy pancakes are served in Café Audrey (on its terrace, weather permitting) before afternoon tea, cocktails and seasonally-led Portuguese meals in Restaurante a Fábrica and Manny's Bar.

PRICE FROM:
€82.50 (per person)

FEATURES:
Restaurant; Wheelchair access

ACTIVITIES:
Shopping; Sightseeing; Walking

NEARBY:
Chiado; Belém; Cascais; Sintra; São Jorge Castle; Santa Justa Lift

GETTING THERE:
Santa Apolónia Railway Station; Lisbon Airport

+351 21 394 1616 ☎
condenastjohansens.com/santiagodealfama 🌐
Rua de Santiago 10-14, 1100-494 Lisbon, Lisbon & Tagus Valley, Portugal

Tivoli Lisboa

A Lisbon city centre favourite with the worldly, discerning set

PRICE FROM:
€150

FEATURES:
Family friendly; Gym; Pool; Restaurant; Wheelchair access

ACTIVITIES:
Shopping; Sightseeing

NEARBY:
Avenida da Liberdade; Restauradores Square and tram to Bairro Alto; Alfama; Chiado

GETTING THERE:
Lisbon Airport

Tivoli Lisboa is everything a city centre hotel should be: perfectly located, full of local character and superbly equipped. In short, it's an attraction in itself. Many stay here for the convenient location on the famous Avenida da Liberdade, great for upscale shopping and exploring the neighbourhoods of Bairro Alto and Chiado. Others are attracted to the old world glamour of the French Brasserie Flo Lisboa, Portuguese Terraço Restaurant and chilled Tivoli Caffe Lisboa. Corporate bigwigs love the extensive business facilities, which include 18 banqueting rooms and a fully-equipped, stand-alone conference centre. No matter the reason for staying at Tivoli Lisboa, everyone's guaranteed a comfortable stay whether sleeping in a Classic Room or extra-ordinary Presidential Suite. Unusual for a city hotel, Tivoli Lisboa has gardens and an outdoor swimming pool. But it's the rooftop Sky Bar with panoramic vistas of the city's rooftops that appeals most to the trendsetting Lisboans and visitors alike who gather up here for evening cocktails before a night on the town. However, before you do anything, it's well worth enquiring about the variety of exclusive T/ Experiences. These range from the Romantic Experience whereby rose petals are strewn across your bed to Challenging Experiences on board a luxury yacht or helicopter along/above the Lisbon coastline.

☎ +351 218 507 708
🌐 condenastjohansens.com/tivolilisboa
🏠 Avenida da Liberdade 185, 1269-050 Lisbon, Lisbon & Tagus Valley, Portugal

Tivoli Palácio de Seteais

A spectacle of palatial greatness on Sintra's hillside

The mad magnificence of the 18th-century Tivoli Palácio de Seteais never ceases to impress. It has it all: romance, majesty and phenomenal scenery. Set on the hillside, the UNESCO town of Sintra is a mere 10-minute walk away. Every which way you turn, there's a fairy-tale image of Moorish architecture and landscaped artistry. And the palace itself is the embodiment of Prince Charming's five-star residence. A step inside and you're transported to a bygone age of regal grandeur showcasing 18th-century fashions. Gilt-edged and intricate wooden inlaid furnishings, frescoed walls and towering ceilings welcome you on in. However, everything feels new and fresh. This is certainly the case in the guest rooms from the Superior Twin Rooms to the extravagant Diplomatic Suite. Period style dominates while the mod-cons (LCD TVs, air con) update. Meanwhile, it's quality ingredients and white glove service that dominate the proceedings at Seteais Restaurant popular with locals, hotel guests and visitors from Lisbon alike. Tuneful tinkles from a grand piano and stunning garden views somehow further enhance the Portuguese and international fare. Outside, in addition to the pretty gardens and their well-tended mazes, a large swimming pool and sleek decking area host sun-seekers, plus there's a tennis court. Travel a little further afield and 19 golf courses are at your disposal.

PRICE FROM:
€270

FEATURES:
Family friendly; Pool; Restaurant

ACTIVITIES:
Horse riding; Sightseeing; Walking

NEARBY:
Pena Palace; Sintra; Estoril; Cascais; Lisbon

GETTING THERE:
Lisbon Airport

+351 218 507 708 ☎
condenastjohansens.com/palaciodeseteais 🌐
Rua Barbosa du Bocage 10, Seteais, 2710 Sintra, Lisbon & 🏠
Tagus Valley, Portugal

The Cliff Bay Hotel

Refined Madeira resort with all the bells and whistles

PRICE FROM:
€160

FEATURES:
Beach access; Gym; Michelin Starred restaurant; Sea views; Spa

ACTIVITIES:
Golf; Tennis; Water sports

NEARBY:
Funchal town centre; Laurisilva of Madeira - UNESCO World Heritage Centre

GETTING THERE:
Madeira Airport

There are many reasons that make this cliff-side resort extra special. Those endless views of the Atlantic Ocean for one. Its glorious gardens for another. And Il Gallo d'Oro, Madeira's one and only Michelin Starred restaurant. They're all here at The Cliff Bay Hotel, a wonderfully romantic and superbly equipped escape. Lush gardens and palm trees encase the 202 guest rooms and suites, three restaurants, two bars, spa and two pools (one is child friendly). The sea views simply add to the majesty of it all. The Cliff Bay Hotel's position atop a natural promontory provides some of the finest views the island has to offer. Plus, the Atlantic's warm, clear waters are just a stroll down a private jetty from where you can swim, dive and snorkel. The Cliff Bay is also a great base for exploring nearby Funchal whose bustling streets will have you occupied for hours. But there's so much to keep you rooted to the resort spot from sunrise to sunset such as the fantastic spa. An eight treatment room centre of well-being, it offers every top-to-toe treatment known to man. There's even an exclusive SPA Suite for two with private Jacuzzi. Then there are the three restaurants: the international à la carte Rose Garden; the poolside Blue Lagoon; and Michelin Starred Il Gallo d'Oro where Mediterranean cuisine meets Iberian produce. Must try: afternoon tea at Le Cliff Bar & Bistro for the finest scones you're ever likely to taste!

☎ +351 291 707 700
🌐 condenastjohansens.com/thecliffbay
🏠 Estrada Monumental 147, 9004-532 Funchal, Madeira, Portugal

Casa da Calçada

Tucked away private treasure in North Portugal's Amarante

A nirvana for avid foodies and Port-loving oenophiles, Casa da Calçada, in the historical city centre of Amarante, is in prime position for enjoying all the spoils of North Portugal's rich land. Sandwiched between Porto and the Douro Valley, close to the UNESCO city centre of Guimarães and set beside the River Tâmega, this is the spine-tingling beauty spot for the 16th-century Casa da Calçada palace. Once the meeting place for politicians and the influential, the Casa was reborn in 2001 as a top-class hotel with Michelin Starred restaurant and a spa room with outdoor adventure activities on its doorstep. Romantic, comfortable and peaceful, not one room or suite is the same but all reflect the hotel's cosy, classic style with palettes of rich burgundys and browns, hanging portraits and ambient lighting. Some have a terrace looking out to the river and St Goncalo's Monastery. Casa da Calçada's recently revamped Largo do Paço restaurant is buzzing with business types meeting, gastronomes salivating and wine aficionados supping in glee. Outside, golfers are swinging with precision on the 18-hole Amarante Golf Course, wine lovers are admiring the hotel's vinho verde Wine Yard and the more leisurely are unwinding in the shady garden or by the pool (open in the summer). Before you book: visit Casa da Calçada's website and chat live with a member of staff about your reservation.

PRICE FROM:
€125

FEATURES:
Michelin Starred restaurant; Pool; Wheelchair access

ACTIVITIES:
Golf; Sightseeing; Walking

NEARBY:
UNESCO historic city of Porto; UNESCO historic city of Guimarães; Douro Valley and Port wineries; Amadeo Souza - Cardoso's Museum; Amarante Golf Course

GETTING THERE:
Porto - Francisco Sá Carneiro Airport

+351 255 410 830 ☎
condenastjohansens.com/casadacalcada 🌐
Largo do Paço 6, 4600-017 Amarante, Porto & Northern Portugal, Portugal 🏠

Pousada Mosteiro de Guimarães

Monastic serenity meets modernistic sensibility in Santa Marinha

PRICE FROM:
€120

FEATURES:
Family friendly; Pet friendly; Pool; Restaurant; Wheelchair access

ACTIVITIES:
Golf; Sightseeing; Walking

NEARBY:
Ponte de Lima; Porto; Amarante; Braga; Gerês

GETTING THERE:
Porto - Francisco Sá Carneiro Airport

The restoration of this 12th-century monastery is so impressive you'd be forgiven for expecting monks from the order of Santo Agostinho to still be in residence. From the outside, there are few clues that belie this exceptional pousada, which remains a retreat for the soul in North Portugal's pretty Santa Marinha. As you saunter along the elegant, whitewashed corridors, passed arched cloisters and towering pillars around the central courtyard, a refined world unfolds before you filled with sink-into sofas, vast salons with vaulted wooden ceilings and cerulean blue Azulejos tiles (depicting scenes from Portuguese history). Pray for a stay in the Pousada's old building where lofty guest rooms have been fashioned from original monks' cells. Dark woods and rich brocades dominate these spaces, while suites feature pastel colours and chinoiserie. Outside, the chorus of birdsong breaks the silence in gardens of mature trees that include a 200-year-old eucalyptus and moss-covered steps leading to a pond where the monks once bathed. There is also a pool area here with breathtaking vistas of the city. In fact, Guimarães was the European Capital of Culture in 2012 and there's much to explore. But come evening you'll be wise to dine in Pousada de Guimarães' D. Mafalda restaurant whose traditional regional cuisine is as spectacular as the view of the UNESCO city it presides over.

☎ +351 253 511 249
🌐 condenastjohansens.com/guimaraes
🏠 Largo Domingos Leite de Castro, Lugar da Costa, 4810-011 Guimarães, Minho, Porto & Northern Portugal, Portugal

Vintage House Hotel

A Douro landmark embraced by the Valley's vineyards

Originally built for the Taylor family, of Taylor's Port fame, Vintage House Hotel is an icon beside the Douro River. Period vestiges and timeless nuances of this once 18th-century home and warehouse remain throughout the property that's now owned by the parent company of Taylor's Port. And a smart revamp has artfully injected a designer, fashionable flair. Public rooms' grand stone fireplaces, wooden beams and vaulted ceilings are now accompanied by dapper fabrics and unfussy lines that all-at-once give a nod to the past, whilst expressing a graceful, modern touch. The undulating vineyards outside are viewed from every balcony of the bedrooms and suites, which also feature bathrooms tiled with intricate, traditional Portuguese Azulejos. More of these hypnotic vistas are captured from The Rabelo Restaurant, the breakfast room (aptly known as the River Room) and the outdoor pool. The tennis courts and pretty gardens also make the most of the privileged location. Ask about river cruises and Vintage House Hotel's Wine Academy, which hosts wine courses, gourmet experiences and introductions to the history, production and flavours of Port. But if putting your feet up and taking in the scenery is all you can muster, drop by the Library Bar, find a deep leather Chesterfield and enjoy.

PRICE FROM:
€150

FEATURES:
Family friendly; Lake views; Pool; Restaurant; Wheelchair access

ACTIVITIES:
Sightseeing; Walking

NEARBY:
Peso da Régua; Mesão Frio; Vila Real; Chaves; Porto

GETTING THERE:
Porto - Francisco Sá Carneiro Airport

+351 254 730 230 ☎
condenastjohansens.com/vintagehouse 🌐
Rua António Manuel Saraiva, 5085-034 Pinhão, Douro, Porto 🏠
& Northern Portugal, Portugal

Vidago Palace

The high life in peaceful Vidago Park

PRICE FROM:
€300

FEATURES:
Family friendly; Gym; Pool; Restaurant; Spa

ACTIVITIES:
Golf; Horse riding; Walking

NEARBY:
Vila Real; Douro Valley; Guimarães; Braga; Porto

GETTING THERE:
Porto - Francisco Sá Carneiro Airport

The mammoth restoration to King Charles I's 100-year-old Vidago Palace is a testament to modern ingenuity. Thanks to the creative minds of interior architects Jose Pedro Lopes Vieira and Diogo Rosa Lã, and architect Alvaro Siza Vieira, every element of this historic site is a contemporary five-star experience. Die-hard romantics, wedding/party planners, spa lovers and golf mad sophisticates are all drawn to Vidago. They're attracted to its serene parkland setting, grand rooms, high-tech spa therapies and challenging course. Every detail in every corner is meticulously finished and sumptuously appointed. But it's possibly the reinvention of Vidago's spa that causes the most excitement, in no small part due to its futuristic, minimalistic design. Built upon an ancient thermal spa that predates the Romans, six natural springs feed this ultra-modern sanctuary. Meanwhile, the redesigned 18-hole championship golf course by Cameron & Powell incites some thrills for its par 72 course with golf academy, driving range, putting greens and informal Club House Bar & Restaurant. This is just one of the three culinary options, which include The Grand Ballroom's traditional Northern Portuguese (organic) fare and the light and airy Winter Garden where elaborate buffet breakfasts are taken.

☎ +351 276 990 920
🌐 condenastjohansens.com/vidago
🏠 Parque de Vidago, 5425-307 Vidago, Porto & Northern Portugal, Portugal

Spain

Please go to condenastjohansens.com/spain

Colonnades and sun rays at Barceló La Bobadilla, page 123

Barceló La Bobadilla

Whitewashed village-style resort in the pretty Granada Hills

PRICE FROM:
€210 (closed mid-November to mid-February)

FEATURES:
Family friendly; Gym; Pool; Restaurant; Spa

ACTIVITIES:
Cycling; Horse riding; Walking

NEARBY:
Oil tastings; Picasso Museum; Alhambra de Granada; Mezquita de Córdoba; Seville

GETTING THERE:
Granada Airport; Málaga Airport

A helicopter ride to the impressive Alhambra in Granada from the palatial Barceló La Bobadilla is just one reason to stay here. High in the Andalucían hills surrounded by an Edenic setting, this eco-conscious, elegant, Moorish-style retreat promises sun-drenched rooms, fabulous food and top-notch facilities. No two of the newly renovated guest rooms and suites are alike, however, all have gardens or balconies that provide extra space for families and private outdoor space for romancing couples. (Honeymooners should book a suite with private Jacuzzi.) Children are particularly well looked after in the Mini Club and there's a dedicated children's pool allowing parents to relax. This is easy at the terrace bar, on a Balinese four-poster bed by the pool or in the U-Spa offering a range of therapies from water to steam treatments. Come mealtime and four restaurants provide varied choice: delicious Spanish and regional cuisine at El Cortijo; light meals and snacks at La Plaza located in the courtyard opposite the chapel; and international and traditional flavours at the formal La Finca. Plus, the casual El Mirador open during the summer, overlooking the landscaped gardens and pools. Week-long gourmet cooking classes show you how to make any one of the dishes on the menus. Romantic bonus: La Bobadilla's private on-site chapel for tailor-made weddings and renewal vow ceremonies.

☎ +34 958 32 18 61
🌐 condenastjohansens.com/bobadilla
🏠 Finca La Bobadilla, Ctra Salinas - Villanueva de Tapia, (A-333) Km 65.5, 18300 Loja, Granada, Andalucía, Spain

Palacio de Úbeda

The embodiment of Andalucía's Renaissance brilliance

There are many reasons why Palacio de Úbeda is Jaén's only five-star hotel. Before you even enter, there's the remarkably maintained 16th-century façade, recognised as one of the finest examples of decorative Plateresque design (specific to this region of Spain). This is the UNESCO World Heritage Site of Úbeda after all, a town of unrivalled centuries-old architectural beauty. However, behind the Palacio's stone exterior, with coats of arms and heraldic symbols, there's a refreshingly light and contemporary hotel spread across three buildings. Clever lighting, ornamental mirrors and splashes of punchy colours propel this former palace into the 21st century while preserving the essence of Renaissance romance. And down below, in its ancient cellars, is a sophisticated spa with hydro-circuit comprising three pools, water fountains, power showers and a hammam. There's even a hairdressing service available, a small gym, rooftop terrace, outdoor pool and three restaurants on-site. Abside Restaurant is Palacio de Úbeda's private dining room for small dinner parties, while Alicún is the main haute cuisine restaurant inspired by flavours of the Med. For sundowners, snacks and tapas, guests head to the terrace at Palacio Gastrónomio with views of the skyline. Note to the newly engaged: the Palacio is attached to a 16th-century church and has a choice of four salons with space for 300.

PRICE FROM:
€250

FEATURES:
Family friendly; Gym; Pool; Restaurant

ACTIVITIES:
Fishing; Horse riding; Walking

NEARBY:
Baeza; Jaén; Cazorla; Granada; Sierra Nevada skiing

GETTING THERE:
Federico García Lorca Airport; Málaga Airport; Adolfo Suárez Madrid–Barajas Airport

+34 953 81 09 73/75 ☎
condenastjohansens.com/palaciodeubeda 🌐
Juan Pasquau 4, 23400 Úbeda, Jaén, Spain 🏠

La Torre del Visco

Natural riches and gourmet dishes in Spain's little-known northeast corner

PRICE FROM:
€195

FEATURES:
Helipad; Pet friendly; Pool; Restaurant

ACTIVITIES:
Cycling; Horse riding; Walking

NEARBY:
Matarranya; Valderrobres; Calaceite; Centre Picasso d'Orta; Parc Natural Els Ports

GETTING THERE:
Barcelona–El Prat Airport; Valencia Airport; Zaragoza Airport

☎ +34 978 76 90 15
🌐 condenastjohansens.com/torredelvisco
🏠 Partida Torre del Visco s/n, 44587 Fuentespalda, Teruel, Aragón, Spain

The Tuscan-like landscape of the Matarranya is an untapped scenic spot in Spain's northeastern corner. And just as Jemma and Piers fell in love with its isolation, romance and beauty over 20 years ago, guests to their 220-acre estate in the heart of it all find themselves falling head over heals too. This exceptionally pretty country retreat ticks all the boxes for rural perfection: green hills, crystal-clear river, rose gardens, olive grove, organic farm and picturesque medieval farmhouse. Inside, (with ever-burning log fires in winter) is a home full of heritage and character. Original artwork, rustic nuances and plush pastoral charm make each room all-at-once cosy and sophisticated. Then there's the long-standing team of staff on-hand to attend to your every need and organise the variety of courses held on-site (cooking, photography, art, bird-watching, astronomy...). Plus, an all-day chef's table offering the chance to meet the remarkable chefs who have placed La Torre on the gourmet map. The traditional Spanish cuisine served at La Torre del Visco celebrates the estate's organic produce and the open-access wine cellar bursts with local choices. La Torre del Visco's setting offers plenty of adventure from swimming under waterfalls and awesome mountain hikes to strolls around nearby medieval villages. Special note: the Starlight Foundation has certified this a prime stargazing spot.

Cas Gasi

Ibizan colour, sizzle and luxury

A former country house-turned-boutique hotel, Cas Gasi in Santa Gertrudis, Ibiza, is one of those up-your-sleeve places you save for the end of the summer (but tell very few about). It's low key loveliness nestled right in the thick of this beautiful island is totally discreet. Get off the beaten track, up into the hills and flop by the pool of this chilled escape to hear your body sing with relief and your skin glow a little more. Surrounded by pine forests, olive groves and organically-fed veggie patches with almond, fig and carob trees trickling down the hillside, Ibiza's Cas Gasi is bursting with all the best spoils of the Med. Nowhere is this more true than in the utterly exclusive restaurant where the ingredients are seasonal, packed with flavour and determined by produce grown at Cas Gasi's very own organic plot. The relaxed and at-home vibe is a favourite among celebrity guests - when not in Balearics' boltholes of their own, Jade Jagger and Kate Moss are huge fans of it here - and no wonder when the intimate 10 rooms and suites are this cosy and comfortable. Each one has its own character, unique décor in a rustic Spanish theme filled with cool terracotta-tiled flooring, striking fabrics and warming chintz-a-copia.

PRICE FROM:
€303.60

FEATURES:
Pet friendly; Pool; Restaurant

ACTIVITIES:
Cycling; Golf; Water sports

NEARBY:
Ibiza's main beaches; St Rafael; Santa Eulalia del Rio; San Antonio; Hippy market in San Carlos

GETTING THERE:
Ibiza Airport

+34 971 197 700 ☎
condenastjohansens.com/casgasi 🌐
Camino Viejo de Sant Mateu s/n, 07814 Santa Gertrudis, 🏠
Ibiza, Balearic Islands, Spain

Son Julia Country House Hotel

Understated elegance and refinement in Mallorca's undisturbed countryside

PRICE FROM:
€225

FEATURES:
Family friendly; Gym; Pool; Restaurant; Spa

ACTIVITIES:
Cycling; Golf; Tennis

NEARBY:
Palma de Mallorca; Es Trenc beach; Son Gual golf course; Maioris Golf Club

GETTING THERE:
Palma de Mallorca Airport

Mallorca's sheltered south-east corner of rural tranquillity is a far cry from Palma's buzzing capital. Immersed in unspoilt nature close to white sandy beaches, this is the idyllic spot the noble Julia family chose to build their home and estate upon. Today, their 15th-century finca is the height of modern sophistication; a boutique retreat with a spa and extensive grounds featuring a vineyard and 300-year-old Arabic-styled gardens. And the best part is, this pocket of peace is only 20 minutes from the beckoning nightlife and sites of the city. When the surrounding scenery is this pretty and the weather this sublime (300 days of sunshine!), you'll want to bask in its glory and Son Julia's many terraces, patios and two outdoor pools allow you to do just that. Some of the rooms and suites (all spacious with big flat-screen TVs) have balconies and terraces. The Superior Garden Rooms have their very own patch of private garden. But for something extra special book the Grand Suite for its romance and pure refinement. Refinement of the gastronomic kind is served at the poolside Son Julia Grill and in the beautifully vaulted Las Bovedas restaurant with views of the vineyard. Their Mediterranean fare is all about fresh, seasonal produce - some picked from Son Julia's fruit trees.

☎ +34 971 669 700
🌐 condenastjohansens.com/sonjulia
🏠 Ctra De S'Arenal a Llucmajor, 07620 Llucmajor, Mallorca, Balearic Islands, Spain

Portals Hills Boutique Hotel

Miami chic and Hollywood glitz in the Mallorcan hills

Bringing Miami-inspired glamour to the Mallorcan hills, the brand new Portals Hills Boutique Hotel is set to become one of the Med's hottest destinations. Perched above the buzzing Puerto Portals marina, this is a sultry, stylish pleasure zone for grown-ups dazzling from on high with its bright white, gilt-framed façade. Inside, the equally gleaming white lobby welcomes you to a world of futuristic art-deco design with a nod to Antoni Gaudí's distinctive shaping (check out the curved, trunk-like columns). From the lobby, a theatrical Hollywood staircase swoops down into La Cabana Poolbar & Lounge where custom-made furniture is embellished by gold and green accents. More rich, jewel colours feature within the cool, South Beach-styled suites and two Fendi-furnished penthouses. These penthouses are the ultimate designer dens, perfectly pitched with high-spec appliances; the two-bedroom Penthouse even has a private lift to a secluded roof terrace. The glamour isn't exclusively decorative at Portals Hills, it's also served on a plate in Collins Restaurant. Seasonal and organic whenever possible, dishes combine Mediterranean favourites with an international flavour paired with the largest and finest Spanish and worldwide wines and champagnes the island has to offer. Don't miss: drinks and music at Portals Hills' SUITE 32 nightclub.

PRICE FROM:
€275

FEATURES:
Pool; Restaurant; Sea views

ACTIVITIES:
Golf; Shopping; Water sports

NEARBY:
Palma de Mallorca; Serra de Tramuntana mountain; Bellver Castle; Numerous golf clubs

GETTING THERE:
Port Portals; Palma de Mallorca Airport

+34 971 679 040 ☎
condenastjohansens.com/portalshills 🌐
Calle Seguí 4, 07181 Portals Nous, Mallorca, Balearic Islands, 🏠
Spain

Blau Privilege Porto Petro Beach Resort & Spa

Mallorca's leisure playground for every generation

PRICE FROM:
€168 (excluding local tourist tax)

FEATURES:
Beach access; Restaurant; Sea views; Spa; Wheelchair access

ACTIVITIES:
Golf; Tennis; Water sports

NEARBY:
Mondragó Natural Park; Cala d'Or; Cala Figuera; Cala Santanyí; Cuevas del Drach (the Caves of Drach)

GETTING THERE:
Palma de Mallorca Airport

☎ +34 971 648 282
🌐 condenastjohansens.com/portopetro
🏠 Carrer des Far 16, 07691 Porto Petro (Santanyí), Mallorca, Balearic Islands, Spain

This mighty resort is somewhere to zone out and zone in on your hobbies and sporting prowess. Tucked away in the fisherman's bay of Porto Petro alongside 900 metres of Mallorca's south-east coastline, you can spend lazy days soaking up the sun around the pool, leisurely afternoons in the spa and evenings feasting on barbecued fare. Or there are endless heart-racing fun and games on-site: volleyball, football, tennis (Nadal's top spin was shaped on Mallorca's red clay), golf, sailing, kayaking, indoor cycling and aqua-fitness. Various classes include Zumba, yoga and aerobics, with the sea just moments away to cool you down and the adults-only pool and Ponent bar encouraging some quite time. Located next to Mondragó Natural Park, Blau Privilege Porto Petro Beach Resort & Spa's setting is not only beautiful but conveniently accessible to the Park's natural beauty, which is a perfect spot for long bike rides and jogs. Thank goodness for the resort's five restaurants that keep your energy levels up! Dishes range from Japanese delicacies to Mediterranean flavours (ask about the private culinary classes), while the five bars offer the chance to wind down and kick back. At the end of the day, Blau Privilege Porto Petro Beach Resort & Spa's contemporary-styled guest rooms provide bright and versatile spaces, well suited to families. Each one benefits from a sun-filled terrace; many overlook the sea.

Gran Hotel Son Net

Modernity meets Mallorcan country house finesse

Fashioning its very own vineyard, Son Net Estate dates back to 1672 and screams quintessential Mallorca. Gran Hotel Son Net's rooms and suites are awash with colonial influences; beautiful four-poster beds and immaculate marble bathrooms big enough to party in! Outside, the wild UNESCO Sierra Tramuntana mountains majestically shape the skyline, seen in all their glory from the casual El Gazebo restaurant. In fact, the resort is so superbly located you could find yourself chilling in the Beauty Lounge within 30 minutes of landing at Palma de Mallorca Airport. It's all about peace and tranquillity at this Spanish bolthole, encouraging you to contemplate and rejuvenate, aided by the second-to-none staff. Be sure to ask them about the rooms and suites because the choice is varied. Some include private pools and/or breathtaking views. Some have a private entrance, twin beds and/or Jacuzzi tubs. When deciding whether to eat at the informal, alfresco El Gazebo or fine-dining Oleum restaurant where gourmet cooking uses fresh local produce, Bar Son Net or the poolside El Mirador will shake you up a pre-dinner cocktail apéritif. Special feature: the ingenious Treehouse where private dinner parties for up to 10 people can be hosted to an impressive panorama of Puigpunyent village in the distance and mountains beyond.

PRICE FROM:
€190

FEATURES:
Family friendly; Gym; Helipad; Pool; Restaurant

ACTIVITIES:
Cycling; Golf; Walking

NEARBY:
Palma de Mallorca; Beaches; Sierra Tramuntana mountains

GETTING THERE:
Palma de Mallorca Airport

+34 971 14 70 00 ☎
condenastjohansens.com/sonnet 🌐
07194 Puigpunyent, Mallorca, Balearic Islands, Spain

CONDÉ NAST
johansens
Luxury Hotels · Spas · Venues
AWARD
WINNER
2016

Gran Hotel Atlantis Bahía Real

Top-notch resort on Fuerteventura's coast

PRICE FROM:
€275

FEATURES:
Beach access; Family friendly; Restaurant; Sea views; Spa

ACTIVITIES:
Sightseeing; Tennis; Water sports

NEARBY:
Natural Sand Dune Park of Corralejo; Island of Lobos; Lanzarote; Fishing village and resort of Corralejo

GETTING THERE:
Fuerteventura Airport

☎ +34 928 537 153
🌐 condenastjohansens.com/bahiareal
🏠 Avenida Grandes Playas 103, 35660 Corralejo, Fuerteventura, Canary Islands, Spain

Wrapped up by Blue Ribbon beaches, Gran Hotel Atlantis Bahía Real, Fuerteventura, is a luxury seaside gift. Utopian white sands and turquoise seas provide breathtaking views from this family-friendly hotel resort, which is part of the UNESCO biosphere. This protected habitat hosts a wonder of natural wildlife. Ask the Atlantis team to organise a trip to explore these volcanic shores. That's if you can tear yourself away from the spa and its spectacular views. Returning from a day of enjoyment and excursion, Gran Hotel Atlantis Bahía Real's private gym is there if you need it but some "me time" in your opulent room may be more appealing. Rooms and suites are decorated with a timeless elegance and combine space and comfort. (Choose a sea-view room or suite for stunning sunset vistas and stellar stargazing nights.) There's fine dining to be enjoyed at La Cúpula de Carles Gaig whose menu of mouth-watering delights is overseen by Gaig's Michelin Starred expertise. And for something a little different, Yamatori presents a fusion of Japanese sushi and teppanyaki whilst the Piano Bar El Mirador is a pocket of romance with a view of the night sky. A Gran Hotel Atlantis highlight: Coco Beach Chill Out and Coco Beach Lounge & Club for relaxing with a glass of Champagne/a cocktail on a cloud-like Balinese bed or alfresco dining with amazing vistas of Lobos and Lanzarote islands.

Bohemia Suites & Spa

Gran Canarian beach-side lounging with style kudos

Bright, bold and daring, Bohemia Suites & Spa, Gran Canaria, evokes 21st-century free spirit. This is one of the island's best hotels - recently revamped with brilliant effect - moments from the stunning, seemingly endless dunes of Maspalomas beach. A poster boy for contemporary, funky modernism, the adults-only Bohemia Suites' use of technicolour and up-to-the-minute design emits a fashionable and laid-back vibe. Locals come here to meet friends while guests retreat to the calm of their thoughtfully decorated guest rooms packed with contemporary furniture and state-of-the-art gadgets (wireless keyboards, Apple Macs, mood lighting). Days at Bohemia are spent lounging by the pool with the heavenly scent of lush bougainvillea and frangipani in the air, which is also the location of Sapphire Pool Bar serving snacks and cocktails. Or you may prefer to take the three-minute walk to the powder-white sand beach. However, there's always Bohemia's Siam Spa for some Eastern-style pampering with an extensive list of Thai and Balinese treatments. In the evening head on up in Bohemia's brightly coloured lift to the fine-dining rooftop 360° restaurant, aptly named for its all-encompassing view of the Dunes of Maspalomas (the biggest dunes in Europe) and azure-blue Atlantic Ocean. This is also where Atelier Lounge & Cocktails is found with more of those eye-popping vistas.

PRICE FROM:
€188

FEATURES:
Gym; Pool; Restaurant; Sea views; Spa

ACTIVITIES:
Cycling; Golf; Water sports

NEARBY:
Maspalomas beach; Campo de Golf de Maspalomas; Las Palmas; The Dunes of Maspalomas; Tejeda

GETTING THERE:
Gran Canaria Airport

+34 928 563 400 ☎
condenastjohansens.com/bohemiasuites 🌐
Avenida Estados Unidos 28, 35100 Playa del Inglés, Gran Canaria, Canary Islands, Spain

Bahía del Duque

Private, refined resort beside Tenerife's beautiful Duque beach

PRICE FROM:
€300

FEATURES:
Beach access; Family friendly; Restaurant; Sea views; Spa

ACTIVITIES:
Cycling; Golf; Water sports

NEARBY:
La Caleta; Adeje; Puerto Colon Marina; Siam Park; Las Cañadas National Park

GETTING THERE:
Tenerife South (Reina Sofia) Airport; Tenerife North (Los Rodeos) Airport

☎ +34 922 746 932
🌐 condenastjohansens.com/bahiaduque
🏠 Avenida de Bruselas s/n, Costa Adeje 38660, Tenerife, Canary Islands, Spain

A testament to colonial architecture, Bahía del Duque in Tenerife is a cluster of impeccable villas. So sublimely luxurious, you needn't step out of the resort into the "Island Of The Eternal Spring". At a consistent 20ºC+, this UNESCO protected plot of forests, majestic cliffs and utopic beaches cries out for exploration. However, in-resort you can relax in the reading lounge or enjoy a plethora of high-adrenaline or family-friendly activities such as relaxing on del Duque's very own yacht, Pámpano. Younger children love the dedicated Ents team while older siblings can relax in their own surf-style beach lounge complete with video consoles and table football. The casas ducales and villas, decorated by prestigious interior designer Pascua Ortega, mix the latest technology with maximum comfort and views of the spectacular Playa del Duque. But for a particularly opulent stay, casas ducales (which have an independent reception) are complete with butler service. Tired muscles? Soothe them with exclusive thalassotherapy treatments at Bahía del Duque Spa. And when hunger strikes, a choice of eight restaurants featuring a medley of global cuisines are available to satisfy the most discerning rumbling tum (and any fussy younger ones too).

Hotel Botánico & The Oriental Spa Garden

Year-round R&R on the lush slopes of north Tenerife

The ultimate go-to for relaxation, Tenerife's Hotel Botánico & The Oriental Spa Garden is located in the north of the island. Surrounding its unfussy 1970s architecture are subtropical gardens and a lake packed with koi carp giving a taster of the volcanic high drama beyond the hotel's borders. Views of which (the ocean, mountains or gardens) are seen through oversized windows from each room and suite, which are sumptuously designed as an oasis of escape. You can be as lazy as you like or as active as you please here. Tennis courts, a driving range and numerous tours beckon you to join in but it's the stonking-great, child-free spa that will make you step back and behold. Decorated with a Far Eastern vibe, it has a pool, Jacuzzi, ice temple, sauna, fitness centre and an eye-popping list of treatments. Four à la carte restaurants serve regional and Asian dishes as well as a super-healthy option known as the Essence of Wellbeing suitable for vegetarians, those that wish to lose weight, simply feel virtuous or have specific dietary requirements. And just a 10-minute walk away is the chilled town of Puerto de la Cruz with colonial buildings and traces of its former fishing village life in narrow, bustling streets.

PRICE FROM:
€270

FEATURES:
Pet friendly; Pool; Restaurant; Sea views; Spa

ACTIVITIES:
Golf; Shopping; Tennis

NEARBY:
Puerto de la Cruz; La Orotava; Santa Cruz; Loro Parque; Buenavista Golf

GETTING THERE:
Tenerife South (Reina Sofia) Airport; Tenerife North Airport

+34 922 38 14 00 ☎
condenastjohansens.com/hotelbotanico 🌐
Avenida Richard J Yeoward 1, 38400 Puerto de La Cruz, 🏠
Tenerife, Canary Islands, Spain

Duquesa Suites

All-suite, all-convenient city pad beside the Old Port of Barcelona

PRICE FROM:
€110 (room only)

FEATURES:
Family friendly; Pool; Sea views; Wheelchair access

ACTIVITIES:
Shopping; Sightseeing; Water sports

NEARBY:
Santa María del Mar Basilica; Picasso Museum; Barcelona Cathedral; Aquarium; Barcelona beach

GETTING THERE:
Port of Barcelona; Barcelona Airport; Gerona Airport

A five-minute stroll from Duquesa Suites and you're basking on the beach, admiring Santa Maria del Mar church, soaking up the atmosphere of El Born Barrio district and browsing along Las Ramblas. This is central Barcelona overlooking the superyachts at Port Vell: convenient, scenic and steeped in history. Duquesa's 30 suites (more akin to apartments) are spread across six floors of a grand 18th-century seafront building. Inside, paintings of the luxury ocean liner, Reina Victoria Eugenia, adorn the walls, paying homage to the Port's bygone nautical past. During her time as a 20th-century cruiser, voyages took her from Port Vell to Buenos Aires and it's the ship's promise of glamorous travel that's so well executed at Duquesa Suites. Each of these spacious, softly-lit home-from-homes has a fully-equipped kitchen/kitchenette, living area and space for up to four to sleep (the sofa beds are ideal for the children). Corner Suites are particularly large with two single sofa beds and double aspect windows of the cityscape. But the two-storey Penthouse is the biggest of them all with a panoramic private terrace. It's all about holidaying at your own pace here and after a day's exploring you always have the rooftop terrace to retreat to, complete with swimming pool and solarium.

☎ +34 937 379 125
🌐 condenastjohansens.com/duquesasuites
🏠 Plaza Antonio López 5, 08002 Barcelona, Cataluña, Spain

Hotel Duquesa de Cardona

Chic, sleek, city boutique hotel beside Barcelona's port

When you've had enough of Barcelona's tourist trail there's Hotel Duquesa de Cardona offering respite from the hustle and bustle. Barcelona's city streets below seem a million miles away when you're hanging out on the roof terrace despite the fact that this marina-front hotel is slap bang in the middle of the action. Las Ramblas and the Gothic Quarter are so close you're in the thick of their pulsing streets in no time. Everything you could want from a city hotel, the Duquesa delivers. Cool, sophisticated and full of character, a glass of cava upon arrival sets the tone. Rooms are light and airy with a crisp modern boutique feel and fear not if your room is located roadside because windows are quadruple glazed so you don't hear one car horn. Hotel Duquesa's 16th-century building was once home to kings and noble types, and much of its grandeur remains. Columns, vaulted ceilings and art-deco windows fuse with wrought iron, contemporary banquettes and Philippe Starck ghost chairs in the restaurant where you can enjoy great à la carte menus. However, the tapas, barbecued plates in the summer and cocktails at the year-round La Terrassa del Duquesa rooftop bar and restaurant are also must-tries (those views!). Don't miss: a flamenco show - just ask a member of staff who will easily organise this for you.

PRICE FROM:
€215

FEATURES:
Family friendly; Pool; Restaurant; Sea views; Wheelchair access

ACTIVITIES:
Shopping; Sightseeing; Water sports

NEARBY:
Port of Barcelona; Gothic Quarter; Las Ramblas; La Boquería market; Picasso Museum

GETTING THERE:
Barcelona Airport; Gerona Airport

+34 93 268 90 90 ☎
condenastjohansens.com/duquesadecardona 🌐
Paseo Colon 12, 08002 Barcelona, Cataluña, Spain 🏛

Hotel Rigat Park & Spa Beach Hotel

Traditional beach-side holidaying on the Gerona coast

PRICE FROM:
€220 (excluding VAT)

FEATURES:
Beach access; Pool; Restaurant; Sea views; Spa

ACTIVITIES:
Golf; Shopping; Water sports

NEARBY:
Santa Clotilde Gardens; Catamaran trips; Golf PGA; Gerona; Barcelona

GETTING THERE:
Gerona Airport; Barcelona Airport

☎ +34 972 36 52 00
🌐 condenastjohansens.com/rigat
🏠 Av Amèrica 1, Playa de Fenals, 17310 Lloret de Mar, Costa Brava, Gerona, Cataluña, Spain

One man's Costa Bravan dream became a reality in 1956 when Hotel Rigat Park & Spa Beach Hotel opened. A family-run operation, the son of ski champion Fillipo Rigat keeps the hotel's traditional spirit alive with cosy, antique-packed interiors and lovingly collected ceramics, tapestries and oil paintings of the Rigat family on the walls. Tucked away behind trees yet a stone's throw from Lloret de Mar's shops and nightlife, this is a perfect escape for a classic beachy break. Its large terrace and pool area are an extension of the ocean whose glorious sheer blue waters are in constant view. Vivid bougainvillea cascades down terracotta-hued hacienda walls and a 300-year-old tamarind tree growing in the bar area brings the tropical vibe inside. If you like subtle bling with your dining, check out the gold ceiling in Hotel Rigat's baroque-style restaurant. Here, Catalan influences mix rice, fish and lots of Mediterranean veggies but the dessert trolley is truly the star. (Tumbling towers of profiteroles, cupcakes and tantalising tartlets!) Of course, eating outdoors is a must and Hotel Rigat serves a mean breakfast alfresco with eggs as you like them and coffee any expert barista would be proud of. Soothe kinks or strains in the spa area (with spa pool, sauna, Jacuzzi and great treatment menu) or whizz off on a boat trip to nearby Tossa del Mar for a little culture and shopping.

Asia Gardens Hotel & Thai Spa

Thailand and Bali converge on Spain's Costa Blanca

Ever imagine stumbling upon a Thai-infused resort on the ever-popular Costa Blanca? No? Meet Asia Gardens Hotel & Thai Spa, Alicante, featuring the finest elements of an Asian resort: a Zen-calm atmosphere, above-and-beyond service and friendly professionalism. Asia Gardens' stunning reception area and atrium (dark wood and woven ceilings with a Chesterfield twist) lead you to Thai-luxe guest rooms dressed in modernist Balinese-style furnishings beside sleek, glamorous bathrooms and dazzling Mediterranean light. Beds are heavenly and the higher the room, the better the view. Techno-fittings, WiFi and iPod docks are standard. A wander around the resort takes in the hot chilli-pink buildings set amidst a tapestry of lush gardens with a number of meandering infinity pools full of private little inlets. Two of the pools are heated and there's also a children's pool; in fact, the kiddies are spoilt with fun at the pirate-themed Miniclub. Feast on Asian-fused Mediterranean cuisine at Udaipur Grand Buffet and reserve a table at restaurant Koh Samui or the sophisticated In Black (over 12s only). Don't miss out on a Thai massage within one of the traditional Thai stilt houses - the spa staff have honed their skills to perfection - and the sizeable gym furnished with Kinesis Personal Heritage equipment that not only gives you a great workout but also looks great.

PRICE FROM:
€240

FEATURES:
Family friendly; Pool; Restaurant; Sea views; Spa

ACTIVITIES:
Golf; Shopping; Water sports

NEARBY:
Finestrat; Altea; Alicante; Theme parks; Nautical Club Campomanes in Altea

GETTING THERE:
Alicante Railway Station; Alicante Airport; Valencia Airport

+34 966 818 400 ☎
condenastjohansens.com/asiagardens 🌐
Rotonda del Fuego s/n, Terra Mítica, Finestrat, 03509 Alicante, Valencia, Spain

Switzerland

Please go to condenastjohansens.com/switzerland

Lakeside divinity at Villa Principe Leopoldo, page 141

The Chedi Andermatt

The new ski scene for the smart set in the Swiss Alps

A big player in re-establishing this charming Urseren Valley village as a world-class ski destination, The Chedi Andermatt is reason enough to visit. Grand Swiss chalet on the outside, with a nod to the Orient on the inside, The Chedi is a happy marriage of super-slick Swiss efficiency and warm Asian hospitality. This is the centre of Europe, equidistant between the cities of Zürich and Milan, so reaching this snowy wonderland is effortless. And plans to connect it to nearby Sedrun in order to create the largest ski resort in central Switzerland are underway. Inside, a plush lobby of polished stone and dark wood welcomes you with a sky high ceiling dripping in shiny chandeliers. Guest rooms and suites are equally lavish and resemble luxury log cabins. They range from the Deluxe to the two-storey, three-bedroom, three-bathroom Furka Suite (complete with wine private spa). Each room and suite is rich in Alpine comfort, high-tech features and has a deep bathtub, rain shower and fireplace. (There are over 200 fireplaces at The Chedi!) When it comes to dining, choices include The Japanese Restaurant, East-West Restaurant serving Swiss, European and Asian dishes and the quaint Chalet eatery. Plus, the elevated Club House with mountain views. Must-visit: the phenomenal spa and wellness centre offering hydrothermal baths, Finnish saunas, a whopping 35-metre pool, Health Club, hair salon and yoga sessions.

PRICE FROM:
€460

FEATURES:
Family friendly; Gym; Pool; Restaurant; Spa

ACTIVITIES:
Golf; Skiing; Walking

NEARBY:
SkiArena Andermatt - Sedrun; 500km of hiking trails; Lucerne; Zürich

GETTING THERE:
Göschenen/Andermatt Railway Stations; Milan Malpensa Airport, Italy; Zürich Airport

+41 41 888 74 88 ☎
condenastjohansens.com/chediandermatt 🌐
Gotthardstrasse 4, 6490 Andermatt, Switzerland 🏠

Villa Principe Leopoldo

Sunny Mediterranean spirit marries warm Swiss hospitality

PRICE FROM:
€312

FEATURES:
Family friendly; Lake views; Pool; Restaurant; Spa

ACTIVITIES:
Golf; Shopping; Sightseeing

NEARBY:
Lake Como, Italy; Golf Club Lugano-Magliaso; Lugano and Campione d'Italia Casinos; UNESCO World Heritage castles of Bellinzona; FoxTown Shopping Outlet

GETTING THERE:
Lugano Railway Station; Lugano Airport; Milan–Malpensa Airport, Italy

☎ +41 91 985 88 55
🌐 condenastjohansens.com/leopoldohotel
🏠 Via Montalbano 5, Lugano 6900, Switzerland

A slice of Prussian royal history, this former summer residence of Prince Federico Leopoldo remains fit for a king. The blissful scene of Lake Lugano below and beyond, with the lush green mountains of the Ticino region all around is where northern Italy meets Switzerland. And since Villa Principe Leopoldo's construction in the early 20th century, this lakeside retreat has hosted countless members of nobility and distinguished guests. Now it's your turn to experience the life once reserved for the select few. Perched high on Collina d'Oro, the views are nothing short of spectacular and the Villa's elegant terrace takes full advantage. Come the evening, relaxed guests sit out here with a glass of local bubbly, watching the twinkling lights in the calm lake water. In the day, this is where they laze by the pool after a bumper breakfast at La Limonaia. Evening meals are taken in Principe Leopoldo Restaurant, which has become a destination in its own right for its Italian and Ticino's fusion cuisine alongside local favourites. But for those visiting Lugano for business the Villa provides all the technology and services needed for successful meetings, corporate retreats, team-building sessions and banquets. Weddings can also be held here with the added bonus of beauty treatments available at the private spa.

Turkey

Please go to condenastjohansens.com/turkey

Watery pleasures at D-Resort Göcek, page 147

CONDÉ NAST
johansens
Luxury Hotels · Spas · Venues
AWARD
WINNER
2016

Cornelia Diamond Golf Resort & Spa

Enormous beach-side pleasure centre on Antalya's coast

PRICE FROM:
€350

FEATURES:
Beach access; Family friendly; Pool; Restaurant; Spa

ACTIVITIES:
Golf; Tennis; Water sports

NEARBY:
Belek; Aspendos Theatre; ESPA Crassula Spa Centre; Cornelia Nick Faldo Championship Golf Course; Antalya city centre

GETTING THERE:
Antalya Airport

☎ +90 242 710 1600
🌐 condenastjohansens.com/corneliadiamond
🏠 Iskele Mevkii, Belek, Antalya, Turkey

Cornelia Diamond Golf Resort & Spa, Belek, is a decadent dream that's been made a reality. Less resort, more miniature kingdom, there's a refreshing emphasis on nature and the environment at this green and pleasant place with accommodation to suit everyone. This includes spacious garden facing family rooms, sleek Lake Houses (connected to the main hotel by a space-age tunnel) and the private Cornelia Azure Villas residence with 33 three and two-bedroom villas, a sea-water pool, restaurant and bar. Every guest is welcome to visit Crassula Spa, a watery playground of Jacuzzis, pools, relaxation areas and traditional hammam. It also happens to host the most indulgent haven of all: the Spa King Suite. Available for private hire, its Turkish bath, sauna, pool, Asian massage and garden can all be exclusively yours. As if this wasn't enough, Cornelia provides additional activities such as golf, entertainment at the hotel's amphitheatre and water sports at the resort's beach. Younger guests haven't been forgotten either thanks to Children's Heaven where there's a waterpark. After all this fun and exercise, room service might be tempting but then you'd be missing out on the taste explosion at the nine restaurants offering everything from traditional Turkish kebabs to the finest seafood.

The House Hotel Cappadocia

Local charm with worldwide appeal in lesser-known Cappadocia

Often overshadowed by its neighbouring towns of Göreme, Ürgüp, Uçhisar and Nevşehir, the little farming village of Ortahisar is a less travelled, authentic taste of the Cappadocia region. A recent addition to the tourist trail, locals go about their business in the cobblestoned streets lined by stone houses and cave dwellings. And off the main square facing the village's lofty fortress, The House Hotel Cappadocia's collection of stone houses and volcanic caves provides rustic-luxe accommodation. Inside is a labyrinthine den filled with original features, fireplaces, domed ceilings, alcoves and age-old frescoes lit by candles and moody lighting. Vaulted corridors lead to guest rooms and suites of different shapes and sizes awash with natural materials, Persian patterns and exposed stone walls. Downstairs there's an underground spa offering yoga classes, a hammam, steam room, adventure showers (with music, lights and water jets), a sauna and four treatment rooms. Up on the roof, a terrace takes in all the glory of Cappadocia's landscape. Fresko Restaurant serves typically Turkish meals on the terrace as well as inside its frescoed walls, plus favourite local delicacies such as pide and lachmacun - stuffed Turkish pizzas - cooked to perfection in a traditional stone oven. Included in your stay: a tour of the village, a local market tour and a climbing tour on Ortahisar Castle.

PRICE FROM:
€129 (excluding tax, including a tour of the village, a local market tour and climbing tour on Ortahisar Castle)

FEATURES:
Family friendly; Restaurant; Spa; Wheelchair access

ACTIVITIES:
Cycling; Horse riding; Walking

NEARBY:
UNESCO Göreme Open-Air Museum; Kaymaklı underground city; Hot-air ballooning; Hiking; Fairy channels aka cave dwellings

GETTING THERE:
Nevşehir Bus Station; Nevşehir Kapadokya Airport; Kayseri Erkilet International Airport

+90 384 3432425 ☎
condenastjohansens.com/househotel 🌐
Eski Mahallesi, Hacı Telgraf Caddesi No 3/1, Ortahisar, Ürgüp, Nevşehir, Cappadocia, Turkey

argos in Cappadocia

Monkish serenity in Cappadocia's age-old stone caves

PRICE FROM:
€210

FEATURES:
Pet friendly; Restaurant

ACTIVITIES:
Cycling; Horse riding; Walking

NEARBY:
Göreme; Nevşehir; Hiking; UNESCO Göreme Open-Air Museum;
Uçhisar Castle

GETTING THERE:
Nevşehir Airport; Kayseri Airport

Your very own ivory tower, argos in Cappadocia (one-time monastery and Silk Road stop-off) is an inspired hotel hewn from volcanic stone. A maze of caves and underground tunnels housing a devilishly decadent wine cellar, argos in Cappadocia is located in the ancient village of Uçhisar. Carved from the volcanic lava emitted from the nearby Mount Erciyes, the city is a spectacular focus for the sunrises and sunsets that illuminate the Cappadocian terrain. Blanketed in snow during the winter and strewn with roses and birdsong come summer, this is about as dramatic as hotel locations get. Rooms have been crafted, rather than built from the local stone and are elegantly simple and stylish with Seljuk and Ottoman touches as a reminder of the centuries-old civilisation surrounding you. Most have views of the lush gardens or sun terraces and some suites have their own underground cave pool for secret subterranean swimming. Above ground, enjoy a drink on the terrace overlooking Pigeon Valley before experiencing argos in Cappadocia's fabulous food. Chefs work their magic with fresh local ingredients combined with cutting-edge techniques giving you a unique flavour of the best of a cuisine that's been a thousand years in the making.

☎ +90 384 2193130
🌐 condenastjohansens.com/argos
🏠 Uçhisar, 50240 Nevşehir (Cappadocia), Turkey

Sacred House

Where fairy tales are brought to life in Cappadocia

A stunning design coup in the heart of Cappadocia's UNESCO World Heritage Site, Sacred House is something from a parallel universe. An ambitious restoration and interior design project, it's the brainchild of host Turan Gülcüoglu, a big romantic with a talent for combining medieval art and contemporary luxury. The former home of a Greek aristocrat, each of the 21 rooms is uniquely decorated with a specific period and culture in mind. These include the Opium room, a decadent den of ancient Greek stonework, gold framed mirrors and an ornate fireplace, the therapeutic Shaman room and opulent Archangel suite whose impressive marble sculpture of the dragon slaying Archangel Michael dominates the room. They're all spacious with a theatrical sense of comfort. Wining and dining takes place in the intimacy of the cellar, home to the formal Angels & The Searchers restaurant and bar where forgotten dishes from the Anatolian and Middle Age cultures are served on chevalier tables with antique crockery. The breakfast is worth waking up early for and the complimentary cake and tea at sundown is certainly worth staying in for. But once you visit Sacred House's Inferno underground spa, you may not want to do anything else other than spend you days luxuriating in its cosseting volcanic cave setting, red-lit pool and authentic Turkish hammam.

PRICE FROM:
€220

FEATURES:
Pool; Restaurant; Spa

ACTIVITIES:
Horse riding; Sightseeing; Walking

NEARBY:
Göreme; Avanos; Nevşehir; Wineries; UNESCO Göreme Open-Air Museum

GETTING THERE:
Nevşehir Airport; Kayseri Airport

+90 384 341 7102 ☎
condenastjohansens.com/sacredhouse 🌐
Dutlucami Mahallesi, Barbaros Hayrettin Sokak, No 25, 🏠
50400 Ürgüp - Nevşehir (Cappadocia), Turkey

D-Resort Göcek
Year-round coastal kicks on the Turkish Riviera

PRICE FROM:
€112

FEATURES:
Pool; Restaurant; Sea views; Spa

ACTIVITIES:
Cycling; Water sports

NEARBY:
Dalyan; Ölüdeniz; Kayaköy; Butterfly Valley; Saklıkent Canyon

GETTING THERE:
Dalaman Airport; Milas–Bodrum Airport

Turkey's Turquoise Coast with pretty marinas and secluded coves is no longer the yachties' big secret. Its talcum-powder sand, brilliant blue water and spectacular forest-covered mountain backdrop is now a flop-and-drop destination for the suave and savvy seeking sun, sea and a dose of culture. 20 minutes from Dalaman Airport, the quiet village of Göcek is as a poster boy for the Turkish Riviera. And next to its yacht-lined, bar-fringed D-Marin marina, D-Resort Göcek is in plum position for admiring all its watery wonderland. Blooming gardens, mountain vistas and sea views face you at every turn, from the fresh crisp-white rooms and suites (check out the sprawling two-bedroom, two-bathroom Presidential Suite with dining room and kitchenette) to The Breeze sea-front restaurant, cool Japanese Q-Lounge and three-floor D-SPA. Jacuzzis, a hammam, vitality pool and saunas provide the space to unwind, while D-Gym's classes and equipment focuses on getting your endorphins flowing. Lazy days spent in D-Resort's three bars or on the private beach may have you itching to hit the ocean waves with a sailing or boat trip, which are easily arranged. Car and bike hire for mountain adventures and visits to the fascinating 2nd to 4th-century Lycian ruins of Caunos can also be organised. Don't miss: dining at the new Günaydin kebab, butcher and steakhouse restaurant.

☎ +90 252 661 09 00
🌐 condenastjohansens.com/dresortgocek
🏠 Cumhuriyet Mahallesi, 48310 Göcek, Fethiye, Muğla, Turkey

Hillside Beach Club

Romance, adventure and fun on Turkey's Mediterranean coast

A seaside resort offering something for everyone, Hillside Beach Club basks in the sun on Turkey's Mediterranean coast, close to the tourist hub of Fethiye. There's never a dull moment here with sports, entertainment and clubs taking place around every corner. But there are also plenty of quiet spots dotted throughout this coastal fun-trap such as the adults-only Silent beach where early morning yoga takes place. Elsewhere, Hillside goes full-on family! Younger guests love KidSide (four to seven-year-olds), Junior Club (eight to 13-year-olds) and Young Club (14 to 17-year-olds) where various age-appropriate programmes take place while mum and dad slope off to one of the seven bars located inside, by the beach and by the pool. Or perhaps one of the two spas. Sanda Spa is a traditional Turkish wellness escape whereas Sanda Nature Spa specialises in Balinese treatments. Water sports are also popular with guests, such as sailing around the bay in the Hillside's private boat. Back at Hillside and two à la carte restaurants provide Italian and Mediterranean meals - reserve a table at Pasha on the Bay for a dose of romance. Some evenings a big screen floats on the sea for movie screenings. Nice touch: a cliff lift to the pretty Tuscan-inspired suites, which is a godsend when carrying a little one to bed.

PRICE FROM:
€134 (per person, including breakfast, buffet lunch, buffet dinner and non-alcoholic beverages)

FEATURES:
Beach access; Family friendly; Pool; Restaurant; Spa

ACTIVITIES:
Fishing; Tennis; Water sports

NEARBY:
Fethiye; Göcek; Öludeniz beach; Kayaköy

GETTING THERE:
Dalaman Airport

+90 252 614 8360 ☎
condenastjohansens.com/hillsidebeachclub 🌐
Belen Mah Belen Cad, No 132, Kayaköy, Fethiye, Muğla, Turkey

CONDÉ NAST
johansens
Luxury Hotels · Spas · Venues
AWARD WINNER 2016

Villa Mahal

An ocean lover's paradise in quiet Kalkan

PRICE FROM:
€250

FEATURES:
Beach access; Pool; Restaurant; Sea views

ACTIVITIES:
Sightseeing; Walking; Water sports

NEARBY:
Kas; Fethiye; Kaputaş beach; Patara beach; Yacht harbour

GETTING THERE:
Dalaman Airport

This little patch of the Lycian Coast honours the few known facts about the ancient Lycian civilisation. Just like these fascinating, mysterious people (who must have been very fit considering this steep mountainous land), Kalkan is enigmatic, independent and free spirited. It remains unspoilt by towering concrete and swarms of tourists, and retains its rugged, natural beauty. Approached from an inconspicuous dusty track, Villa Mahal in Kalkan Bay suddenly materialises as a welcome mirage in the blinding sun. Instantaneously it's evident that Villa Mahal's world is all about kicking back, relaxing and rejuvenating. This is a refuge from the daily grind where decisions revolve around the rooftop restaurant's Turkish/Mediterranean menu, beach restaurant's à la carte options, the perfect sunbathing spot (Beach Club? Infinity pool? Private terrace?) and water-sport pursuits. (Snorkelling? Kayaking? Scuba diving? Sailing? Private gulet tours?) If the lack of stress doesn't have you in a zombie-like state, then a restorative massage in the shade of a natural cave beside a twinkling emerald green and dark blue watery scene assuredly will. Full-height windows from bedrooms and suites bring the meditative powers of the setting in; all have terraces making the most of the view. Indulgent tip: book one of the Sunset Rooms or the two-storey Pool Room with its very own pool and unbeatable view.

☎ +90 242 844 32 68
🌐 condenastjohansens.com/villamahal
🏠 Kalkan, 07960 Antalya, Turkey

Nirvana Lagoon Villas Suites & Spa

VIP lifestyle on the Turkish Riviera

On Turkey's south Mediterranean coast, below the rugged Taurus mountains, this service-led seaside resort brings new meaning to VIP. Within a pine tree forest, wedged between a golden stretch of sand and the towering mountains, Nirvana Lagoon Villas Suites & Spa lives up to its name. Close to all the region's attractions (Stone Age caves, wild forest, water sports), Nirvana is quietly tucked away in lesser-known Beldibi. And it's a polished, glam and wonderfully family-friendly newcomer focused on indulging its guests in a life of privilege. Accommodations are categorised as Standard family rooms and VIP suites with the two-bedroom Villa Nirvana appointed the Top VIP option (complete with sauna, steam room, Turkish bath, five TVs, dressing room, sitting room and dining room). Endless sun terraces, huge sun loungers, a Jacuzzi and private beach pavilions encourage hours of relaxation. But Nirvana's colossal Aquapark with 11 water slides is a must-visit for children of all ages - mums and dads too - for when the family's not taking part in aerobics classes, beach volleyball, watery pursuits such as banana boating and activities at the children's Crispy Mini Club. When hunger strikes, the nine ocean-side restaurants take you on a whistle-stop tour of the globe. And for some re-energising pampering, the Ottoman-inspired Nirvana Spa & Wellness obliges with a plethora of treatments.

PRICE FROM:
€360

FEATURES:
Beach access; Family friendly; Restaurant; Sea views; Spa

ACTIVITIES:
Shopping; Tennis; Water sports

NEARBY:
Beldibi Beach Park; Dino Park; Moonlight Park; Antalya's city centre; Kemer

GETTING THERE:
Antalya Airport

+90 24 28 24 99 15 ☎
condenastjohansens.com/nirvanahotel 🌐
Atatürk Cad No 141, 07985 Beldibi, Kemer, Antalya, Turkey 🏠

UK/ England

Please go to condenastjohansens.com/england

The lovely welcome at Chewton Glen, page 189

Luton Hoo Hotel, Golf & Spa

Grade I listed hotel in endless acres of Bedfordshire parkland

Where horse-drawn carriages and chugging automobiles once stood, golf buggies and London-style cabs transport guests around Luton Hoo Hotel, Golf & Spa's 1,000-acre estate. Famed architect Robert Adam and landscaper "Capability" Brown designed this masterpiece in the late 18th century that today gives a glimpse into the aristocratic life of yesteryear. As you step into the imposing Grand Hall and through to the elegant lounges (where afternoon tea is a boom) take time to soak up the details: towering ceilings; chandeliers; precious paintings; tapestries; restored stonework; and marquetry. Then admire the views out to the green parkland, lake, rock garden, 18-hole golf course and immaculate formal gardens. Staying at The Mansion House is a taster of a bygone high-life while more contemporary rooms are next door in The Parkland. A short stroll away are The Flower Garden rooms beside the spa and The Club House (former stables) popular with the golfing set. This is also where you'll find Adam's Brasserie offering an informal alternative from The Mansion's fine-dining Wernher Restaurant whose menus offer exciting flavours (Black Gold fillet of Scottish beef with parsley gnocchi) and carefully selected wines from both internationally renowned and smaller, boutique vineyards.

PRICE FROM:
£320

FEATURES:
Gym; Helipad; Pool; Restaurant; Spa

ACTIVITIES:
Golf; Tennis; Walking

NEARBY:
Cathedral city of St Albans; Warner Bros Studio Tour London – The Making of Harry Potter; Hatfield House and gardens; Knebworth House; Woburn Safari Park

GETTING THERE:
M1 jct 10; Luton Parkway Railway Station; Luton Airport

+44 (0)1582 734437 ☎
condenastjohansens.com/lutonhoo 🌐
The Mansion House, Luton Hoo, Near Luton, Bedfordshire 🏠
LU1 3TQ, England

Coworth Park

A British charmer through and through in Berkshire's fair countryside

PRICE FROM:
£288 (room only, excluding VAT)

FEATURES:
Family friendly; Gym; Helipad; Restaurant; Spa

ACTIVITIES:
Golf; Horse riding; Walking

NEARBY:
Windsor Great Park; Legoland; Windsor Castle; Ascot Racecourse

GETTING THERE:
A30; M3 jct 3; London Heathrow Airport

Coworth Park, just outside Ascot, is redefining the country house hotel for the 21st century. While upholding all that's great about the English countryside, Coworth Park's estate (The Mansion House, Stables, Cottages, The Dower House, Polo Centre) is a fresh take on the luxury country house hotel where nothing is formulaic. Peppered with surprises, this is a country retreat for the discerning hankering for something out of the ordinary. On the borders of Windsor Great Park, Coworth Park is idyllically set within far-reaching, photo-pretty parkland (visit during the summer to see the beautiful wildflower meadow in bloom) including two polo fields. It's also home to a luxury spa and three restaurants featuring expert pastry chefs who create sweet treats of the heavenly variety alongside culinary creations from one of the UK's most talented chefs, Adam Smith. Adam oversees the modern interpretation of classic British dishes in Restaurant Coworth Park. Plus, the traditional afternoon teas taken in the Drawing Room and the welly-boot glamour and relaxed rustic dining in The Barn. Meanwhile, The Spatisserie in The Spa welcomes bathrobe wearing guests to enjoy a little indulgence. Noteworthy credential: Coworth Park is a member of Dorchester Collection.

☎ +44 (0)1344 630540
🌐 condenastjohansens.com/coworthpark
🏠 Blacknest Road, Ascot, Berkshire SL5 7SE, England

Cliveden House

One of Britain's best, presiding above the River Thames in Berkshire

Reborn further to a full restoration, the epic Cliveden House is reliving its glory days. Almost SO grand, opulent and downright English it seems too fantastic to believe but here it is, in Berkshire beside the River Thames, conveniently near London and Heathrow Airport. During Cliveden's 350-year history, royal guests from George I to Queen Victoria have graced its stately walls and as home to the wealthy Astors, many politicians, celebrities and artists including Winston Churchill, Charlie Chaplin and George Bernard Shaw have also visited. Today, Cliveden's hundreds of acres and formal gardens belong to the National Trust. Inside, the equally mind-blowing Great Hall sets an imposing welcome with incredibly ornate fireplace, oak panelling and priceless artworks. Rooms and suites are dashing with plush velvets, jewel colours and homely comfort with a clue or two pertaining to the famous guests that stayed here before you. In fact, the new Churchill function room is now available for dinner receptions and business meetings. However, if the occasion requires some fine-dining treatment, André Garrett at Cliveden doesn't disappoint (traditional, elegant, romantic), whilst The Astor Grill located in the former stables keeps matters more casual. Don't forget: the idyllic river cruises and Waldo's Private Dining Room and Screening Room designed for presentations and special occasions.

PRICE FROM:
£445

FEATURES:
Family friendly; Gym; Pet friendly; Pool; Restaurant

ACTIVITIES:
Sightseeing; Tennis; Walking

NEARBY:
Windsor Castle; Windsor Great Park; Ascot Racecourse; Henley; Legoland

GETTING THERE:
M4 jct 7; Taplow/Burnham Railway Stations; London Heathrow Airport

+44 (0)1628 668561 ☎
condenastjohansens.com/clivedenhouse 🌐
Taplow, Berkshire SL6 0JF, England 🏠

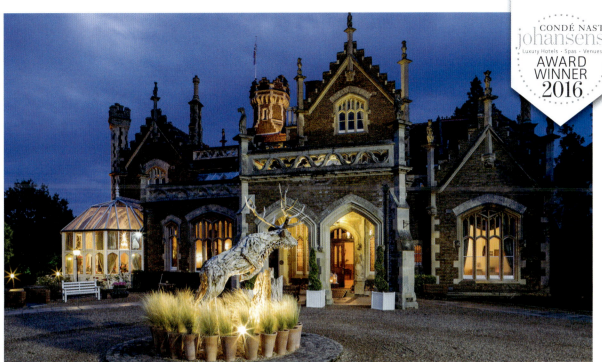

The Oakley Court

Victorian gothic timepiece with a modern sensibility on the River Thames

PRICE FROM:
£160

FEATURES:
Gym; Pool

ACTIVITIES:
Cycling; Golf; Tennis

NEARBY:
Windsor Castle; Ascot Racecourse; Legoland; Henley; Savill Garden

GETTING THERE:
A308; M4 jct 6; London Heathrow Airport

If it's an English classic you're after, look no further than Berkshire's Oakley Court. Set beside the Thames, just downwind of Windsor, you can almost hear the chukkas from the Great Park. And with Oakley fielding its own polo team there's even more reason to visit, catch a match and join them in a glass of celebratory/commiserating bubbly. Adorned with more pointed arches and decorative turrets than you can count, the hotel's Victorian façade is a true gothic beauty. Host to movies such as Count Dracula, The Rocky Horror Picture Show and most recently, the Oscar and BAFTA-winning Theory of Everything, Oakley Court is a country manor with a modern sensibility. Bedrooms are spread across the Courtyard, East Wing, West Wing and Mansion House (reserve a river-viewing room) and options for dining include the river-facing Terrace Restaurant during the summer months. The beating culinary heart of Oakley is The Scullery where the team of passionate chefs serve up a storm. The kitchen's refreshingly unfussy dishes allow the quality ingredients to shine through. Plus, the afternoon teas in the Drawing Room are to die-for. Sporty types appreciate the fitness centre complete with gym, pool, Jacuzzi, sauna, steam room and nine-hole golf course, while the little ones are kept busy with golf or tennis camp (available during the school holidays).

☎ +44 (0)1753 609988
🌐 condenastjohansens.com/oakleycourt
🏠 Windsor Road, Water Oakley, Windsor, Berkshire SL4 5UR, England

Danesfield House Hotel and Spa

Victorian proportions in rural Buckinghamshire

The Victorians knew a thing or two about show-stopping architecture. Cue: the wedding-cake white Danesfield House Hotel and Spa, Buckinghamshire. Built at the end of the 19th century, its arresting beauty is matched by the swathes of stunning gardens that encase it and the views out to the River Thames and Chiltern Hills beyond. For a special occasion book the most spoiling Tower Suite set within the clock tower of the house spanning three floors. Or there are the Deluxe Rooms richly decorated and furnished in a classic style. The only rooms not in-keeping with the timeless, traditional design favoured throughout Danesfield are the two Feature Rooms and the newly refurbished stable courtyard wing where modernity rules the day. Before taking dinner in The Restaurant at Danesfield House it's pleasant to soak up your surroundings and suppress pre-dinner hunger pains with a drink in the chandelier-clad Grand Hall with minstrels' gallery, the sun-lit atrium or comfortable bar. Sublime modern British cuisine can be enjoyed in either The Restaurant, or in the warmer months, The Terrace with its stunning views of the River Thames and surrounding countryside. If you feel the need to burn off some of those well-worth-it calories, leisure facilities include Spa Illuminata at Danesfield House with its 20-metre pool, sauna, Jacuzzi and steam room.

PRICE FROM:
£214

FEATURES:
Family friendly; Helipad; Pet friendly; Pool; Spa

ACTIVITIES:
Golf; Shooting; Shopping

NEARBY:
Marlow; Henley; Windsor; Ascot; River walks

GETTING THERE:
A4155; M40 jct 4; London Heathrow Airport

+44 (0)1628 891010 ☎
condenastjohansens.com/danesfieldhouse 🌐
Henley Road, Marlow-on-Thames, Buckinghamshire SL7 2EY, 🏠
England

Carlyon Bay Hotel

Golfing, spa-ing and romancing on Cornwall's coast, St Austell

PRICE FROM:
£80 (including one round of golf per person, per night)

FEATURES:
Family friendly; Helipad; Restaurant; Sea views; Spa

ACTIVITIES:
Golf; Tennis; Walking

NEARBY:
The Eden Project; Lost Gardens of Heligan; Charlestown; Fowey; Mevergissey

GETTING THERE:
A391; St Austell Railway Station; Newquay Airport

☎ +44 (0)1726 812304
🌐 condenastjohansens.com/carlyonbay
🏠 Sea Road, St Austell, Cornwall PL25 3RD, England

When Percy Brend opened a butcher's shop in Barnstaple in the 1920s it was a seemingly ordinary event. But it marked the beginning of the Brend family's presence in England's South West, who are now the owners of a hotel empire based in Cornwall and Devon. Perched above the cliffs of St Austell, Carlyon Bay Hotel is their pride and joy. As a family-run property, families are welcome at Carlyon and those seeking a luxury break away, some pampering spa time and excellent golf need look no further. In fact, one free round of golf per night is included in each guest's stay, so just as the little ones enjoy the family entertainment programme or time in the playroom, mums and dads are well-catered for with the cliff-side 18-hole championship golf course. The views of St Austell Bay are spectacular from here and the Club House where meals and drinks are served until dusk. Alternatively, there's the holistic spa and its indoor and outdoor pools, heated stone loungers, spa bath, steam room, sauna and experience shower. (With over 40 treatments choose in advance to save deliberation time.) Bedrooms range from singles to larger, luxurious state rooms, however, it's well worth opting for a panoramic sea-view room. And for more of those hypnotic views, the fine-dining Bay View Restaurant doesn't disappoint. For more informal evenings try Taste brasserie.

The Nare

Beach-side getaway on Cornwall's south coast

Hailing from a well-respected family in Cornish hospitality, it's second nature for owner Toby Ashworth to be a hands-on host at The Nare. His grandmother Bettye Gray purchased this characterful house in 1989 and since then it's evolved into one of Cornwall's most comfortable hotels. In a prime position, The Nare is situated beside the endless sandy beach of Gerrans Bay. Most bedrooms look out to this idyllic scene and have patios and balconies where you can while away the hours. More sea views are the backdrop to The Nare's two restaurants. The main Dining Room is traditional with table d'hôte menus that specialise in classic English cuisine. The Quarterdeck Restaurant is more informal with the opportunity to have breakfast, lunch or dinner on the terrace overlooking Gerrans Bay or inside where floor-to-ceiling windows bring the scenic views to your table. Both serve local seafood dishes such as Portloe lobster and crab, and delicious home-made puddings with lashings of Cornish cream. Make the most of your time in Cornwall and explore the glorious Roseland Peninsula's villages and gardens or the stunning coastline from The Nare's own classic 38' motor launch.

PRICE FROM:
£290

FEATURES:
Family friendly; Pet friendly; Pool; Sea views; Spa

ACTIVITIES:
Shooting; Tennis; Walking

NEARBY:
Many of The Great Gardens of Cornwall including Lost Gardens of Heligan; National Maritime Museum; St Mawes; The Eden Project; Lanhydrock Country House and Estate

GETTING THERE:
M5; Truro Railway Station; Newquay Airport

+44 (0)1872 501111 ☎
condenastjohansens.com/nare ⊕
Carne Beach, Veryan-in-Roseland, Truro, Cornwall TR2 5PF, ⌂
England

The Royal Duchy Hotel

Seaside action and total relaxation on Falmouth Bay

PRICE FROM:
£74 (per person)

FEATURES:
Family friendly; Pool; Restaurant; Sea views

ACTIVITIES:
Sightseeing; Walking; Water sports

NEARBY:
National Maritime Museum; Pendennis Castle; The Eden Project; Lost Gardens of Heligan; St Ives

GETTING THERE:
A39; Falmouth Railway Station; Newquay Airport

☎ +44 (0)1326 313042
🌐 condenastjohansens.com/royalduchy
🏠 Cliff Road, Falmouth, Cornwall TR11 4NX, England

Popular for its polished service, cosseting comfort and sea views across Falmouth Bay and to Pendennis Castle, The Royal Duchy Hotel promises a relaxing getaway. However, there's plenty of active pursuits in surrounding Cornwall and the West Country such as deep sea fishing, fly-fishing, yachting, sailing, pony trekking and numerous water sports to keep days interesting if and when you feel sprightly. Families are more than welcome to The Royal Duchy with designated family rooms and large interconnecting rooms as well as deluxe with sea-front views. Thoughtful touches include binoculars, fresh flowers, slippers and chocolates, and careful consideration is made for those requiring extra beds, cots and bunk beds. On-site there's ample to keep you (and the children) busy with an indoor heated pool, snooker room, sauna and treatment room, not to mention an entertainment programme during the school holidays. Then, come mealtimes, The Pendennis Restaurant offers up an eclectic mix of classic and inventive dishes alongside a children's menu, all prepared from fresh Cornish produce. For a less formal affair, meals and snacks can be served to you in the Terrace Lounge or bar (try a Duchy cocktail or local beer while you're here). It's entirely up to you.

Armathwaite Hall Hotel and Spa

The Lake District manor with its very own wildlife park

Armathwaite Hall Hotel and Spa in the English Lake District is a mighty impressive stately home oozing period drama with a modern sensibility. Set in no less than 450 acres of parkland, this 4 Red Star hotel faces not only the pretty Bassenthwaite Lake but also the imposing Skiddaw Mountain and Lake District Fells (don't forget the camera!). Armathwaite Hall is privately owned by the Graves family who in recent years added a luxury spa with a 16-metre infinity pool, thermal suite, outdoor hot tub and 10 treatment rooms. Guest rooms are categorised into numerous groups such as studio suites (with lake views), deluxe rooms (aptly named double rooms), spa rooms (convenient for spa breaks) and deluxe family rooms (some have bunk beds). Each is individually furnished and most have lake, park or garden views. Mealtimes are something to remember thanks to Armathwaite Hall's two dining options. The Courtyard Bar and Brasserie offers informal, contemporary dining while the Rosette-awarded, fine-dining Lake View Restaurant showcases seasonal local produce. Within the estate's grounds is The Lake District Wildlife Park, home to hundreds of rare breeds and endangered species, where conservation work is paramount. The Park includes a Bird of Prey Centre where half and full day experiences for the whole family take place.

PRICE FROM:
£205

FEATURES:
Helipad; Lake views; Pet friendly; Pool; Spa

ACTIVITIES:
Fishing; Shooting; Walking

NEARBY:
The Lake District Wildlife Park; Bassenthwaite Lake; Lake District National Park; Wordsworth House and Garden; Ullswater Steamers

GETTING THERE:
M6 jct 40; Carlisle Railway Station; Newcastle Airport

+44 (0)17687 76551 ☎
condenastjohansens.com/armathwaite 🌐
Bassenthwaite Lake, Keswick, Cumbria CA12 4RE, England 🏠

Sharrow Bay

The "jewel of the Lakes" continues to dazzle beside Ullswater

PRICE FROM:
£150

FEATURES:
Lake views; Pet friendly; Restaurant

ACTIVITIES:
Cycling; Fishing; Water sports

NEARBY:
The Ullswater Way; Ullswater Steamers; The Lakeland Bird of Prey Centre; Dalemain House and Garden; Lowther Castle & Gardens

GETTING THERE:
M6; Penrith Railway Station; Newcastle Airport

☎ +44 (0)1768 486301
🌐 condenastjohansens.com/sharrowbay
🏠 Ullswater, Penrith, Cumbria CA10 2LZ, England

Sharrow Bay is an English Lakes legend. Idyllically located directly on the lakeshore, at the foot of Ullswater's wild and quiet Eastern Fells, the panoramic views from here are utterly breathtaking. Heralded as the very first "country house hotel" following its launch in the late 1940s by Francis Coulson, his subsequent business partnership with Brian Sack became an industry-changing event. Sharrow Bay was also where the original recipe for Sticky Toffee Pudding was created by Francis in the 1970s. Today, private ownership of the hotel ensures that Brian and Francis' polished hospitality lives on, with a reputation for fine dining and an excellent, extensive wine cellar. A refreshing makeover of the rooms has updated the original décor, whilst keeping its highly unique and eclectic character. Guest rooms are located in the Main House, Garden Wing and Edwardian Gate Lodge; each one individually styled and as comfortable and reassuringly traditional as the next. Most enjoy those spectacular views. Sharrow Bay is the perfect base for a leisurely break or exploring all the outdoor activities the Lakes are becoming famed for. These include a cruise along the Lake on an Ullswater Steamer making it back in time for a guilt-free, mouth-watering à la carte dinner or exceptional tasting menu.

Cedar Manor Hotel and Restaurant

Rural elegance in Cumbria's Windermere

Cedar Manor Hotel and Restaurant in the Lake District may be chocolate-box-pretty from the outside but inside there's nothing twee or cutesy about it. Everything is high-end and country home chic, in-keeping with its original Victorian gothic style yet refreshingly smart. It's easy to imagine the original Victorian gentleman of the house surveying his garden and resting by the dominating cedar tree; perhaps admiring the house's brickwork and tall arched windows. Today, it's eco-conscious owners Jonathan and Caroline Kaye who care for this romantic boutique retreat with 10 newly refurbished bedrooms (available for exclusive hire) just half a mile from Lake Windermere. Sofas are sink-into cosy, the armchairs are reading-the-paper-perfection and each room contains locally crafted furnishings; some have views to the Lake and Langdale Pikes. Considered one of the finest suites in the Lake District, Cedar Manor's two-storey Coach House Suite is packed with "wow" factors (super-king-size bed, huge double bathroom with stand-alone air bath and walk-in wet room) whilst special touches such as spa baths grace the rooms and suites in the main house. This is also where you'll find the fine-dining restaurant for breakfast, lunch and dinner with a seasonally-led menu that's become a local attraction. New to Cedar Manor: the all-day snack menu and front patio for relaxing during warmer months.

PRICE FROM:
£135

FEATURES:
Lake views; Restaurant

ACTIVITIES:
Fishing; Golf; Walking

NEARBY:
Lake Windermere and town; Blackwell, The Arts & Crafts House; The World of Beatrix Potter Attraction; Dove Cottage

GETTING THERE:
A591; M6 jct 36; Windermere Railway Station

+44 (0)1539 443192 ☎
condenastjohansens.com/cedarmanor 🌐
Ambleside Road, Windermere, Cumbria LA23 1AX, England 📧

Gilpin Hotel & Lake House

Two outstanding country houses - one family's gift to Cumbria

PRICE FROM:
£335 (including four-course dinner)

FEATURES:
Helipad; Lake views*; Restaurant

ACTIVITIES:
Cycling; Golf; Walking

NEARBY:
Lake Windermere; The Lake District Fells; Blackwell, The Arts & Crafts House; Hill Top, Beatrix Potter's home; Dove Cottage, William Wordsworth's home

GETTING THERE:
M6 jct 36; Oxenholme/Windermere Railway Stations; Manchester Airport

*Lake House only

☎ +44 (0)15394 88818
🌐 condenastjohansens.com/thegilpin
🏠 Crook Road, Windermere, Cumbria LA23 3NE, England

When a property is run with the unwavering passion that's expressed by the Cunliffes, it shows in every detail. Owned and managed by the family since 1988, Gilpin Hotel & Lake House in Windermere spans across two estates. The 20-acre Gilpin Hotel estate is where you'll find 25 country chic bedrooms, Junior Suites, Garden Suites (each with their own outdoor cedar wood hot tub) and the recently opened Spa Lodges. The Spa Lodges each have an open-plan bedroom with huge windows, a treatment area, steam room, rain shower, stone bath and a walled garden with sauna and hydrotherapy hot tub. They're exceptionally romantic and provide an indulgent spa experience. Gilpin Hotel is also where the restaurants are located. In the main restaurant, Hrishikesh Desai delivers Lake District produce showcasing incredible textures and flavours of modern British cuisine with a twist. In contrast, the recently opened informal restaurant focuses on the spice trail with dishes from the Indian sub-continent, Japan, China and South East Asia. Located one mile from Gilpin Hotel, within 100 acres of grounds, is the utterly private six-suite Lake House on the shore of a small lake with boat house and jetty (exclusive to Lake House guests). Each evening, chauffeurs ferry Lake House guests to and from the restaurants at Gilpin Hotel. Take note event planners: the Lake House can be booked for exclusive use.

Holbeck Ghyll

Gourmet food, outdoor adventure and epic scenery in the Lake District

It's all about staggering scenery, culinary genius and profound peace at Holbeck Ghyll, a former hunting lodge perched high above Lake Windermere. Now a warm and inviting hotel where old world grace meets modern sensibility, service is instinctive, friendly and thoughtful (expect a welcoming hot water bottle in your bed on a cold night). Rooms and suites are spread across three locations: the main house with Arts and Crafts décor, oak-panelled walls, classic William Morris prints and roaring fires; the contemporary eight-bedroom Lodge comprising interconnecting and dog-friendly rooms; and two cottages (Renee Zellweger stayed in the Miss Potter Suite while filming Miss Potter, the Beatrix Potter biopic). These smart cottages are perfect for mini-breaks and include special touches such as spa baths. Foodie heaven is dished up on a plate in Holbeck's oak-panelled restaurant from breakfasts of Cumbrian air-dried ham and free-range eggs, and afternoon teas with delicate cakes to five-course gourmet dinners featuring tian of crab and Cumbrian lamb. Outside, the natural playground of the Lakes presents endless opportunities to cycle, climb, walk and sail. But for lazier days, there's always the escape of the health spa offering LaStone therapy, ESPA enzyme facials and reflexology.

PRICE FROM:
£280 (including dinner)

FEATURES:
Helipad; Lake views; Pet friendly; Restaurant; Wheelchair access

ACTIVITIES:
Cycling; Sightseeing; Walking

NEARBY:
Lake Windemere; Lake District National Park; The World of Beatrix Potter Attraction; Climbing/walking trails of Coniston Old Man, the Langdale Pikes and Scafell Pike

GETTING THERE:
A591; M6 jct 36; Oxenholme Lake District Railway Station

+44 (0)15394 32375 ☎
condenastjohansens.com/holbeckghyll 🌐
Holbeck Lane, Windermere, Cumbria LA23 1LU, England 🏠

Lakeside Hotel & Spa

Overlooking nothing but Lake Windermere

PRICE FROM:
£179

FEATURES:
Gym; Lake views; Pool; Spa

ACTIVITIES:
Cycling; Sightseeing; Walking

NEARBY:
Windermere Lake cruises; Lake District Aquarium; Lakeland Motor Museum; Lakeside and Haverthwaite Steam Railway; Holker Hall and Gardens

GETTING THERE:
M6 jct 36; Oxenholme Railway Station; Manchester Airport

☎ +44 (0)15395 30001
🌐 condenastjohansens.com/lakeside
🏠 Lakeside, Newby Bridge, Cumbria LA12 8AT, England

Sensationally picturesque and uniquely located, Lakeside Hotel & Spa on the edge of Lake Windermere is a reassuringly classic and relaxed luxury Lake District hotel. From the moment you step through the doors its enchanting spell is cast and lingers long after your visit is over. Many of the bedrooms and suites look out to the lovely lake vistas and ground floor rooms open onto private patios. Families are welcome here with a selection of suites and interconnecting rooms. In the kitchen, Cumbrian favourites are the order of the day served in the highly-applauded Lakeview Restaurant and contemporary John Ruskin's Brasserie & Bar. Dishes at John Ruskin's also showcase traditional fare, the ingredients of which are sometimes divulged within the Chef's blog so you can try it out at home. To achieve an authentic Lake District experience, cruises are available adjacent to the hotel ready for your exploration and adventure but in case of inclement weather, Lakeside Hotel's pool and spa (exclusive to hotel residents) provides a pampering alternative. The huge indoor pool, gym, sauna, steam room and Aveda treatment rooms complete the picture. For business travellers: Lakeside's Windermere Suite is a business and events venue located opposite the hotel available for private use offering delegates privacy and first-rate hotel services.

Linthwaite House

Getting country house hospitality perfectly right in the Lake District

These are exciting times for Linthwaite House in the Lake District. As a recent addition to the Leeu Collection's portfolio of three South African boutique hotels, Linthwaite is its one and only British retreat. Of course, the showroom-perfect bedrooms and seriously good restaurant continue to wow guests and those Lake Windermere vistas (over to Belle Isle), endless acres of flowering garden and woodland never cease to impress. The nine-hole putting green and par three practice hole also attract attention. So centrally located at the heart of the Lake District, walkers love it here, while culture vultures can follow in the footsteps of William Wordsworth and Beatrix Potter. But stepping out of Linthwaite's cosseting world isn't easy. By marrying on-trend interior fashions with homely comfort (very House & Garden) and providing the finest hospitality, you never want to leave! The pretty lake, garden and fell views from most of the bedrooms keep you rooted to the cushioned spot too. If you've reserved the popular Luxury Lake View Room with outside hot tub, just try and remember to check the time. It would be a crying shame to miss out on Linthwaite's modern British food meticulously prepared from fresh, local produce. The list of fine wines is equally outstanding. In fact, Leeu Collection's founder Analjit Singh is a partner in the award-winning winery, Mullineux & Leeu Family Wines.

PRICE FROM:
£154

FEATURES:
Helipad; Lake views; Pet friendly; Restaurant; Wheelchair access

ACTIVITIES:
Fishing; Golf; Walking

NEARBY:
Windermere; The World of Beatrix Potter Attraction; Dove Cottage; Lake District National Park; Brantwood

GETTING THERE:
M6 jct 36; Oxenholme Railway Station; Manchester Airport

+44 (0)15394 88600 ☎
condenastjohansens.com/linthwaitehouse 🌐
Crook Road, Windermere, Cumbria LA23 3JA, England 📧

Fischer's Baslow Hall

Michelin-Starred restaurant with rooms on the edge of Chatsworth house estate

PRICE FROM:
£200

FEATURES:
Michelin Starred restaurant

ACTIVITIES:
Cycling; Fishing; Walking

NEARBY:
Chatsworth house; Haddon Hall; Market towns of Bakewell and Buxton; Peak District National Park

GETTING THERE:
A623; M1 jct 29; Manchester Airport

☎ +44 (0)1246 583259
🌐 condenastjohansens.com/fischers
🏠 Calver Road, Baslow, Derbyshire DE45 1RR, England

As scrumptiously delightful as a Bakewell tart, Fischer's Baslow Hall sits only four miles from where the teatime fancy originates. A beautiful Edwardian manor house, this is an intimate, pleasure-inducing, cosy country house a-flurry with soft furnishings, plump pillows and fluffy white towels. Gorgeous floral prints, parquet flooring and pretty leaded windows embrace the character and warmth of this listed building. Max and Susan Fischer acquired Baslow Hall in 1989 and lovingly renovated the property with pride. Their hospitality is unparalleled alongside a carefully chosen team of dedicated staff. They all go to great lengths to ensure your visit is memorable. Front of house is in the safe hands of General Manager John Cooper, while Head Chef Rupert Rowley's instinctive approach creates Michelin Starred dishes from locally sourced ingredients (some of which are grown in the hotel's garden). He showcases the best of British produce in his Taste of Britain menu, which is out of this world, and now offers a Kitchen Tasting Bench experience. This allows for up to four diners to watch the masters at work from the centre of the kitchen. Baslow Hall also offers private dining options perfect for wedding and business receptions. With Chatsworth house nearby and an array of activities such as great cycling routes, your stay will be a satisfying mix of English heritage and traditions.

Cary Arms

Seaside adventure for everyone on South Devon's coast

Lana de Savary's passion and talent for establishing high quality hotels, clubs and resorts with husband Peter led her to the picturesque Babbacombe Bay on the South West Coast Path. Based on the concept of creating a place of fun for everyone, maintaining the essence of a quintessential English inn and the luxury of a boutique hotel, Cary Arms was born. It's wholesome, hearty and comforting. It's also a hotspot for water-sport enthusiasts. The whole family is welcome here, including the dog. There's not only a family suite but a dog friendly one too complete with dog bed and bowl. Each guest room is an expression of designer Kathleen Fraser whose chic seaside living décor brings a fresh, New England flavour. They all overlook the sea and luxury rooms have a private balcony or terrace. Six new Beach Huts and two Beach Suites also convey a cool New England vibe and contain sitting rooms with contemporary feature fires, wet bars and first-floor bedrooms looking out to the watery vistas. For utter seclusion, three to five-bedroom cottages are available. Weather permitting, dinner is taken alfresco otherwise the Conservatory is a great viewing point. The ever-changing menus present simple, seasonal, English Heritage Dining from local produce and line-caught seafood. Don't miss: the new spa with plunge pool fitted with massage jets, a steam room, mini gym and sun deck.

PRICE FROM:
£195

FEATURES:
Family friendly; Pet friendly; Restaurant; Sea views; Spa

ACTIVITIES:
Golf; Horse riding; Water sports

NEARBY:
Babbacombe Cliff Railway; Cockington Court; Torre Abbey; Greenway, former home of Agatha Christie

GETTING THERE:
M5; Newton Abbot Railway Station; Exeter International Airport

+44 (0)1803 327110 ☎
condenastjohansens.com/caryarms 🌐
Babbacombe Beach, South Devon TQ1 3LX, England 🏢

Saunton Sands Hotel

Holidaying by the sea from stunning art-deco surrounds on the North Devon Coast

---

PRICE FROM:
£140

FEATURES:
Beach access; Gym; Helipad; Pool; Spa

ACTIVITIES:
Golf; Tennis; Walking

NEARBY:
Braunton and District Museum; The Tarka Trail; RHS Rosemoor Garden; Dartington Crystal Visitor Centre; UNESCO World Biosphere Reserve of Braunton Burrows

GETTING THERE:
M5; Barnstaple Railway Station; Exeter/Bristol Airports

☎ +44 (0)1271 890212
🌐 condenastjohansens.com/sauntonsands
🏠 Saunton, Braunton, North Devon EX33 1LQ, England

Four hours from London the North Devon Coast offers the ultimate breath of salt-tinged fresh air and escape from the hustle and bustle of the urban haze. On these immaculate golden sandy shores Saunton Sands Hotel stands against the dramatic backdrop of the famous South West Coastal Path. This is postcard perfection. The beach Saunton faces is big (three miles to be precise) but the breakers are even bigger. As a surfer's paradise, things get going in June with the arrival of surf and music festival, Gold Coast Oceanfest, held in neighbouring Croyde Bay. However, activities for the whole family abound all year such as horse riding, cliff-top walking, cycling trails and sand dune frolicking. Thanks to the West Coast's natural larder (Lundy lobster, Devonshire crab, Exmoor venison) you can expect superb locally sourced meals in Saunton's restaurant, acknowledged by an AA Rosette. Full English breakfasts begin the day and are somehow made even better by the panoramic views. Draped in aquamarine coloured silk as striking as the ocean outside, guest rooms are spacious and versatile. Then there are the indoor and outdoor pools, spa, tennis and squash courts, mini-gym and nearby golf courses that cement the hotel's status as one of England's chicest seaside retreats. Don't miss a spot of famous Devonshire cream tea.

The Old Rectory Hotel

A North Devon escape from the daily grind

A place for contemplation, relaxation and rejuvenation, The Old Rectory Hotel, North Devon, keeps things uncomplicated. Caring hospitality, stylish elegance and great cuisine are its hallmarks run by perfectionists Huw Rees and Sam Prosser. High up on the cliffs of Exmoor National Park on North Devon's coast, The Old Rectory looks out to undulating National Trust land from acres of an impossibly immaculate garden with trout pond and Victorian maze. The hotel was originally a Georgian rectory and has undergone a beautifully executed refurbishment to provide all the modern comforts discerning travellers expect (free super-fast WiFi for one). Each bedroom has a character of its own and a tasteful country chic style. Eight are located in The Old Rectory while three exceptionally spoiling suites are next door in the Coach House. When it comes to mealtimes, Huw and Sam's ethos of doing things well is most evident. The excellent dishes are created from local seasonal produce (North Coast fish and seafood, meat from an ethical local farm) served alongside an expertly chosen wine list that's won high acclaim. If you feel the need to burn off some of these calories, The Old Rectory's garden leads to the Coastal Path where some of the most spectacular scenery England has to offer is found.

PRICE FROM:
£210

FEATURES:
Restaurant; Wheelchair access

ACTIVITIES:
Fishing; Golf; Walking

NEARBY:
South West Coastal Path; Lynmouth; Woolacombe; Exmoor; Lundy Island

GETTING THERE:
M5 jct 25; Barnstaple Railway Station; Bristol Airport

+44 (0)1598 763368 ☎
condenastjohansens.com/oldrectoryexmoor 🌐
Martinhoe, Exmoor National Park, Devon EX31 4QT, England 🏠

Hotel Endsleigh

Genteel Regency grace in the outstanding Devonshire landscape

PRICE FROM:
£190 (minimum two-night stay during weekends)

FEATURES:
Family friendly; Pet friendly; Restaurant

ACTIVITIES:
Fishing; Horse riding; Shooting

NEARBY:
Cothele House; North Cornish coast; 4×4 driving; Tree-surfing;
Adrenaline Quarry

GETTING THERE:
A388; Gunnislake Railway Station; Exeter Airport

Hotel Endsleigh still feels like the private sporting retreat it once was, set in rural perfection. Reminders of the past include baronial shields in the wood-panelled dining room and the formal terrace overlooking all 108 acres of rolling woodland. 200-year-old landscaped gardens designed by Humphry Repton immediately surround the hotel and are an attraction in their own right. These feature follies, grottos, streams and an arboretum. Inside the hotel, everything has been brought gently up to 21st-century date to offer country house comfort without the chintz. This is a continually evolving labour of love with a revamped living room and library, plus two new suites in the Grade I listed former stable block. Each room and suite showcases Olga Polizzi décor, antiques and vintage 1950s' English fabrics; the new family suite has bunk beds and a wood-burning stove. In summer, the fabulous local cuisine tastes even better when eaten on the terrace. In winter, cosying up to the fire in the library is even more relaxing with a tipple from the impressive wine list. Known as the prettiest spot in Devon, the River Tamar flows through the grounds and Hotel Endsleigh's ghillie can transform you into a fly-fishing pro within hours! Croquet, canoeing, archery and shooting are all here and Dartmoor is on the doorstep. For some "me time" visit the nearby country club with spa or book an in-room spa treatment.

☎ +44 (0)1822 870000
🌐 condenastjohansens.com/hotelendsleigh
🏠 Milton Abbot, Devon PL19 0PQ, England

Soar Mill Cove Hotel & Spa

South Hams coastal escape-from-it-all

Outdoor-loving families, hopeless romantics and friends escaping the daily grind all flock to Soar Mill Cove Hotel & Spa for some good old-fashioned wholesome fun, scenic beauty and warm hospitality. Beside the south Devon coast, this remote getaway faces the golden sands of a private beach and feels a world away from the urban rat race. Sporty types love the sailing, snorkelling and tennis opportunities while others revel in the exceptional restaurant, swish Bollinger bar and serene Discovery Spa. This is the Makepeace family's home, business and passion, and the importance of family is evident at every turn (you're welcome to bring Fido too). The atmosphere is friendly, the service is polished and the amenities are diverse. It's also a convenient location for exploring nearby Salcombe and numerous National Trust houses and gardens. Well-appointed rooms include family suites and come with sea-facing patios. Two additional self-catering villas, plus the five-bedroom West Soar House (with hot tub) are also located within the grounds for exclusive escapes. The heart of Soar Mill Cove is the 2 Rosette-awarded restaurant with Head Chef Ian MacDonald at the helm who uses fresh, local ingredients to dictate his seasonal menu (don't miss the cooking demos). Top tip: enquire about the latest short break offers and take the little ones to the relaxed café for high tea.

PRICE FROM:
£199

FEATURES:
Beach access; Family friendly; Pool; Restaurant; Spa

ACTIVITIES:
Golf; Walking; Water sports

NEARBY:
Salcombe; Totnes; Dartmouth; South West Coast Path; Thurestone and Dartmouth Golf Courses

GETTING THERE:
A38; Totnes Railway Station; Bolt Head landing strip

+44 (0)1548 561566 ☎
condenastjohansens.com/soarmillcove 🌐
Soar Mill Cove, Near Salcombe, South Devon TQ7 3DS, England 🏠

Hotel Riviera

The pride of Sidmouth's Regency England

PRICE FROM:
£198 (including five-course table d'hôte dinner)

FEATURES:
Beach access; Family friendly; Restaurant; Sea views;
Wheelchair access

ACTIVITIES:
Golf; Tennis; Walking

NEARBY:
Killerton House and Gardens; Exeter Cathedral; Powderham
Castle; Dartmoor

GETTING THERE:
M5 jct 30; Honiton/Exeter St David's Railway Stations; Exeter
International Airport

☎ +44 (0)1395 515201
🌐 condenastjohansens.com/riviera
🏠 The Esplanade, Sidmouth, Devon EX10 8AY, England

Poet Laureate John Betjeman described Sidmouth as "a town caught still in a timeless charm." Full of Regency splendour, seaside fun and dramatic (protected Jurassic) red cliff coastline, his words continue to ring true today. Perfectly located at the centre of Sidmouth's historic Georgian esplanade is Hotel Riviera overlooking Lyme Bay. Its bright Regency façade with bow-fronted windows foretells the elegance within whose handsome public rooms and classically appointed bedrooms (many with sea views) are arguably some of the most comfortable and hospitable in the region. This prestigious and welcoming coastal hotel - awarded 4 Stars by both the AA and Visit Britain - is also a proven success story of traditional service and know-how. Owned and run by the Wharton family for more than 40 years, Hotel Riviera places comfort and professional service above all else, committed to providing the very highest standards of excellence. Nowhere is this more evident than in the fine-dining salon where cuisine prepared by English and French trained chefs is paired with exceptional wines from the cellar. The Cocktail Bar is open until midnight most evenings where the resident pianist can be found playing for your pleasure. Look out for: Hotel Riviera's annually anticipated festive programme and seasonal breaks.

The Horn of Plenty

Tavistock proves that the best things really do come in small packages

Somewhere to escape to, nestle in and breathe out, this is a retreat for the soul on the scenic Devon/Cornwall border. You're not far from Tavistock, Dartmoor and the Eden Project here but the surrounding five acres of skilfully crafted gardens allow you to hole up with a lover, take some time-out for a well-deserved break or simply drink in the natural beauty around you with uninterrupted tranquillity. The refinement of the house (awarded Silver in the VisitEngland Awards for Excellence 2015) is perfectly matched by its setting with breathtaking views of Tamar Valley below. Foodies come to The Horn of Plenty Country House Hotel & Restaurant for a fine-dining experience, which has upheld an exemplary reputation for more than 40 years. The kitchen is genuinely passionate about creating superb food from seasonal produce that's locally sourced whenever possible and creates menus that often include Newlyn crab, rump of Devonshire lamb and Cornish turbot. It's known as one of the best in Devon, if not the South West. As for the 16 guest rooms - six of which were recently added - each individually styled refuge is decorated to showroom perfection. Those in the main house are classic in character whilst Coach House rooms reflect a more contemporary design.

PRICE FROM:
£110

FEATURES:
Helipad; Pet friendly; Restaurant

ACTIVITIES:
Cycling; Sightseeing; Walking

NEARBY:
Dartmoor National Park; Buckland Abbey; Devon coastline; Eden Project; Cotehele

GETTING THERE:
Just off A390; M5 jct 31; Exeter International Airport

+44 (0)1822 832528 ☎
condenastjohansens.com/thehornofplenty 🌐
Gulworthy, Tavistock, Devon PL19 8JD, England 🏠

Orestone Manor Hotel & Restaurant

Very English, very pretty, very charming South Devon getaway

PRICE FROM:
£110

FEATURES:
Family friendly; Restaurant; Sea views

ACTIVITIES:
Fishing; Golf; Walking

NEARBY:
Babbacombe Model Village; Kents Cavern; Award-winning beaches; Greenway, former home of Agatha Christie; Dartmoor

GETTING THERE:
M5 jct 30; Newton Abbot Railway Station; Exeter International Airport

☎ +44 (0)1803 897511
🌐 condenastjohansens.com/orestonemanor
🏠 Rockhouse Lane, Maidencombe, Torquay, Devon TQ1 4SX, England

Gently warmed by the gulf stream and overlooking some of England's most beautiful coastline is the Georgian delight of Orestone Manor Hotel & Restaurant. A country house home-from-home, this family-run escape sings with English charm complete with a pretty English garden and magnificent sea views over Lyme Bay. Located a stone's throw from some of Devon's loveliest beaches, it's well worth visiting Maidencombe beach whose red cliffs shelter a sandy cove and for some bucket and spade action there's nearby Teignmouth for traditional English seaside fun. The local cognoscenti know Orestone as a hotspot for some of Devon's best food. Whether it's fine-dining or bistro-style fare that tickles your fancy, Orestone's cuisine excels because of its use of local ingredients from Brixham scallops to locally produced cheeses. Food is served in the elegant restaurant or conservatory, while in summer, Orestone's chic veranda is just the place for alfresco feasting. 14 flamboyant bedrooms including two new Coach House Suites (family-friendly, split-level cottages each with a lounge, balcony and outdoor hot tub) provide a welcoming retreat at the end of your day. Before booking: check out Orestone's schedule of events and catch one of their much-loved Seafood Nights, Pudding Tasting Evenings and comedy dinner theatre experiences.

Watersmeet Hotel & Restaurant

North Devon's premier coastal escape

From an elevated position above Combesgate beach, just moments from the South West Coastal Path, Watersmeet Hotel & Restaurant seemingly floats above the North Atlantic coast. Considered one of the most dramatic locations in the South West, Watersmeet resides between the seaside village of Mortehoe and Woolacombe beach. A fresh, contemporary retreat ideal for romantic getaways and short breaks, this is also a walker's and rambler's paradise with various National Trust coastal trails (Morte Point, Baggy Point) nearby. Golfers enjoy two world-class links courses close by. Watersmeet has direct access to the sandy shore below via a set of steps but for the best bird's eye views of this ever-changing coastline over to Lundy Island, gaze through the wall of windows onto the hotel's brand new terrace spread across two levels. From here, you may dine alfresco and/or enjoy a cocktail. Many of the guest rooms have balconies facing these sea views too; one has a four poster and the top-floor suite is a cosy, romantic option. Weather permitting, alfresco lunch and tea in the tea garden is a must, and dining by candlelight at the pavilion restaurant is essential. Dishes are well balanced, imaginative and contain local ingredients. Alternatively, the Bistro serves classic British favourites. Additional facilities: a heated outdoor pool, indoor pool with hot spa and steam room.

PRICE FROM:
£150

FEATURES:
Family friendly; Pool; Restaurant; Spa; Wheelchair access

ACTIVITIES:
Fishing; Golf; Walking

NEARBY:
Barnstaple; National Trust coastal walks; Arlington Court; Coastal footpaths to Morte Point and Baggy Point; Watermouth Castle

GETTING THERE:
A361; M5 jct 27; Bristol Airport

+44 (0)1271 870333 ☎
condenastjohansens.com/watersmeet 🌐
Mortehoe, Woolacombe, Devon EX34 7EB, England 🏨

The Woolacombe Bay Hotel

Wholesome seaside fun with a sophisticated touch in North Devon

PRICE FROM:
£160

FEATURES:
Beach access; Family friendly; Pool; Restaurant; Sea views

ACTIVITIES:
Cycling; Horse riding; Tennis

NEARBY:
Barnstaple; Exmoor; National Trust coastal walks; Lynton; RHS Garden Rosemoor

GETTING THERE:
A361; M5 jct 27; Barnstaple Railway Station

☎ +44 (0)1271 870388
🌐 condenastjohansens.com/woolacombebay
🏠 South Street, Woolacombe, Devon EX34 7BN, England

If the Lancaster family were inclined to wax lyrical about their North Devon Victorian retreat, they might say that its location is unbeatable, its yesteryear charm is timeless and its facilities are second-to-none. But there's simply no need, for The Woolacombe Bay Hotel speaks for itself. Facing the Atlantic Ocean from the surfers' spot of Woolacombe beach with Lundy Island in the distance, this seaside sojourn has been coined Britain's Best Beach and is considered one of Europe's finest stretches of coast. Between these golden shores and The Woolacombe Bay Hotel is the Bay Lido, exclusive to guests where (weather permitting!) poolside barbecues take place. The hotel is also surrounded by acres of landscaped grounds, which many of the bedrooms look out to. It's well worth booking a Luxury Sea View Room with private balcony or a Luxury Suite whose on-trend décor and generous proportions are perfect for romantic getaways or extended family breaks. And as a hub of activity both indoors and out, there's plenty to keep adults and children of all ages occupied with tennis, squash, snooker, The Den and The Hothouse Health Club and Haven Spa. Come mealtimes, there are two restaurants to choose from. Doyle's seasonal, locally sourced menu features tasty seafood dishes and inspired vegetarian meals, whilst the Bay Brasserie is your casual, Mediterranean-inspired option.

The Green House

Eco-cred with creative finesse in beachy Bournemouth

This Grade II listed Victorian villa may be white on the outside but it's green through and through. Setting new standards in eco-tourism, the owners of the 32-room Green House in Bournemouth scoured the area for the all that's green and clean. This resulted in rooms filled with wooden furniture crafted from storm-felled trees, beds dressed in fairtrade cotton sheets, low-impact power supplies and walls covered in sustainable paper. The décor is quirky, sophisticated and luxurious; and each member of staff is knowledgeable and genuinely friendly. Drinks at the cosy bar are followed by refreshingly unpretentious meals at Arbor restaurant (a member of the 2 AA Rosette club). And as you would expect from The Green House, all ingredients are locally sourced: many of Dorset's farms and the New Forest coastline are close by so Chef Andy Hilton has the pick of the crops, finest seafood and fairtrade produce. Daily deliveries of meat, veg and dairy keep everything fresh and seasonal. Arbor and the adjoining bar have become the go-to destination for locals in-the-know hankering a spot of afternoon tea, a cocktail or two and Sunday roasts as well as the hearty dinners enjoyed under the branches of the wooden tree sculpture that dominates the dining room. (Arbor is Latin for "tree".) Pamper bonus: in-room beauty treatments can be arranged.

PRICE FROM:
£109

FEATURES:
Restaurant; Wheelchair access

ACTIVITIES:
Cycling; Walking; Water sports

NEARBY:
Eight miles of sandy beach; Sandbanks; Brownsea Island; The New Forest; Christchurch Castle ruins

GETTING THERE:
A338; Bournemouth Railway Station; Bournemouth Airport

+44 (0)1202 498900 ☎
condenastjohansens.com/greenhousehotel 🌐
4 Grove Road, Bournemouth, Dorset BH1 3AX, England 🏠

Captain's Club Hotel and Spa

Timeless nautical style near Christchurch, Dorset

PRICE FROM:
£289

FEATURES:
Family friendly; Pet friendly; Restaurant; Spa; Wheelchair access

ACTIVITIES:
Fishing; Golf; Walking

NEARBY:
Christchurch Priory; Christchurch Harbour; River and sea cruise; New Forest National Park

GETTING THERE:
A35; Christchurch Railway Station; Bournemouth International Airport

☎ +44 (0)1202 475111
🌐 condenastjohansens.com/captainsclubhotel
🏠 Wick Lane, Christchurch, Dorset BH23 1HU, England

Maritime fever at Captain's Club Hotel and Spa is contagious. If the nautically themed bedrooms and suites, fresh fish and seafood in the Restaurant and deckchairs on the CCSpa's terrace fail to have you reaching for your deck shoes, then the riverside views from every room just might. Trips on Captain's Club's private 34-foot cruiser, Orchid, most certainly will. For this is where the Rivers Avon and Stour meet, a short stroll from the age-old coastal town of Christchurch (whose Priory Church has choir stalls older than those in Westminster Abbey). Captain's Club Hotel moors alongside the river like a mighty cruise liner overseeing its active comings and goings. Inside, it's sleek and contemporary, awash with neutral colour schemes and ever-present, watery-related elements in each of the State Rooms (doubles) and suites. For longer stays or visits with the family, the two and three-bedroom, two-bathroom suites (kitchen too!) are perfect. And just as the hotel's style is elegantly uncomplicated, fresh and innovative, so too is the Restaurant's cuisine. Full of traditional favourites, just-caught shellfish and grilled fare, there's something for everyone. Chef will even prepare baby food on request. The award-winning cocktail bar and mixologists also draw a crowd but it's the afternoon Tea Club selections that are a must.

Summer Lodge Country House Hotel

Traditional English charm in pretty Evershot village

For an escape to the English countryside in distinguished style, it's got to be Summer Lodge Country House Hotel in Evershot, West Dorset. Complete with a pretty English garden spanning four acres, this idyllic scene borders a deer park teeming with wildlife and natural beauty all year-round. A private residence for almost 200 years, Summer Lodge was built as a dower house in 1798 for the second Earl of Ilchester. (Local architect and novelist Thomas Hardy was commissioned to extend the house in 1893.) And it wasn't until 1979 that Summer's charms opened up to the public. Now, it's a small country house hotel setting new heights in comfort, style, relaxation, courteous hospitality and exceptional cuisine; it feels more like a (genteel) home than a hotel. The bedrooms, suites and cottages are exceptionally tasteful and combine the finest English furnishings with all the modern amenities you would expect, including free WiFi. Meals in the restaurant (whose credentials are too many to list) are the creation of Head Chef Steven Titman, and world-renowned Sommelier Eric Zwiebel lends his expertise to the proceedings. Steven's lip-smacking cuisine uses an abundance of fresh local produce and herbs grown on-site. His traditional Dorset cream teas are legendary. For active guests: a conservatory-style pool, spa, gym, croquet lawn, tennis court and bicycles are all at your disposal.

PRICE FROM:
£215

FEATURES:
Family friendly; Pet friendly; Pool; Restaurant; Spa

ACTIVITIES:
Fishing; Golf; Walking

NEARBY:
Thomas Hardy country; Cerne Abbas; Abbotsbury; Jurassic Coast; Sherborne

GETTING THERE:
A37; M5 jct 25; Bristol Airport

+44 (0)1935 482000 ☎
condenastjohansens.com/summerlodge 🌐
9 Fore Street, Evershot, Dorset DT2 0JR, England ✉

Alexandra Hotel and Restaurant

Reassuringly traditional Dorset seaside hotel and foodie favourite

PRICE FROM:
£185

FEATURES:
Family friendly; Gym; Restaurant; Spa

ACTIVITIES:
Fishing; Golf; Horse riding

NEARBY:
South West Coast Path; Beaches; Fossil walks

GETTING THERE:
On the A3052; M25 jct 25; Exeter International Airport

A breath of fresh air, Alexandra Hotel and Restaurant in Lyme Regis is poised on the Jurassic Coast overlooking the picturesque Cobb Harbour. Distinctly devoid of any pretention or formality, Alexandra has found a balance between comfortable seaside holiday home and charming boutique hotel. Like the countess for whom the residence was built in 1735, this grande dame is reassuringly old fashioned, elegant and well maintained with just a hint of eccentricity. The place eeks of windswept romance and is set in beautiful gardens that lead you down to the beach; the perfect place to unfurl. The fresh sea air, rock-pooling and sandcastle building, coupled with treats such as beer crab and cucumber sandwiches are the stuff innocent Enid Blyton-esque childhood memories are made of. But Alexandra is a foodie destination at heart with Chef Ian Grant keeping it simple. Local and in-season, the menus are always a recipe for success. The recurring scallops with roasted cauliflower purée and truffle oil, and exceedingly good Dorset apple cake speak for themselves. Seemingly a million miles away from it all, the essence of Alexandra is so good you'll want to bottle it up and take it home with you.

☎ +44 (0)1297 442010
🌐 condenastjohansens.com/hotelalexandra
🏠 Pound Street, Lyme Regis, Dorset DT7 3HZ, England

Seaham Hall

Five-star R&R in County Durham

Poet, Romantic and hedonist Lord Byron married Anne Isabella Milbanke at Seaham Hall in 1815 and their daughter, celebrated mathematician and writer Ada Lovelace was born here. As a hub of historic significance this gracious Georgian manor on the Durham Heritage Coast has seen several incarnations: aristocratic home, military hospital and Prohibition-era whisky storehouse. Now, it's a leading spa hotel. Behind its 18th-century white walls, Seaham Hall has a refreshingly contemporary-luxe interior where distressed/retro furniture and bold patterns meet plush linens and high-tech gadgetry. An all-suite hotel ranging from juniors, gardens with hot tubs and executives, there is also a penthouse with lounge and dining area. Whether you're here to detox or retox, the Seaham experience isn't complete without a visit to the highly impressive Serenity Spa (17 treatment rooms, 25-metre pool) where inspiring up-to-the-minute treatments feature alongside ancient therapies. Ozone at Seaham Hall is the Pan-Asian restaurant with views of the pretty gardens. The main dining room, Byron's Restaurant, is as opulent as its namesake. Inspired by its coastal location, the menu fuses classical dishes with contemporary twists prepared from local produce to create mouth-watering dishes.

PRICE FROM:
£235

FEATURES:
Beach access; Helipad; Pool; Sea views; Spa

ACTIVITIES:
Cycling; Sightseeing; Walking

NEARBY:
Durham Castle and Cathedral; Durham Heritage Coastal trail; Beamish Museum; Hadrian's Wall; Bamburgh Castle

GETTING THERE:
A1M jct 62; Durham Railway Station; Newcastle Airport

+44 (0)191 5161400 ☎
condenastjohansens.com/seahamhall 🌐
Lord Byron's Walk, Seaham, County Durham SR7 7AG, 🏠
England

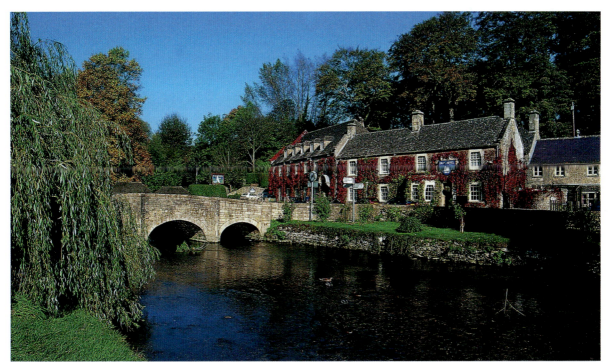

The Swan Hotel

Smart, stylish and ever-so "Cotswold" village inn

PRICE FROM:
£170

FEATURES:
Family friendly; Pet friendly; Restaurant; Wheelchair access

ACTIVITIES:
Fishing; Horse riding; Walking

NEARBY:
Cheltenham; Bath; Oxford; Cotswold Wildlife Park; Bibury Trout Farm

GETTING THERE:
A429; M4 jct 15/M5 jct 11; Birmingham International Airport

Bibury is the archetypal Cotswold village. Honey-hued terraced cottages, hilly green scenery and a tranquil riverside location all sound too perfect to be true yet this is Bibury, home to The Swan Hotel, a 17th-century coaching inn. Recommended by Condé Nast Johansens for more than 30 years, The Swan always delivers the perfect Cotswold experience for country lovers, anglers (fishing on the trout-filled River Coln can be arranged) and walkers. It's also an unashamedly romantic spot where winding down comes easy. Understanding the desires of the modern-day traveller, The Swan's interiors are an inspired mix of classic country living and dynamic contemporary flair. Oak panelling, plush carpets and sumptuous fabrics dress the eclectic rooms whose fine paintings, artwork and antiques add additional special touches. If you're bringing the family choose the two-bedroom Family Suite but if some romancing is on the agenda Superior Four Poster Rooms and the secluded Garden Cottage Suites (situated a short walk from the main hotel) are perfect. Warm and graceful, The Swan Brasserie is the inn's trump card. Dictated by fresh local produce, the seasonally influenced menu features European-style favourites alongside fine wines. If it's a lighter bite you're craving, the convivial Swan Bar is at your disposal all day. Their afternoon teas are something to write home about.

☎ +44 (0)1285 740695
🌐 condenastjohansens.com/swanhotelbibury
🏠 Bibury, Gloucestershire GL7 5NW, England

Barnsley House

Designer interiors and legendary gardens in Barnsley, the Cotswolds

Placing the Cotswold village of Barnsley on the map with its enchanting gardens and ancient meadows, Barnsley House's setting is a hard one to beat. Designed by former owner Rosemary Verey, OBE, VMH, the gardens' collection of intimate, artistic nooks and crannies met with admiration upon its opening to the public in 1970. Notably from HRH the Prince of Wales and Sir Elton John (who employed Rosemary) and they continue to attract thousands of paying visitors today. Inside, an original approach to the traditional concept of comfort and luxury has resulted in unfussy, soothing rooms whose 17th-century origins have been given a 21st-century transformation. Stone fireplaces, wooden floors and exposed beams add authenticity to the country atmosphere whilst high-tech equipment such as cinema surround-sound hi-fi systems and wide-screen plasmas bring the House firmly up-to-date. However, for total privacy stay in the three-bedroom Home Farm Cottage across the road from the House - very cosy. The Barnsley Spa & Skincare Centre is well worth a visit and to complete the pampering, meals at The Potager Restaurant are a must. Head Chef Francesco Volgo can often be seen picking vegetables from the gardens to produce English classics with Italian inspiration. Calling all film lovers: Barnsley House has a big screen cinema room showing films at selected times.

PRICE FROM:
£209

FEATURES:
Helipad; Pet friendly; Restaurant; Spa

ACTIVITIES:
Golf; Tennis; Walking

NEARBY:
Bibury village; Cirencester; Cheltenham

GETTING THERE:
M4 jct 15; Kemble Railway Station; Bristol Airport

+44 (0)1285 740000 ☎
condenastjohansens.com/barnsleyhouse 🌐
Barnsley, Cirencester, Gloucestershire GL7 5EE, England 📧

Burleigh Court Hotel

Gentleman's manor-turned-charming Cotswold hotel

PRICE FROM:
£175

?heated

FEATURES:
Family friendly; Pet friendly; Pool; Restaurant; Wheelchair access

ACTIVITIES:
Fishing; Golf; Shooting

NEARBY:
Cirencester; Cheltenham; Bath; Slimbridge Wildfowl Trust; Westonbirt Arboretum

GETTING THERE:
A419; M4; London Heathrow Airport

Swashbuckling vistas from every room of Burleigh Court Hotel's elegantly dressed rooms take in the Cotswolds and Golden Valley. This is a country retreat of a bygone era - a hidden gem in the truest sense: hard to find but utterly worth the search. Near Stroud, Burleigh Court is a small but perfectly formed and divinely serviced hotel with romantic country weekend written all over it. Located within an equestrian triangle of Gatcombe Park, Badminton and Cheltenham, it's a horse lover's haven minus the pomp and ceremony. Following a countryside outing, sashay onto the terrace and tuck into a very English afternoon tea looking out to more of those views. At the restaurant, Burleigh Court's Mediterranean/French fusion food is packed with local produce including rainbow trout if you're lucky (courtesy of Chef Adrian Jarrad, a keen fisherman). And room for dessert is not just advisable but absolutely necessary! Red apple cheesecake anyone? After dinner, curl up into a deep leather sofa or armchair and unwind by the roaring log fire with an after-dinner brandy.

☎ +44 (0)1453 883804
🌐 condenastjohansens.com/burleighgloucestershire
🏠 Burleigh, Minchinhampton, Near Stroud, Gloucestershire GL5 2PF, England

The Manor House Hotel

A Cotswold treasure highlighting the finer things in life

Market day at the 13th-century market town of Moreton-in-Marsh is a Tuesday. The goods on sale may have altered since trading began in 1227 but the buzz is undoubtedly the same. And at the pulsing heart of this historic High Street is the 16th-century Manor House Hotel, a former coaching inn-turned-upscale boutique escape charming guests with tales of yesteryear. King George VI and Queen Elizabeth The Queen Mother stayed here during World War II and the town itself inspired scenes in J R R Tolkien's Lord of the Rings. Sensitively refurbished with plush fabrics, elegant furnishings and contemporary convenience, The Manor House's atmosphere is informal and friendly. Its rooms and suites are the essence of chic country style with views to the picturesque High Street or The Manor's pretty garden, at the bottom of which is the Apple Cottage Suite with private hot tub. Filled with sweet scented flowers and meandering pathways, the garden features a 300-year-old mulberry tree and mature evergreen oak complete with a sun terrace. This is a favourite spot for afternoon teas, drinks and small gatherings. Breakfasts, lunches and dinners highlighting local produce with seasonal twists are served in The Mulberry Restaurant whilst the laid-back Beagle Bar & Brasserie whips up equally fine fare and snacks too.

PRICE FROM:
£158

FEATURES:
Family friendly; Pet friendly; Restaurant; Wheelchair access

ACTIVITIES:
Golf; Sightseeing; Walking

NEARBY:
Cheltenham Races, Blenheim Palace; Bath; Oxford; Stratford-upon-Avon

GETTING THERE:
On the A429; M40 jct 8/15; Birmingham International Airport

+44 (0)1608 650501 ☎
condenastjohansens.com/manorhousemoreton 🌐
Moreton-in-Marsh, Gloucestershire GL56 0LJ, England 🏠

The Mill at Gordleton

Quaint riverside escape for foodies, just outside the New Forest

PRICE FROM:
£99

FEATURES:
Family friendly; Restaurant

ACTIVITIES:
Fishing; Golf; Walking

NEARBY:
Lymington; Southampton; New Forest; Exbury Gardens; Beaulieu National Motor Museum, House and Garden

GETTING THERE:
A337; M27 jct 1; Southampton Airport

The ivy-clad Mill at Gordleton is a masterpiece in informal elegance. Small and perfectly formed, with just eight comfortable country house-style bedrooms, the soporific sound of the adjacent river transports you to another time entirely. The Mill lies on the outskirts of the New Forest with every type of outdoor adventure on your doorstep. However, if adventures of the gastronomic kind are more to your liking, the chic yet relaxed dining room where traditional British food (including gluten-free and vegetarian options) is served with a sublime lightness of touch. The Mill at Gordleton's menu is largely locally sourced, from New Forest venison to fresh crab caught from the Georgian sailing town of Lymington just a five-minute drive away. In summer there are few more beautiful dining spots than overlooking the pretty garden, complete with Monet-style bridges and intriguing local sculptures. Come winter, the pale oak-panelled bar is just the place for a warming snifter in front of a roaring fire. It's the small touches that make The Mill at Gordleton extra special, whether it's a rainy day box of entertainment for children or the atmospheric lanterns that light up the terrace as you relax with a glass of bubbly.

☎ +44 (0)1590 682219
🌐 condenastjohansens.com/themillatgordleton
🏠 Silver Street, Hordle, Near Lymington, New Forest, Hampshire SO41 6DJ, England

Lime Wood

The New Forest's fresh, new spin on the traditional English country house hotel

The secret behind Lime Wood's brilliance is simple: source and acquire the best. Thanks to the creative juices of sought-after architects and interior designers such as Martin Brudnizki, Lime Wood in the New Forest has become a byword for deft design. And in the kitchen, Luke Holder and Angela Hartnett are creating exciting foodie waves with their home-cooked style that's all about fine Italian fare with an attitude of sharing and provenance. Likewise, the three-storey Herb House Spa leads the way in sophisticated spa-ing alongside cutting-edge technology and healthy cuisine at the Raw & Cured food bar. Beyond the bedrooms and suites in the main Regency-style country house (17th-century charm and character still intact with high-end amenities, hand-picked artwork, some log fires and wood-burning stoves), the Coach House, Crescent and self-contained Forest Lodges, Cottages and Cabin are alternative locations. All are great for family-friendly breaks, romantic getaways and good old fashioned relaxation. If you're invited to the Kitchen Table, go! It's a chance to chat with the chefs and taste the highlights of Hartnett Holder & Co's seasonal menu. Now available: fun and informative classes at HH&Co Backstage cookery school ranging from mastering the art of party food to learning the tools of professional baking. The children are welcome to join in too.

PRICE FROM:
£330

FEATURES:
Family friendly; Pet friendly; Pool; Restaurant; Spa

ACTIVITIES:
Fishing; Golf; Walking

NEARBY:
New Forest National Park; Beaulieu; Lepe Country Park; Lymington; Winchester

GETTING THERE:
A31; M27; Southampton/Bournemouth Airports

+44 (0)23 8028 7177 ☎
condenastjohansens.com/limewood 🌐
Beaulieu Road, Lyndhurst, Hampshire SO43 7FZ, England 🏠

Chewton Glen

Ultimate luxury and on-trend style on the edge of the New Forest

PRICE FROM:
£325

FEATURES:
Family friendly; Helipad; Pool; Restaurant; Spa

ACTIVITIES:
Fishing; Golf; Shooting

NEARBY:
New Forest National Park; Isle of Wight; Bournemouth; Lymington; Beaches

GETTING THERE:
M27 jct 1; Southampton Central Railway Station; Southampton Airport

☎ +44 (0)1425 275341
🌐 condenastjohansens.com/chewtonglen
🏠 New Forest, Hampshire BH25 6QS, England

When a hotel's received as many accolades as Chewton Glen expectations run high on arrival. But despite this, you'll still be blown away, even if you're a returning guest because Chewton Glen is always improving (even when it doesn't seem possible) and evolving. There's certainly no restriction with space thanks to the acres of gardens and parkland at the edge of the New Forest; the sea's only a gentle 10-minute stroll away too. (Bring your camera for those awesome seascapes across to the Isle of Wight.) Inside, each bedroom and suite is nothing short of utter luxury with marble bathrooms and views over the grounds. Eco-conscious Treehouses offer alternative accommodation tucked away in Chewton Glen's wooded valley. These spacious suites are set on stilts, and are hugely private complete with kitchenettes - romantic for couples and fun for the family. However, you're missing out if you bypass the fresh, new-look restaurant where Executive Chef Luke Matthews whips up clever dishes from fresh local produce alongside an impressive wine list. That's if you can haul yourself away from the heavenly spa with steam room, sauna and hydrotherapy pool. Outside, there's another pool, a sun terrace, croquet lawn, tennis and nine hole par three course, plus alfresco dining whatever the weather!

Tylney Hall Hotel and Gardens

Endless fun in the Hampshire countryside

Romantics love Tylney Hall Hotel's red brick beauty. Historians relish in the period details. Golfers mosey on over to the adjacent 18-hole course. Foodies flock to the Oak Room Restaurant while pleasure-seekers head to the Health Suite (five treatment rooms, a gym, saunas and a whirlpool). Even the children and teenagers are occupied (treasure hunts, board games, swimming, a DVD film library…). The family dog too, with walking routes within the estate. So, looking beyond its grand façade and acres of land featuring ornamental gardens, water gardens, a lake and parkland, this impressive Grade II listed Mansion is more resort-hotel than stately home. Yes, traditional comfort of squishy sofas, panelled walls and shelves stacked with books maintain Tylney's classic style, yet a modern gloss keeps this Hampshire escape slick and fresh. Luxuriously appointed, some bedrooms and suites have four-poster beds and spa baths but all are filled with masses of natural light and old school elegance. For lunch and dinner, the much-talked-about Oak Room Restaurant is Head Chef Stephen Hine's gift to the world. Placing a modern twist on classic dishes, it's become a leader in Hampshire's dining scene and during the summer a terrace opens up for alfresco dining facing the wooded trails, lake, orchard and Victorian greenhouses. Note to party planners: Tylney has 12 banqueting rooms.

PRICE FROM:
£250

FEATURES:
Gym; Pet friendly; Pool; Restaurant

ACTIVITIES:
Tennis

NEARBY:
Antiquing at Hartley Wintney and West Green House and Gardens; Jane Austen's house; Winchester Cathedral; Watercress Line Steam Railway; Basingstoke

GETTING THERE:
M3 jct 5; Farnborough Airport; London Heathrow Airport

+44 (0)1256 764881 ☎
condenastjohansens.com/tylneyhall 🌐
Rotherwick, Near Hook, Hampshire RG27 9AZ, England 🏠

Castle House

Make-yourself-at-home Hereford town house hotel

PRICE FROM:
£150

FEATURES:
Family friendly; Restaurant; Wheelchair access

ACTIVITIES:
Golf; Sightseeing; Walking

NEARBY:
Mappa Mundi; The Chained Library at Hereford Cathedral; Ludlow; Hay-on-Wye; Cheltenham

GETTING THERE:
M4 jct 15; Hereford Railway Station; Birmingham Airport

In the middle of Hereford, just a hop, skip and a jump from Hereford Cathedral, Castle House is a smart town house hotel with a 2 AA Rosette-awarded restaurant to match. A testament to luxury boutique style, the Castle's immaculate Georgian façade gives way to a warm welcome and bright lobby area. From here, a dominating grand staircase leads you to individually designed luxury suites and bedrooms while eight more guest rooms, suites and a penthouse family room are located in Castle House's additional town house known as Number 25, a few yards from the main hotel. Here, the rooms uphold the refined ambience but feature a more contemporary feel. The restaurant, overseen by Head Chef Claire Nicholls, is predominantly an English affair, however, an international twist brings an interesting element to the dishes (Claire loves Asian flavours). Locally sourced produce and home-grown vegetables have a huge role to play on the menu. In fact, some of the beef and lamb that appear on it have been reared on the owner's nearby farm (tours of the farm can be easily arranged). Lighter bites, pastries and cocktails are the Ballingham Bar and Bistro's speciality. The hotel's pretty terraced garden runs beside the old Hereford Castle's moat and is the perfect spot for a relaxed traditional afternoon tea - brewed from tea leaves of course.

☎ +44 (0)1432 356321
🌐 condenastjohansens.com/castlehse
🏠 Castle Street, Hereford, Herefordshire HR1 2NW, England

The Grove

Rural Hertfordshire with a close London connection

Just 18 miles from central London, The Grove is referred to as "London's Country Estate". This was originally the rural seat for the Earls of Clarendon who were residents until the 1920s and entertained famous guests including Queen Victoria and Edward VII. After the Clarendons' departure, The Grove underwent several transformations from girls' boarding school to the railway's wartime headquarters before becoming this fun, family-friendly country escape set in hundreds of acres of Hertfordshire's countryside with its very own urban beach. Today, the 18th-century Mansion houses numerous newly refurbished meeting and event spaces, and 26 rooms and suites decorated with a 21st-century spin on vintage glamour. Choose from one of the three themes: fresh and classic; cool and contemporary; hot and sexy. Or stay in the thoroughly modern West Wing with a further 189 deluxe, superior and family rooms. Many of these rooms have balconies/terraces looking over the immaculate Formal Gardens. Inside the four-acre Victorian Walled Garden, fruit and veg are grown for use in the seasonally-led fare of the fine-dining Colette's, buffet-style The Glasshouse and rustic The Stables restaurant. The Stables faces the Kyle Philips-designed championship golf course, host of The British Masters 2016. But if you'd rather take a soak than a swing, visit Sequoia health club and spa.

PRICE FROM:
£265

FEATURES:
Family friendly; Gym; Pool; Restaurant; Spa

ACTIVITIES:
Cycling; Golf; Tennis

NEARBY:
Warner Bros Studio Tour London – The Making of Harry Potter; Cassiobury Park; Whipsnade Zoo; Knebworth House, Gardens and Park

GETTING THERE:
M25 jct 19/20; Watford Junction Railway Station; London Heathrow Airport

+44 (0)1923 296010 ☎
condenastjohansens.com/thegrove 🌐
Chandler's Cross, Hertfordshire WD3 4TG, England 🏠

Sopwell House

Dashing Georgian splendour meets modern-luxe in historic St Albans

PRICE FROM:
£134

FEATURES:
Gym; Pool; Restaurant; Spa

ACTIVITIES:
Golf; Sightseeing; Walking

NEARBY:
St Albans Cathedral; Butterfly World Project; Willows Farm Village and Park; Warner Bros Studio Tour London – The Making of Harry Potter

GETTING THERE:
M1 jct 8; St Albans Railway Station; Luton Airport

☎ +44 (0)1727 864477
🌐 condenastjohansens.com/sopwellhouse
🏠 Cottonmill Lane, St Albans, Hertfordshire AL1 2HQ, England

Illustrious characters Francis Bacon, King Henry VIII and Lord Mountbatten all play a part in the history of Sopwell House. Today, notable guests include premier league football teams and celebrities, hosted by the Bejerano family who bought this 128-room hotel in 1986. Located five minutes from St Albans, Sopwell House stands in acres of Hertfordshire countryside and is a sought-after venue for weddings, special events and business meetings. It's also a superb leisure break destination thanks to its luxurious day spa with pool, sauna, steam room, Jacuzzi and 14 recently refurbished treatment rooms. For some heart-pumping action, there's a cardio gym (with Technogym equipment), weights gym and state-of-the-art studio with classes including Zumba and Pilates. Plus, there's a par 72 golf course on the doorstep. The fine-dining restaurant serves a modern British and European menu while the all-day, casual Brasserie presents flavour-packed international dishes. Relaxing in the sumptuous Cocktail Lounge is popular (try the Lord Mountbatten cocktail and afternoon tea) and the garden-viewing Conservatory or terrace are ideal spots for a drink. Faithful to its Georgian heritage, each recently revamped bedroom, suite and apartment is a fusion of classic British style and modern comfort. For extra privacy stay in a spacious Mews Suite set in its own gardens.

Eastwell Manor

Classic gentility in the Garden of England

Kent's Eastwell Manor is everything you would want an elegant country house hotel to be. Packed to its dark-wood rafters with old world charm, the origins of this grand estate have been traced back to the Norman Conquest. Today, it's a family-owned business, run by people who really care about you having a memorable stay. Just outside Ashford (and its great transport links), this eyebrow-raising neo-Elizabethan manor is reached via a long tree-lined drive. Within 3,000 acres (including a nine-hole golf course), the landscape is beautified by gardens, which are idyllic settings for traditional outdoor pursuits such as croquet, boules and a spot of tennis. 23 classically styled, homely rooms and suites are located in the Manor, while a further 39 are within 19 Mews Cottages, formerly the Victorian stables. The Cottages are ideal for families or small groups and are available on a full hotel service basis or self-catering. Dining at Eastwell is a traditional affair in the wood-panelled Manor Restaurant where a resident pianist tinkles the ivories. However, a more casual brasserie is situated in the Pavilion. Drinks are served in The Manor Bar and Lounge, which is where Eastwell Manor's unmissable afternoon teas are enjoyed. Must visit: The Dreams Spa with Roman-style bath, hydrotherapy pool, sauna, steam room, 15 treatment rooms, a heated indoor and heated outdoor pool (during the summer months).

PRICE FROM:
£145

FEATURES:
Gym; Helipad; Pet friendly; Pool; Spa

ACTIVITIES:
Cycling; Golf; Walking

NEARBY:
Canterbury; Leeds Castle; White Cliffs of Dover; The North Downs; Battle of Britain Memorial at Capel-le-Ferne

GETTING THERE:
M20; Ashford International Railway Station - Eurostar; London Gatwick Airport

+44 (0)1233 213000 ☎
condenastjohansens.com/eastwellmanor 🌐
Eastwell Park, Boughton Lees, Ashford, Kent TN25 4HR, 🏠
England

Rowhill Grange Hotel & Utopia Spa

The Garden of England's smart, grown-up retreat

PRICE FROM:
£105 (per person, including dinner)

FEATURES:
Gym; Pool; Spa

ACTIVITIES:
Golf; Horse riding; Shopping

NEARBY:
Jack Nicklaus-designed London Golf Club; Hop Farm Country Park; Canterbury; Rochester Castle; Leeds Castle

GETTING THERE:
Dartford Crossing; Swanley Railway Station; London Gatwick Airport

☎ +44 (0)1322 615136
🌐 condenastjohansens.com/rowhillgrange
🏠 Wilmington, Dartford, Kent DA2 7QH, England

Enveloped by the Garden of England's green beauty, Rowhill Grange Hotel & Utopia Spa is a boutique sanctuary for everyone, for every occasion. Some retreat here for a good old-fashioned peaceful getaway, while others visit for some spa pampering, a gourmet break, corporate function or wedding. You can reach Rowhill Grange in just over an hour from central London. But the bright lights of the capital feel a million miles away from this 19th-century manor house. The 38 guest rooms and suites are straight from the pages of an interior design magazine with huggable cushions and throws adding warmth to the clean lines, neutral colours and polished finishes. The Groombridge Suite is perhaps the most spectacular with a super-king bed, walk-in power shower and enormous Victorian bathtub. This sumptuous comfort continues in the two-storey, Roman-style spa comprising swimming and hydrotherapy pools, a sauna, steam room, 21 treatment rooms and superb gym. Outside, an open-air terrace is a great sun trap for whiling away the hours. Treat yourself to an indulgent lunch at Elements Bar & Lounge or a classic afternoon tea and don't miss a meal at Rowhill Grange's signature restaurant, RG's. Taking quality ingredients such as locally caught seafood, the skilled chefs elevate the produce to a new level of taste with modern techniques and refined presentation.

Cheval Three Quays at the Tower of London

Luxury lifestyle apartments beside London's River Thames

As the leaders in luxury serviced apartments, Cheval Residences has outdone itself again. New to London's Square Mile, beside the Tower of London and overlooking the River Thames, Tower Bridge and City Hall, Cheval Three Quays is making waves. A great base for exploring The City of London's ancient history and landmarks, it's also ideal for discovering the copious attractions and exhibitions of the South Bank. Cheval Three Quays' studios, penthouses, one, two, three and recently opened four-bedroom interconnecting apartments are suitable for both short and extended stays, for business or pleasure. Each one is a celebration of cutting-edge interior design with clever lighting, shiny surfaces, clean lines and geometric shapes. Original artworks by Barnaby Gorton and an elegant water feature by the renowned William Pye add an artistic grace. At the heart of Cheval Three Quays lies exceptional management and service, which is delivered through a dedicated team of Concierge, Housekeeping and Maintenance. And facilities include a state-of-art fitness room. Those who prefer to simply relax can enjoy the café and restaurant facilities on the ground floor but getting around couldn't be easier with Tower Hill Underground Station just minutes away and the Thames Clipper at Cheval Three Quays providing transport along the river from Greenwich and The O2 arena to Putney and Chelsea Harbour.

PRICE FROM:
£220 (excluding VAT)

FEATURES:
Family friendly; Gym; Pet friendly; Restaurant; Wheelchair access

ACTIVITIES:
Shopping; Sightseeing; Walking

NEARBY:
Tower of London; Tower Bridge; South Bank; Canary Wharf; Westminster Abbey

GETTING THERE:
Tower Hill Underground Station; London Liverpool Street Railway Station; London City Airport

+44 (0)20 3725 5333 ☎
condenastjohansens.com/chevalthreequays 🌐
40 Lower Thames Street, London EC3R 6AG, England 🏛

The Great Northern Hotel

King's Cross St Pancras' first luxury boutique hotel

PRICE FROM:
£209

FEATURES:
Restaurant; Wheelchair access

ACTIVITIES:
Shopping; Sightseeing; Walking

NEARBY:
Gagosian Gallery; King's Place; The British Library; King's Cross Square; Granary Square

GETTING THERE:
King's Cross St Pancras Railway Station - Eurostar; London Gatwick Airport; London City Airport

☎ +44 (0)20 3388 0800
🌐 condenastjohansens.com/gnhlondon
🏠 King's Cross St Pancras Station, Pancras Road, London
N1C 4TB, England

The utterly transformed London's King's Cross is now one of the city's most vibrant and culturally exciting quarters. And just 25 metres from the Eurostar terminal at St Pancras, beside the main concourse of King's Cross (served by six underground lines), is The Great Northern Hotel. A re-imagined five-star boutique hotel, this is one of London's finest upscale retreats offering exceptional service. Long and wide curved corridors lead to 91 rooms where original Italianate architecture has been sensitively renovated with elegant interiors. High ceilings and large "6-over-6" sash windows bring in natural light to rooms featuring bespoke artisan-made furniture and warm, natural materials and colours. The Couchette rooms are an innovative interpretation of the railway sleeper carriage, while on the top floor, Wainscot rooms are sultry spaces lined with rich walnut. Cubitt rooms, named after the Victorian master-architect Lewis Cubitt, epitomise the charm and graceful spirit of the hotel. On each floor a Pantry is stocked with complimentary newspapers, Nespresso machines, home-made cakes and iconic candies. However, leave room for a meal at the celebrated Plum + Spilt Milk whose modern British cuisine is prepared by the highly-acclaimed Chef Mark Sargeant. GNH Bar is its adjoining glamorous cocktail bar, while the hugely popular hole-in-the-wall KIOSK serves freshly carved hot-roast meat sandwiches.

Mondrian London at Sea Containers

A masterclass in visionary design and hospitality on London's South Bank

Reflecting the great city in which it resides, Mondrian London at Sea Containers emits dynamic energy from the capital's South Bank. Design Research Studio - under the creative direction of Tom Dixon - has overseen the building's transformation from 1970s' office space to futuristic hotel with an ocean liner spirit. Every aspect is inspired by the golden age of transatlantic travel, fusing the nautical with new wave. Striking examples of this is a beaten copper hull sculpture running through the lobby and into the restaurant, and the subtle references to luxury 1920s' liners in the guest rooms. These radiate urban chic with painted wood panelling segueing into gleaming white marble bathrooms featuring bold black accents. Combining Stateside flair with the best of British in Sea Containers restaurant, Head Chef Gus Crosby (from Smith of Smithfields and Launceston Place) combines all that's great about UK and US dining. And the multi-award-winning Dandelyan bar keeps the mood lively as the resident mixologist creates cocktails influenced by the botanical wilds of the British countryside. Plus, there's the glamorous rooftop Rumpus Room serving Champagne any which way you wish. There's always tomorrow to detox in the gleaming subterranean agua Bathhouse & Spa. Bonus feature: the 56-seater Curzon Mondrian London cinema showing new releases on weekends.

PRICE FROM:
£195

FEATURES:
Family friendly; Gym; Restaurant; Spa

ACTIVITIES:
Shopping; Sightseeing; Walking

NEARBY:
Tate Modern; London Eye; Globe Theatre; Borough Market; Covent Garden

GETTING THERE:
Blackfriars Underground Station; Southwark Underground Station; Waterloo Railway Station

+44 (0)20 3747 1000 ☎
condenastjohansens.com/mondrianlondon 🌐
20 Upper Ground, London SE1 9PD, England 🏠

The Royal Horseguards

A central London time capsule of Victorian splendour

PRICE FROM:
£199

FEATURES:
Family friendly; Gym; Restaurant

ACTIVITIES:
Shopping; Sightseeing; Walking

NEARBY:
Covent Garden; London Eye; Trafalgar Square; The Houses of Parliament; The West End

GETTING THERE:
Embankment Underground Station; Charing Cross Railway Station; London City Airport

☎ +44 (0)207 523 5062
🌐 condenastjohansens.com/royalhorseguards
🏠 2 Whitehall Court, London SW1A 2EJ, England

Rich in history and old school class, The Royal Horseguards is a timepiece of grandiose Victoriana with a Digital Age edge. Superbly positioned on the capital's Embankment beside the River Thames, this iconic Whitehall address has seen several incarnations. None more interesting than its days as headquarters for the British Secret Service during World War I. The first Secret Intelligence Service chief, Sir Mansfield Cumming, lived and worked here (the inspiration for Ian Fleming's "M") and a sense of mystery and intrigue still pervades these well-dressed walls that supposedly hide a network of underground tunnels once used by Sir Winston Churchill. Behind its French château-styled façade, interiors are a mass of dark woods, bronzes, high ceilings, impressive chandeliers and rich red fabrics all brought up-to-date with smart modern finishings. Swathes of natural light pour into the guest rooms and suites and some have spectacular views such as the grand Tower Suite's 270-degree river panorama. Afternoon tea in the Lounge is a must and dining at One Twenty One Two is essential on a Sunday when a traditional British roast graces the ever-changing seasonal menu. The Royal Horseguards also has an outdoor Terrace - a rare commodity in London - facing Whitehall Gardens where you can sip a cocktail or two from Equus Bar.

41

The pad you wished you had in London's royal district

Talking about getting the royal treatment is irresistible when discussing 41. On the doorstep of Buckingham Palace with views of The Royal Mews, it's a two-minute dash to the Queen's Gallery or the Changing of The Guard. From the guest preference forms to the aromatherapy pillow menu, in-room treatments and even Pet Concierge, nothing is too big an ask for the exceptionally attentive staff. In the heart of London's sovereign quarter, 41 presents a home-away-from-home experience. And what a home it is! It's a boutique retreat from the frenzy of the Big Smoke. The discreet private entrance, stylish monochrome décor, opulent rooms and apartments (all crisp white linen and welcoming fireplaces), smart technology and elegant mahogany-panelled Executive Lounge, all give this little gem the air of a private members' club. The Executive Lounge's "Plunder The Pantry" invitation (complimentary snacks are laid out throughout the day) sums up 41's character: thoughtful, clever and classy. Diamond-sharp service is always on the agenda, however, the location is the jewel in the crown. Step outside and London's parks, palaces and parades are at your feet.

PRICE FROM:
£329

FEATURES:
Family friendly; Pet friendly

ACTIVITIES:
Cycling; Shopping; Sightseeing

NEARBY:
Buckingham Palace; Westminster Abbey; Houses of Parliament; Hyde Park; Green Park

GETTING THERE:
Victoria Underground Station; London Heathrow Airport; London Gatwick Airport

+44 (0)20 7300 0041 ☎
condenastjohansens.com/41buckinghampalaceroad 🌐
41 Buckingham Palace Road, London SW1W 0PS, England 🏢

Cheval Phoenix House

Exclusive fully-serviced apartments with luxury hotel style in Chelsea

PRICE FROM:
£240 (excluding VAT)

FEATURES:
Family friendly; Gym; Pet friendly

ACTIVITIES:
Shopping; Sightseeing

NEARBY:
Royal Court Theatre; Sloane Square; Saatchi Gallery; Duke of York Square; Canvas Restaurant

GETTING THERE:
Sloane Square Underground Station; Victoria Railway Station; London Heathrow Airport

☎ +44 (0)20 7259 8222
🌐 condenastjohansens.com/phoenixhouse
🏠 1 Wilbraham Place, Sloane Street, London SW1X 9AE, England

Home to the well-heeled and a film star or two, London's affluent Chelsea is a rare mix of high-end and high-street shopping, artistic influence (Saatchi Gallery) and football (home to the Premier League's Chelsea Football Club). Aiming and succeeding to charm whomever walks through its doors, Cheval Phoenix House is at the core of everything Chelsea has to offer. Located minutes from the boutiques and galleries of Sloane Square, the pedestrianised Duke of York Square and Chelsea Harbour, Cheval Phoenix is your exclusive gateway to one of the capital's most desirable neighbourhoods. Extremely private, it houses 33 fully-serviced apartments with fully-equipped kitchens ranging from open-plan one and two-bedroom apartments and loft suites. Attentive 24-hour concierge service and security, and housekeeping Monday through to Sunday means that not only is this your London home-from-home but also a spoiling retreat delivering world-class hotel services. There'll even be a Well-Being Welcome Tray to greet you upon arrival. Ideal for nightly stopovers, short breaks and longer stays for individuals, couples and families, Cheval Phoenix House is smart, modern and stylish where you can just as easily entertain guests as kick back and relax in comfort. Don't miss: dining at Canvas restaurant.

Sofitel London St James

A fusion of British class and French finesse in London's elite St James's

On the corner of Waterloo Place and Pall Mall, Sofitel London St James proudly stands in a prime City of Westminster position. Moments from the flashing lights of Piccadilly Circus and the lions guarding Nelson's Column in Trafalgar Square, this is London's buzzing St James's area known for its high-end and popular commercial appeal. As with many buildings in this area, the Sofitel London St James's imposing Grade II listed structure is owned by the Crown Estate (Buckingham Palace is a five-minute walk away), and behind its regal façade is a stylish interior blending classic British design with contemporary French flair. Formerly the headquarters to the Cox's & King's bank (whose original artwork still hangs on the walls today), you're led through the smart lobby and into your plush room or suite. Each is utterly serene decorated in tones of chocolate, almond and olive fitted with high-def TVs (110 channels), WiFi and sleek black and white marble bathrooms. French-British fusion cuisine is the trademark of the brasserie, The Balcon, while sultry St James Bar is where you'll find a large selection of Champagnes and vintage cocktails. For afternoon tea with a French twist head to The Rose Lounge. Don't miss: the stunning SoSPA and Technogym-equipped SoFIT gym.

PRICE FROM:
£425

FEATURES:
Family friendly; Gym; Restaurant; Spa; Wheelchair access

ACTIVITIES:
Shopping; Sightseeing; Walking

NEARBY:
Trafalgar Square; Buckingham Palace; Royal Parks; National Gallery; Upscale Bond Street shopping

GETTING THERE:
Piccadilly Underground Station; King's Cross St Pancras Railway Station - Eurostar; London Heathrow Airport

+44 (0)20 7747 2200 ☎
condenastjohansens.com/stjames 🌐
6 Waterloo Place, London SW1Y 4AN, England 🏠

Claverley Court

Fashionable apartments in upscale Knightsbridge

PRICE FROM:
£300

FEATURES:
Family friendly

ACTIVITIES:
Shopping; Sightseeing

NEARBY:
Hyde Park; Science Museum; Victoria and Albert Museum; Harrods

GETTING THERE:
Knightsbridge Underground Station; South Kensington Underground Station; London Heathrow Airport

☎ +44 (0)20 7938 5930
🌐 condenastjohansens.com/claverleycourt
🏠 Beaufort Gardens, London SW3 1PS, England

Dreaming of the ultimate London pied-à-terre? Welcome to Claverley Court, a collection of spacious and chic studio, one, two and three-bedroom apartments in a quiet, tree-lined Knightsbridge square where guests enjoy all the benefits of a first-class London hotel. This is London living at its five-star best. Potter along the pavements in your new Jimmy Choos (the boutique is seconds from Claverley Court) or pop into Harvey Nichols for the best designer ware this side of Milan. Close to some of London's finest museums, there's plenty of cultural delights in the vicinity to experience too. For a particularly special occasion stay in the Beaufort Suite, a beautifully designed, marble and walnut-clad penthouse where your only care will be making plans for the evening. Will it be a short taxi hop to the West End for world-renowned theatre? Or a trip to one of Knightbridge's acclaimed restaurants? If travelling with the family, Claverley Court's split-level, three-bed, three-bathroom Knightsbridge Suite is a home-from-home sumptuously furnished complete with Jacuzzi in the master suite. And for solo guests or couples, a one-bed apartment finished to the highest standard is unbeatable. Whatever your choice, take your pick of an east or west-facing pad; early birds can watch the sunrise, night owls can toast the sunset before hitting the clubs and bars moments from the front door.

The Egerton House Hotel

Enchanting Victorian house in residential Knightsbridge

The Egerton House Hotel resides in one of London's most prestigious neighbourhoods. In a quiet tree-lined street in the heart of fashionable Knightsbridge, this elegant town house hotel (built in 1843) is a short walk from Harrods, Harvey Nichols, Sloane Street and King's Road. The ideal base for experiencing the best London has to offer, it's also within walking distance of some of the capital's best loved museums including the Victoria and Albert, Science and Natural History Museums. Each bedroom at The Egerton House Hotel has been individually decorated and showcases a personal collection of original artwork and Italian antique furnishings. Service, quality and luxury are the hallmarks of its charming boutique style where you can relax in the cosy drawing room and indulge in a traditional afternoon tea. Feast on freshly baked scones covered in thick clotted cream and home-made fruit preserves, and a tempting assortment of delicate finger sandwiches and pastries. For a classic treat, sample one of Esley's martinis, lauded as the finest in London. The Egerton House Hotel is a real country house in the city welcoming families and pets with a passionate, professional hospitality that considers no request too large and no detail too small.

PRICE FROM:
£295

FEATURES:
Family friendly; Pet friendly

ACTIVITIES:
Shopping; Sightseeing; Walking

NEARBY:
Harrods; Victoria and Albert Museum; Hyde Park; Buckingham Palace

GETTING THERE:
Knightsbridge Underground Station; Victoria Railway Station; London Heathrow Airport

+44 (0)20 7589 2412 ☎
condenastjohansens.com/egertonhouse 🌐
17-19 Egerton Terrace, Knightsbridge, London SW3 2BX, 🏠
England

11 Cadogan Gardens

Vintage drama with a fashionable edge in London's prestigious Chelsea

PRICE FROM:
£225

FEATURES:
Gym; Restaurant

ACTIVITIES:
Shopping; Sightseeing

NEARBY:
Saatchi Gallery; Harrods; Harvey Nichols; Buckingham Palace; London Eye

GETTING THERE:
Sloane Square Underground Station; Victoria Railway Station; London Heathrow Airport

Once frequented by 19th-century aristocrats and bon viveurs, Lord Chelsea's four red and white brick town houses now accommodate the wonderfully eccentric and oh-so British 11 Cadogan Gardens. Interconnected via winding hallways and staircases, this intriguing luxury hotel is located in the heart of London's most talked about neighbourhood: Chelsea, with King's Road shopping, the avant-garde Royal Court Theatre, Kensington, Natural History Museum and V&A all with walking distance. There are 56 rooms in total, including 25 suites (five have a private entrance). All suites are decadent, sumptuous and full of character. Rich fabrics, sash windows, soaring ceilings and opulent four-poster beds are matched by marbled bathrooms with cavernous bathtubs. And the especially indulgent Sloane Suite is the epitome of high-class living from a bygone era. For when the rain comes, the Library offers shelter lined with Victorian classics, and the speakeasy-esque bar provides expertly prepared libations. Then there's always the great British pastime of afternoon tea to be taken, between 12pm and 6pm, in the lavish Drawing Room. But for when the sun does shine on London (it does happen!), head on over to 11 Cadogan Gardens' terrace.

☎ +44 (0)20 7730 7000
🌐 condenastjohansens.com/11cadogangardens
🏠 11 Cadogan Gardens, Chelsea, London SW3 2RJ, England

Mayflower Hotel

Your swanky West London home

Full of originality, Mayflower Hotel is the convenient West London crash pad you wish you had. Located in the favoured neighbourhood for a string of the rich and rare over the years (Freddie Mercury, Alfred Hitchcock, a young Diana, Princess of Wales and currently Gary Barlow), this boutique town house hotel marries vibrant Eastern design with Western contemporary comfort. It's the perfect retreat if travelling alone or on business, not to mention great value for money. Earls Court Exhibition Centre, Knightsbridge, Chelsea and various attractions such as the Natural History and Science Museums are all nearby. It's worth noting that Mayflower's guest rooms located on the ground floor are small but stylish, rich in pale stone, vibrant fabrics and Indian and Oriental antiques. Upstairs on the first floor, larger bedrooms are refurbished in light, fresh colours with sparkling glass lighting and mirrors. Each has a smart bathroom made from marble, slate and chrome complete with a walk-in shower. Continental buffet breakfast is laid out in the beautifully refurbished downstairs dining room every morning and when the weather is fine, Mayflower's extended patio garden opens out for some alfresco action. The hotel's café also provides an endless flow of coffee and juice throughout the day.

PRICE FROM:
£120

FEATURES:
Family friendly

ACTIVITIES:
Shopping; Sightseeing; Walking

NEARBY:
Earls Court Exhibition Centre; Harrods; King's Road; Hyde Park; Madame Tussauds

GETTING THERE:
London Heathrow Airport; London Gatwick Airport; Earls Court Underground Station

+44 (0)20 7370 0991 ☎
condenastjohansens.com/mayflower 🌐
26-28 Trebovir Road, London SW5 9NJ, England 🏠

Twenty Nevern Square

Discreet, chic residence in the centre of London's Kensington and Chelsea

PRICE FROM:
£130

FEATURES:
Family friendly

ACTIVITIES:
Shopping; Sightseeing; Walking

NEARBY:
Victoria and Albert Museum; Natural History Museum; Harrods; King's Road; Hyde Park

GETTING THERE:
Earls Court Underground Station; London Heathrow Airport; London Gatwick Airport

Twenty Nevern Square in London's Earls Court is a town house home-hotel with a high-end residential vibe. Set beside the very smart Nevern Square Garden (privately owned by Garden Members from neighbouring town houses), Earls Court and Olympia Exhibition Centres are minutes away. Harrods, Harvey Nichols, King's Road and High Street Kensington are a short walk, as are theatres and attractions such as the Victoria and Albert Museum and Science Museum. Inside, European and Oriental furnishings harmoniously fuse together to furnish the irregularly shaped rooms with surprising nooks and crannies cleverly made into sumptuous features (see: the Mezzanine Double Room's cushioned snug). The bedrooms may be compact but with clever use of neutral coloured walls set against delicate silks, bold patterns and intricate touches such as hand-carved headboards, the quirkiness and designer flair of each room has you settling in and cosying up. Book one of the three suites for some extra space and if you're looking to really spoil someone, opt for the grandeur of the Ottoman Suite with free-standing bath beside a log fire and private balcony looking across to the manicured Nevern Square Garden. Breakfast is served in the light, bright Conservatory opening onto a decked balcony area. Gym facilities are available by arrangement.

☎ +44 (0)20 7565 9555
🌐 condenastjohansens.com/twentynevernsquare
🏠 20 Nevern Square, London SW5 9PD, England

Cheval Knightsbridge

Fully-serviced apartment living, Knightsbridge style

With Harrods, Harvey Nichols and the flagship stores of Manolo Blahnik and Jimmy Choo, London's Knightsbridge is serious shopping territory. It's also an essential stop on London's tourist trail for Hyde Park and the Victoria and Albert Museum. In plum position for exploring this assembly of attractions, the residences of Cheval Knightsbridge allow you to temporarily reside in this exclusive neighbourhood on extended stays. Spread across several sought-after locations in the highly exclusive Brompton Road, Montpelier Mews (just off Brompton Road) and Cheval Place (parallel to Brompton Road), Cheval Knightsbridge is a collection of two and three-bedroom mews houses, apartments, town houses and a city cottage (which is available for three months or more). Created with families, groups of friends and corporate trips in mind, each accommodation has been designed as a private home with the added benefits of pampering hotel services. These include maid service Monday to Sunday, a 24-hour concierge, CCTV and health club membership. Intended for nightly, week-long, monthly or even longer stays, each one is full of individual style and character fitted with modern kitchens and the latest techy gizmos. So, treat Cheval Knightsbridge as your luxury London pad and do as the local rich-set do and immerse in the city high life.

PRICE FROM:
£400 (excluding VAT)

FEATURES:
Family friendly; Gym; Pet friendly

ACTIVITIES:
Horse riding; Shopping; Sightseeing

NEARBY:
Harrods; Harvey Nichols; Victoria and Albert Museum; Kensington Gardens

GETTING THERE:
Knightsbridge Underground Station; Victoria Railway Station; London Heathrow Airport

+44 (0)20 7225 3325
condenastjohansens.com/chevalknightsbridge
15 Cheval Place, London SW7 1EW, England

130 Queen's Gate Apartments

South Kensington super-luxe town house apartments

PRICE FROM:
£300

FEATURES:
Family friendly; Gym

ACTIVITIES:
Shopping; Sightseeing

NEARBY:
Royal Albert Hall; Hyde Park; Victoria and Albert Museum; Science Museum; Natural History Museum

GETTING THERE:
South Kensington Underground Station; Gloucester Road Underground Station; London Heathrow Airport

☎ +44 (0)20 7938 5930
🌐 condenastjohansens.com/queensgate
🏠 130 Queen's Gate, Kensington, London SW7 5LE, England

One thirty isn't the time but rather the place for the ultimate city getaway. Surrounded by top London attractions, this is the capital's Royal Borough of Kensington and Chelsea, all leafy streets lined with 19th-century town houses. Mary Poppins territory. There's a continental vibe to the neighbourhood that wows fashionistas and foodies alike, and 130 Queen's Gate Apartments is very much part of this ever-so European high-end style. Shiny Italian marbles and ergonomically-friendly soft furnishings fill each studio, one to four-bedroom apartment and penthouse suite. And modern amenities such as dishwashers and washer dryers are standard conveniences (you can simply ignore them of course – the housekeeper will blitz the apartment daily Monday to Saturday). At 130 Queen's Gate Apartments the emphasis is on home comforts with 24-hour multi-lingual staff on hand to take the stress of planning away from you. It's also more than prepared for England's typically inclement weather. If the rain sets in, root yourself to the sumptuous spot and enjoy the apartment's state-of-the-art audio-visual system, Jacuzzi bath and services of a private chef in your very own kitchen. Don't forget, if you need anything, anything at all, there's the all-knowing concierge at your service.

The Kensington

Your South Kensington base for days filled with afternoon teas and museum trips

Around the corner from the Natural History, Victoria and Albert and Science Museums (all free!), The Kensington is perfectly situated to enjoy them all. The Royal Albert Hall, Hyde Park, Kensington Palace, Harrods and Harvey Nichols are all within walking distance too. One of London's most elite addresses, South Kensington is the savvy choice for culture vultures. Spanning across several Regency town houses, The Kensington offers a taste of London's affluent urban lifestyle. Inside, the dazzling chandelier above and red velvet reception alcove in front of you appear like the inside of a jewellery box. From here to the Morning Room, along to the Drawing Room (afternoon teas here are a must), varying colour schemes and eclectic furnishings create distinctive atmospheres as you pass through one town house to the next. Artwork from all over the world dresses the walls alongside objets d'art, which also appear in the guest rooms and suites; many of which have oversized windows (sound-proofed) bringing in rays of natural light. If it's space you need, book The Kensington Suite, London's largest town house suite. When hunger sets in, head to the Town House for some casual, all-day dining. Added bonuses: WiFi is free and every guest room has a Nespresso machine.

PRICE FROM:
£235

FEATURES:
Family friendly; Gym; Restaurant; Wheelchair access

ACTIVITIES:
Shopping; Sightseeing

NEARBY:
Natural History Museum; Victoria and Albert Museum; Science Museum; Harrods; Hyde Park

GETTING THERE:
South Kensington Undergound Station; Victoria Railway Station; London Heathrow Airport

+44 (0)20 7589 6300 ☎
condenastjohansens.com/kensington 🌐
109-113 Queen's Gate, South Kensington, London SW7 5LR, 🏠
England

The Marylebone

Urban cool and cosmopolitan flair in the heart of fashionable Marylebone village

PRICE FROM:
£235

FEATURES:
Family friendly; Gym; Pool; Restaurant; Spa

ACTIVITIES:
Shopping; Sightseeing

NEARBY:
Oxford Street; Bond Street; Hyde Park; Theatreland; Madame Tussauds

GETTING THERE:
Bond Street Underground Station; Paddington Railway Station; London City Airport

☎ +44 (0)20 7486 6600
🌐 condenastjohansens.com/marylebone
🏛 47 Welbeck Street, Marylebone, London W1G 8DN, England

London's district of Marylebone is where village-style character meets vibrant city life. With Theatreland, Madame Tussauds, Regent's and Hyde Parks, high-street and high-end shopping at Oxford and Bond Streets all close by, it offers the best of both worlds: a brilliant base for the tourist trail and a fashionable residential address. Spanning across an entire block of the neighbourhood, The Marylebone is a reflection of its affluent location. Despite its vast size (257 bedrooms, restaurant and bar, six conference suites, business centre, health club, pool and spa), an intimate atmosphere travels through The Marylebone. This is apparent as soon as you enter the glamorous lobby where Parisian furnishings, Italian ceramics and a hand-laid mosaic floor set the scene. All at once exclusive yet comfortable, it doesn't matter if you're travelling with the family (check out the children's concierge service), on business (WiFi is complimentary) or for pleasure, The Marylebone's resort facilities cater for all. The impressive Third Space Gym with 18-metre pool and spa is an attraction in its own right. So too is 108 Brasserie where the menu features traditional favourites, fine wines, spirits and cocktails. No stay is complete without an afternoon tea in 108 Pantry, or one of the lounges, with a glass of English sparkling wine.

The Arch London

London life at its finest

The Arch London at Marble Arch gets it just right in every way: West End location; knockout design; superior hospitality; and sublime food and drink. It's London at its swanky (yet never pretentious) best. Sleek and on-trend, The Arch throws a curveball at the meaning of boutique hotel with the result being a sophisticated, intimate and highly stylish retreat. And despite its central location, the quiet residential address means that noisy traffic and the day-to-day buzz of city life isn't a concern from your peaceful room. However, the damage you'll do to your wallet might be. The three-pronged attack from Oxford (Selfridges!), Regent (Liberty!) and Bond (Fenwicks!) Streets leave you defenceless. So, back to your guest room or suite to assess the damage to your credit cards where maybe the bespoke colour scheme, ultra-sumptuous bathroom, high-techery, vibrant art, crisp linens and rich textiles and furnishings will help soften the blow. To start an evening off in style, there's the glam Bar whose cocktail menu is only matched by the elegance of Le Salon de Champagne and open kitchen of the lively Hunter 486 Restaurant (named after the 1950s' district dialling code for Marylebone).

PRICE FROM:
£255

FEATURES:
Gym; Restaurant; Wheelchair access

ACTIVITIES:
Shopping; Sightseeing

NEARBY:
Selfridges; Hyde Park; Oxford Street; Bond Street; Kensington High Street

GETTING THERE:
King's Cross St Pancras Railway Station - Eurostar; London Heathrow Airport; London Gatwick Airport

+44 (0)20 7724 4700 ☎
condenastjohansens.com/thearchlondon 🌐
50 Great Cumberland Place, Marble Arch, London W1H 7FD, 🏠
England

The Athenaeum Hotel & Residences

Short and long-stay London Mayfair home-from-home

PRICE FROM:
£260

FEATURES:
Family friendly; Gym; Restaurant; Spa

ACTIVITIES:
Shopping; Sightseeing

NEARBY:
Buckingham Palace; Hyde Park; Green Park; Bond Street;
Oxford Street

GETTING THERE:
Green Park Underground Station; Hyde Park Corner
Underground Station; King's Cross St Pancras Railway Station
- Eurostar

☎ +44 (0)20 7499 3464
🌐 condenastjohansens.com/athenaeum
🏠 116 Piccadilly, Mayfair, London W1J 7BJ, England

London's Piccadilly isn't just an iconic address, it's one of the capital's most important thoroughfares. In the heart of Mayfair it stretches from Piccadilly Circus to Hyde Park with some of the city's most recognisable landmarks lining the way. These include The Royal Academy, Green Park and the family-owned, five-star, art-deco treasure: The Athenaeum Hotel & Residences at no. 116. A private, understated hotel where discretion and first-rate service are guaranteed, The Athenaeum underwent a recent renovation to its ground floor, introducing floor-to-ceiling windows to the open-plan lobby and lounge, and new all-day dining menus from Michelin Starred chefs, The Galvin Brothers now at the culinary helm. Rooms, suites and full-service residences with kitchens, living and dining areas are contemporary but homely, unfussy yet inviting, practical whilst stylish. And are equally convenient for business travellers as they are for families staying for a flying visit or year-long sabbatical. Children are so welcome there's a Children's Concierge and many of the fully-serviced residences were designed with families in mind. But it's perhaps the views that leave the lasting impression, taking in Royal Green Park, the spires of Buckingham Palace and London Eye beyond. Must visit: THE BAR, a stylish and intimate retreat featuring pioneering craft spirits and signature cocktails.

Mayfair House

Serviced apartments/suite accommodation in London's Mayfair

Location is everything in London therefore Mayfair House has it all. From here, Hyde Park is found in one direction, Bond Street shopping in the other, Green Park this way and Berkeley Square that. Then there's Mayfair House's address in the Shepherd Market neighourhood; a London hotspot tucked between Piccadilly and Curzon Street. This was the site of the annual 15-day "May Fair" that took place during the 17th and 18th centuries. Today, it attracts a well-heeled, in-the-know, diverse crowd seeking out the eclectic eateries, pubs and boutique shops that line its narrow streets and alleyways. For those requiring a luxury crash pad for seven nights or more (three months max), Mayfair House's assortment of apartments and suites is the sublime solution. On the top floor is the whopping Presidential Penthouse Suite, a four-double bedroom, four-bathroom beast with private entrance and rooftop terrace. The glossy three-bedroom, two-bathroom Executive Suite also has a private entrance. And one and two-bedroom apartments offer a choice of Classic, Contemporary and Executive categories. Call on the obliging concierge if you need help deciding and if you need a parking space during your stay; mention this prior to arrival and one shall magically be reserved on-site.

PRICE FROM:
£332

FEATURES:
Family friendly; Gym; Wheelchair access

ACTIVITIES:
Shopping; Sightseeing; Walking

NEARBY:
Green Park; Upscale Bond Street shopping; Piccadilly Circus; Oxford Street shopping; Royal Academy of Arts

GETTING THERE:
Green Park Underground Station; King's Cross St Pancras Railway Station - Eurostar; London Heathrow Airport

+44 (0)20 7938 5930 ☎
condenastjohansens.com/mayfairhouse 🌐
22-28 Shepherd Street, Mayfair, London W1J 7JH, England 🏠

The May Fair Hotel

London Mayfair's stylish and spirited trend-setter

PRICE FROM:
£240

FEATURES:
Gym; Restaurant; Spa; Wheelchair access

ACTIVITIES:
Shopping; Sightseeing

NEARBY:
Green Park; Bond Street shopping; Royal Academy;
Buckingham Palace; Piccadilly Circus

GETTING THERE:
Green Park Underground Station; Victoria Railway Station;
London Heathrow Airport

Mayfair is the London neighbourhood where designer label junkies come to shop, where food fans enjoy fine eateries and art aficionados flock for the galleries and world-famous Christies and Sotheby's. And in the thick of it is The May Fair Hotel, totally in-keeping with its grand, high-styling London setting. It also offers that other very British trait: a touch of eccentricity. As you would expect, all the staple services of a leading city hotel are here, however, The May Fair stands apart for many reasons. Yes, the suites are bag-swinging spacious but it's their vibrant colour schemes, surprising detail and good old fashioned decadence that all come together to make even the most moneyed oil baron happy. Then there's the electric blue-lit May Fair Bar. On the surface, it's an extremely hip watering hole but look a little closer to uncover its seriously fine selection of wines, Champagnes, malts and spirits. And let's not forget The Terrace (an exclusive enclave at the heart of the hotel that recreates the outdoors), the Italian leather trimmed 201-seat private cinema, the exclusive casino and poker room, and inner sanctum that is the spa. Plus, the newly revamped May Fair Kitchen where Mediterranean flavours dictate the menu of Spanish and Italian small plates complemented by the finest wines.

☎ +44 (0)20 7769 4041
🌐 condenastjohansens.com/mayfair
🏠 Stratton Street, Mayfair, London W1J 8LT, England

The Westbury

Central London location with worldwide appeal

London's your oyster at The Westbury, Mayfair. A matter of moments and you're in Bond Street, Regent Street, Oxford Street and Piccadilly Circus. Soho, Leicester Square, Covent Garden, Green Park and Buckingham Palace are a short walk away. Simply put, The Westbury is central. In the beating heart of the capital's fashionable Mayfair, it's a five-star sophisticate in an enviable location. Personal service (often lacking in large city hotels) is a trademark of The Westbury where each and every member of staff displays a marked passion to ensure every guest has a memorable stay. Complete with expert concierge and extremely knowledgeable, multi-lingual staff, guests from around the world each receive the star treatment and stay in bedrooms or suites graced with luxury touches. Each is an interior design masterclass on how to create a warm, comforting, homely space with the finest of fabrics, elegant muted colour schemes and on-trend fashion. Since 2011, Alyn Williams at The Westbury has been drawing a crowd for its fine-dining feats of flavour, while the Japanese Tsukji Sushi Restaurant provides an alternative dining option with dishes prepared from organic ingredients. All the while, the casual, welcoming Polo Bar presents an impressive cocktail list and tasty bar menu.

PRICE FROM:
£439

FEATURES:
Gym; Michelin Starred restaurant

ACTIVITIES:
Cycling; Sightseeing; Walking

NEARBY:
Mayfair shopping; West End theatres; Royal Academy of Arts; National Gallery; London Eye

GETTING THERE:
Bond Street Underground Station; King's Cross St Pancras Railway Station - Eurostar; London Heathrow Airport

+44 (0)20 7629 7755 ☎
condenastjohansens.com/westburymayfair 🌐
Bond Street, Mayfair, London W1S 2YF, England 🏠

Sanderson London

London's otherwordly escape in the thrum of the West End

PRICE FROM:
£263

FEATURES:
Gym; Restaurant; Spa

ACTIVITIES:
Shopping; Sightseeing; Walking

NEARBY:
Oxford Street shopping; Bond Street shopping; West End theatres; Soho; Covent Garden

GETTING THERE:
Oxford Street Underground Station; London Heathrow Airport; London Gatwick Airport

☎ +44 (0)20 7300 1400
🌐 condenastjohansens.com/sanderson
🏠 50 Berners Street, London W1T 3NG, England

Walk past Sanderson London's unassuming façade and you miss out on a revolutionary hotel experience. Behind its urban grey concrete belies a dream-like universe that instantaneously transports you out of central London and into a fantastical realm. As much art gallery as hotel, wide-open spaces showcase trippy design features and artwork while the newly renovated guest rooms reveal avant-garde quirks (Philippe Starck industrial elements, beds aligned askew). Spread across the entire eighth floor is Sanderson's magnificent Penthouse reached by private lift. This vast suite is an exercise in designer innovation with no interior walls but glowing glass panels covered by sheer curtains. Back downstairs and Sanderson's signature restaurant infuses its dishes with equally clever design. Weather permitting, these meals may be taken in the courtyard garden accompanied by artisan cocktails made to complement the refined, elegant flavours by talented mixologists. Drinks are also served in the dark and moody Purple Bar and iconic Long Bar where an 80-foot long counter is resplendent in glowing onyx. In contrast, agua Spa is an all-white sanctum dressed in flowing white curtains. Must do: the Mad Hatter's Afternoon Tea beginning with a search for the menu amongst vintage books.

The Mandeville Hotel

Boutique panache in London's Marylebone

Quirky yet sophisticated, progressive whilst old school, blissfully quiet but centrally located, The Mandeville Hotel in London's Marylebone Village cleverly manages it all. Funky enough for the fashionistas and retro glam enough for the traditionalists, The Mandeville is a central London hotel for everyone offering a highly personalised service. Harley, Oxford, Bond and Regent Streets are all within walking distance; Regent's and Hyde Parks too. Inside, the expertly furnished guest rooms and suites are dressed in nothing but the finest fabrics put together by some of the leading London design houses. These include the new Deluxe Riviera Rooms by Maison Christian Lacroix, exclusive to the fifth floor. Each one is breathtaking and tells a story of drama, exuberance and grandeur. However, if sprawling space is your priority, book the two-storey, apartment-style Terrace Suite with two bathrooms and roof terrace. Achieving an equally high level of hospitality is The Mandeville's Reform Social and Grill. Channelling a gentleman's club vibe, its typically British menu includes classic favourites alongside elegant dishes for breakfast, Sunday brunch, lunch and dinner. No visit is complete without enjoying a superb Vintage or Gentleman's Afternoon Tea (Festive Afternoon Teas from November also) and browse through the cocktail list made with some of the finest spirits distilled in the UK.

FEATURES:
Family friendly; Restaurant; Wheelchair access

ACTIVITIES:
Shopping; Sightseeing

NEARBY:
The Wallace Collection; Selfridges; Wigmore Hall; Regent's Park; Hyde Park

GETTING THERE:
Bond Street Underground Station; Victoria Railway Station; London Heathrow Airport

+44 (0)20 7935 5599 ☎
condenastjohansens.com/mandeville 🌐
Mandeville Place, Marylebone, London W1U 2BE, England ✉

New Linden Hotel

Your designer Notting Hill digs with an Oriental flair

PRICE FROM:
£120

FEATURES:
Family friendly

ACTIVITIES:
Shopping; Sightseeing

NEARBY:
Portobello Road Market; Hyde Park; Kensington Palace and Gardens; Oxford Street; Madame Tussauds

GETTING THERE:
Notting Hill Underground Station; Paddington Railway Station; London Heathrow Airport

New Linden Hotel in Notting Hill is a little gem with instant appeal. Spread across three pretty white town houses in a peaceful residential street, you're in the heart of London's cosmopolitan Notting Hill neighbourhood, a short walk from Portobello Road Market and within easy reach of various tourist hotspots. You're also just a few steps from the fashionable Westbourne Grove where the annual Notting Hill Carnival passes through. Transformed into a 50-bedroom bolthole, none of the buildings' Victorian charm has been lost. Beyond the ornate entrance pillars are stylish bedrooms and suites in palettes of cream, brown, red and black with an Oriental panache alongside trendy minimal furnishings, high-tech entertainment units and stunning marble, limestone and slate bathrooms. Clever interior design uses every inch of the building with some bedrooms particularly cosy. However, the high-end finishes and use of lavish fabrics and materials such as silk, velvet and the finest cotton create an incredibly lavish and comfortable setting. If staying with friends or the children, Triple and Family Rooms are ideal while the Honeymoon Suite is New Linden's crowning glory complete with Jacuzzi bath and private terrace. Head on down to the lower ground floor for a freshly prepared breakfast each morning or weather permitting, outside on the communal terrace.

☎ +44 (0)20 7221 4321
🌐 condenastjohansens.com/newlindenhotel
🏠 58-60 Leinster Square, Notting Hill, London W2 4PS, England

The Milestone Hotel & Apartments

London Kensington's premier address and premier hotel

Opposite Kensington Palace and gardens (the London residence of the Duke and Duchess of Cambridge), just a five-minute walk from the Royal Albert Hall and around the corner from Harrods and Harvey Nichols, is The Milestone Hotel & Apartments. The pulsing heart of the capital's most exclusive neighbourhood, this is the Royal Borough of Kensington with Hyde Park, upscale shopping, popular museums and endless tourist attractions on the doorstep. The Milestone's blend of personal service (complete a guest preference form prior to arrival), family and pet-friendly policies, opulent comfort and inspired cuisine see it winning accolades year after year. With a staff to guest ratio of 2:1 it's no wonder. Each room, suite and apartment is unique, fashioned with fine fabrics, fresh flowers, antique furnishings and rare works of art. The Milestone's luxury two-bedroom apartments have full access to the hotel's facilities and are perfect for families or longer stays. The club-like Stables Bar is a cosy spot for a drink (try the Old Fashioned), while the Park Lounge serves prize-winning afternoon teas. Cheneston's Restaurant showcases fine British cuisine while lighter snacks can be savoured in the black and white conservatory. All these well-worth-it calories may be burnt off in the hotel's resistance pool, gym and on-site spa treatment room.

PRICE FROM:
£354

FEATURES:
Family friendly; Gym; Pet friendly; Pool; Restaurant

ACTIVITIES:
Horse riding; Shopping; Sightseeing

NEARBY:
Kensington Palace and gardens; Royal Albert Hall; Victoria and Albert Museum; Harrods

GETTING THERE:
Paddington Railway Station; London Heathrow Airport; London Gatwick Airport

+44 (0)20 7917 1000 ☎
condenastjohansens.com/milestone 🌐
1 Kensington Court, London W8 5DL, England 🏨

The Bloomsbury

Neo-Georgian timeless elegance in central London's leafy Bloomsbury

PRICE FROM:
£235

FEATURES:
Family friendly; Gym; Restaurant; Wheelchair access

ACTIVITIES:
Shopping; Sightseeing

NEARBY:
British Museum; Oxford Street; Covent Garden; West End theatres; Soho

GETTING THERE:
Tottenham Court Road Undergound Station; King's Cross St Pancras Railway Station - Eurostar; London City Airport

Reassuringly traditional whilst refreshingly fashionable, The Bloomsbury is minutes from London's Theatreland, Covent Garden and Oxford Street. It's also around the corner from the British Museum in the district of Bloomsbury, a mass of formal green squares and architectural significance. The Bloomsbury is located within a neo-Georgian building designed by the renowned British architect, Sir Edwin Landseer Lutyens (renowned for the Cenotaph in Whitehall). As such, an essence of orderliness and classic British style permeates throughout but there's nothing stuffy or pretentious about it with an interior that's all about refined yet comfortable living accompanied by friendly, professional service. Bold fabrics, striking colours and geometric lines in the rooms and suites lend a contemporary edge with luxury details such as duck down pillows and duvets, underfloor bathroom heating, Nespresso coffee machines and free WiFi. Studio Suites are the spacious, king-size option for the ultimate experience. Just like the traditional spirit of the building itself, the Bloomsbury Club Dining Room celebrates traditional British dishes with a gourmet flair by Exec Chef Paul O'Brien. Afternoon tea in the Dalloway is the quintessential English treat. Check out: the hidden Chapel that can be hired for special events and the Dalloway Terrace for alfresco dining and private parties.

☎ +44 (0)20 7347 1000
🌐 condenastjohansens.com/bloomsbury
🏠 16-22 Great Russell Street, Bloomsbury, London WC1B 3NN, England

The Lamb Inn

The quintessential English inn within the archetypal Cotswold village

It doesn't take too much imagination to picture Burford in its 15th-century sheep market town heyday. Little has changed to its medieval streets lined with distinctive Cotswold stone cottages and green lawns, except maybe the antique shops and exclusive boutiques that now trade their wares instead. On Sheep Street, a collection of former weavers' cottages has provided the setting for the picture-postcard Lamb Inn since 1718. And today, it's the embodiment of what a top-rate inn should be: cosy comfort, historic nuance, good food, fine drink and outstanding service. A contemporary punch complements the original features such as centuries-old flagstone flooring, antiques and beckoning log fires with a fresh, chic country home style of bold colour pairings and richly patterned fabrics. Each of the 17 bedrooms is a romantic spot, however, families or groups of friends, perhaps visiting for a party or special occasion, are wise to reserve The Allium Room and connecting Rosie Room to create a two-floor apartment. Facing the pretty courtyard, The Lamb Inn Bar celebrates locally sourced produce (don't forget to sample its English real ales on tap) while the coveted, more formal Lamb Restaurant specialises in fresh fish and offers a fantastic vegetarian menu option. In the summer you can eat outside in the walled garden.

PRICE FROM:
£165

FEATURES:
Pet friendly; Restaurant

ACTIVITIES:
Fishing; Golf; Horse riding

NEARBY:
River Windrush; Oxford, Cheltenham, Stow-on-the-Wold;
Cheltenham Racecourse

GETTING THERE:
A40; M40; London Heathrow Airport

+44 (0)1993 823155 ☎
condenastjohansens.com/lambinnburford 🌐
Sheep Street, Burford, Oxfordshire OX18 4LR, England 🏠

Old Swan & Minster Mill

Charm of the past and convenience of the present meet at Minster Lovell

PRICE FROM:
£175

FEATURES:
Family friendly; Helipad; Pet friendly; Restaurant; Wheelchair access

ACTIVITIES:
Fishing; Horse riding; Tennis

NEARBY:
Oxford; Blenheim Palace; Cheltenham Racecourse; Cotswold Wildlife Park and Gardens; Sudeley Castle and Gardens

GETTING THERE:
A40; M40 jct 8/9; London Heathrow Airport

The de Savary family's latest gift to the boutique hotel scene is the Old Swan & Minster Mill. Their authority on unpretentious, upscale hospitality combined with the idyllic village setting of Old Minster has succeeded in setting new heights of traditional English accommodation and gastro-pub dining. Spread across two buildings, the 15-room Old Swan has an inherent centuries-old charm with oak beams, log fires and the essence of a bygone era; all coming together to create the archetypal Cotswold scene. Next door at the 37-room Minster Mill, a contemporary flair keeps matters fresh and cushiony comfortable. Set alongside the River Windrush (fishing can be arranged), over 65 acres of prize-winning floral and kitchen gardens, and wild-flower meadows envelop the hotel. An apiary, tennis court, children's activity area, playroom and the new Windrush Spa with indoor/outdoor pool, sauna, steam room and superb treatment menu complete the picture. All the while, a laid-back vibe permeates throughout the dining rooms that comprise large halls, cosy snugs, saloons, a garden terrace and the Malt House. They range in size and can cater various occasions from wedding receptions to romantic meals for two. (The Malt House can host up to 100.) Whichever you choose you'll enjoy fresh local ingredients crafted into hearty dishes. Note to dog lovers: canine companions are welcome.

☎ +44 (0)1993 774441
🌐 condenastjohansens.com/milloldswan
🏠 Minster Lovell, Near Burford, Oxfordshire OX29 0RN, England

The Feathers

Cotswold character with contemporary pizzazz

Somewhere to whisk your loved one away to, take in a little culture and relish heavenly food and drink, The Feathers has you instantly refreshed and leaving with a smile on your face. This is in no small part due to the restaurant's incredible seasonal dishes, boutiquey accommodation and Cotswold charm at every turn. You're in Oxfordshire's famously pretty Woodstock after all, with Winston Churchill's place of birth, Blenheim Palace, a mere walk away. Although this collection of Cotswold town houses and cottages date back to the 17th century, a revamp in recent years has made sure that there's nothing outdated here. Splashes of colour, striking artwork and funky touches keep matters on-trend yet the history within these coaching inn walls is ever-present. Romancing couples, history buffs, foodies and families are all drawn to The Feathers' metropolitan, stylish flair but for lovers of the juniper berry, there's one outstanding reason to stay: The Feathers' record-breaking (in accordance with the Guinness Book of Records™) Gin Bar stocked with no less than 280 labels and exotic list of tonics. Not to be outdone, the fine-dining restaurant offers five and seven-course tasting menus accompanied by carefully chosen wine flights. Lunch is a casual affair in the friendly bar and coffee breaks in The Courtyard allow you to kick back and relax with the papers.

PRICE FROM:
£159

FEATURES:
Family friendly; Restaurant

ACTIVITIES:
Shopping; Sightseeing; Walking

NEARBY:
Oxford; Bicester Village; Blenheim Palace; Cotswold Wildlife Park; Waddesdon Manor

GETTING THERE:
A34; M4/M40; London Heathrow Airport

+44 (0)1993 812291 ☎
condenastjohansens.com/feathers 🌐
Market Street, Woodstock, Oxfordshire OX20 1SX, England 🏠

The Mandolay Hotel

Personalised hospitality in Surrey's largest privately owned hotel

PRICE FROM:
£109

FEATURES:
Restaurant

ACTIVITIES:
Shopping; Sightseeing

NEARBY:
Polesden Lacey; G Live; RHS Wisley; The Yvonne Arnaud Theatre; Thorpe Park

GETTING THERE:
A3100; M25 jct 9; London Road (Guildford) Railway Station

☎ +44 (0)1483 303030
🌐 condenastjohansens.com/mandolay
🏠 36-40 London Road, Guildford, Surrey GU1 2AE, England

The handsome Mandolay Hotel regally resides at the top of Guildford's pretty high street (great shopping!). It's also just a short drive from the breathtaking Surrey Hills and only 35 minutes from London Waterloo Station. Relaxed, inviting and managed with personal care, it's always buzzing with discerning diners and business types meeting. Everything has been carefully thought out from the on-trend interior design with a traditional sensibility to the wholesome, locally sourced (and 2 AA Rosette-awarded) British cuisine in the restaurant. Leisurely getaways here revolve around days filled with shopping, visits to the nearby countryside, country estates and gardens with cushiony comfort waiting your return in guest rooms that guarantee deep sleeps and a chance to recharge. Located in the main hotel or private coach house, each one is decorated in bold wallpapers alongside classic, top quality fabrics. The Mandolay is also home to a conference centre comprising eight purpose-built conference and meeting spaces; exclusive use of the entire hotel can be arranged. Don't miss: afternoon tea on the restaurant's heated outdoor terrace and a concert, dance show or comedy act at the nearby G Live entertainment, conference and hospitality venue, a mere 140 metres from the hotel.

Langshott Manor

A pocket of peace and sophistication minutes from Gatwick Airport

Langshott Manor is a vision of loveliness. Glorying in a leafy, elegant setting of incredibly pretty formal gardens, it's surprising to learn that this rambling Elizabethan hideaway is just a few minutes from the hubbub of Gatwick Airport. While some stay here for an indulgent, spoiling respite after a long-haul flight, others visit for the renowned afternoon teas and smart Mulberry Restaurant's fine dining and tasting menus. A slice of Elizabethan splendour with an ancient moat, leaded windows, fireplaces, four posters and beamed ceilings, Langshott is also one step ahead with its distinctly modern interior design, service and amenities. The 22 bedrooms and suites are slick, bright and up-to-the-minute, kitted out with techy gadgets that make all the difference (iPod docking stations, Nespresso coffee machines, speedy WiFi). Each has an individual style all of its own; some offering a balcony overlooking the beautiful grounds, a working fireplace and/or a double walk-in shower. Whether sampling Exec Chef Phil Dixon's seasonal fare in Mulberry Restaurant or a tempting little something in a cosy corner of a lounge, quality ingredients dictate the menu – herbs, fruits and veggies are grown in Langshott's garden. Come summer, the flower-scented terrace opens up for alfresco lunches and teas.

PRICE FROM:
£85 (per person, including dinner)

FEATURES:
Lake views; Restaurant; Wheelchair access

ACTIVITIES:
Cycling; Sightseeing; Walking

NEARBY:
Leonardslee; Wakehurst Place; Chartwell House; Brighton; Bluebell Railway

GETTING THERE:
M23 jct 9; Horley Railway Station; London Gatwick Airport

+44 (0)1293 786680 ☎
condenastjohansens.com/langshottmanor 🌐
Ladbroke Road, Horley, Near Gatwick, Surrey RH6 9LN, 🏠
England

The Grand Hotel

Seaside high life on Eastbourne's Victorian parade

PRICE FROM:
£240

FEATURES:
Family friendly; Pool; Restaurant; Sea views

ACTIVITIES:
Fishing; Golf; Horse riding

NEARBY:
South Downs Way National Park; The English Wine Centre; Theatres; Glyndebourne Opera

GETTING THERE:
A22; M23 jct 11; London Gatwick Airport

☎ +44 (0)1323 412345
🌐 condenastjohansens.com/grandeastbourne
🏠 King Edward's Parade, Eastbourne, East Sussex BN21 4EQ, England

Officially Britain's "sunniest place" thanks to its sheltered south-easterly position, Eastbourne is a go-to destination for a spot of sea air. It's also a fascinating illustration of a Victorian seaside town as commissioned by wealthy landowner William Cavendish in 1859. The idea of a resort built "for gentlemen by gentlemen" resulted in grand, sprawling feats of architecture such as The Grand Hotel along Eastbourne's sea front. Behind The Grand's crisp-white façade lies an interior filled with natural light (thank you oversized windows and tall ceilings) flush with rich fabrics, fresh flowers and antique furnishings that appear brand new. Many of the 152 bedrooms are nothing less than vast, each one refurbished to include every comfort the demanding guest requires. But there are so many places within The Grand where you can simply kick back and while away the hours, not just your room. The choice of mealtime options is impressive too. Try The Mirabelle Restaurant for fine dining at its modern European best and The Garden Restaurant for British classics with a modern twist. Cocktails, afternoon tea, private dining… it's all here. There is also the opportunity to burn off some of those devoured calories in The Grand's Health Club with indoor and outdoor pools, a gym, sauna, spa bath, steam room, snooker tables and eight spa treatment rooms.

Ashdown Park Hotel and Country Club

The ultimate de-stresser in rural East Sussex

Ashdown Park Hotel and Country Club, East Sussex, breaks the mould of the traditional, grand country hotel. Yes, it has all the hallmarks of a stately, plush, sprawling estate but it's also somehow intimate, comfortable and unpretentious. It's a clever balancing act pleasing those seeking classic British hospitality and others hankering for up-to-the-minute spa and wellness facilities. The setting alone of everlasting green countryside (where deer roam freely) is enough to place a content smile on anyone's face. In fact, regaining perspective and finding inner calm comes easy here, with woodland walks (or jogging trails if you're feeling athletic) in the surrounding Ashdown Forest whose meditative powers are undeniable. Whether visiting with family or getting away with a loved one, Ashdown's eight room categories suit every occasion; each one an immaculate chic retreat. Head to the Country Club for some adrenaline-pumping action where the gym, tennis courts and aerobics studio reside alongside The Spa, which helps takes the edge off. Treatments have been specifically created for men and women. Complimentary amenities include a heated indoor pool, steam room, sauna and 18 hole par 3 golf course. Perfect days end with dinners at the Anderida Restaurant where a resident pianist and wonderful views set the scene.

PRICE FROM:
£250

FEATURES:
Lake views; Pet friendly; Pool; Restaurant; Spa

ACTIVITIES:
Fishing; Golf; Tennis

NEARBY:
Bluebell Railway; Lingfield Park Racecourse; Wakehurst Place; Hever Castle

GETTING THERE:
M23 jct 10; East Grinstead Railway Station; London Gatwick Airport

+44 (0)1342 824988 ☎
condenastjohansens.com/ashdownpark 🌐
Wych Cross, Near Forest Row, East Sussex RH18 5JR, England 🏠

Horsted Place Country House Hotel

Serene Sussex Downs country estate

PRICE FROM:
£145

FEATURES:
Helipad; Restaurant

ACTIVITIES:
Golf; Tennis; Walking

NEARBY:
Lewes; Glyndebourne Opera; Sheffield Park gardens; Bluebell Railway; East Sussex National Golf Course

GETTING THERE:
A26; M23 jct 10; London Gatwick Airport

☎ +44 (0)1825 750581
🌐 condenastjohansens.com/horstedplace
🏠 Little Horsted, East Sussex TN22 5TS, England

Horsted Place Country House Hotel is a splendid Victorian gothic house built in 1850. Set in rolling Sussex countryside, on the edge of the South Downs, it's perfectly placed for two championship golf courses and the 600-year-old Glyndebourne. The enchanting grounds and formal gardens offer tennis and croquet, and a nugget of royal history: a myrtle tree grown from a sprig of Queen Victoria's wedding bouquet. (You'll also be walking in the steps of Queen Elizabeth II and Prince Philip who have frequented this once private estate.) Horsted is a country house hotel with all the accoutrements one would expect from a sumptuous period drama. 24-hour room service, silver cloches and Egyptian cotton sheets, a log fire in the Drawing Room, canapés on the terrace and a pianist at dinner being just some of the luxuries available. Complimentary use of Horsted Health Club, just a two-minute drive away, allows you to keep to your fitness regime before tucking into traditional afternoon tea guilt-free. This is certainly something to write home about; lavish and elegantly indulgent with finger sandwiches, crumbly scones and the lightest meringues. Everything is home-made on the restaurant's à la carte daily changing menu. That's the key to Horsted: the extra touch.

Bailiffscourt Hotel & Spa

The Middle Ages meets fanciful decadence near the Sussex coast

Time travel is possible after all, or at least it is at Bailiffscourt Hotel & Spa in Climping. However, before you brush up on your flux-capacitor knowledge, it's worthwhile knowing that Baillifscourt was the vision of Lady Moyne (wife of Lord Moyne, aka Walter Guinness of the famed stout empire), brought to reality by Amyas Phillips in 1933. By using authentic material salvaged from age-old buildings, this most-convincing Medieval House with six outbuildings (complete with gnarled 15th-century beams, gothic mullioned windows) and private parkland featuring a moat, resulted in a playground for the rich and famous of its day. Host to many a-bopping party, Baillifscourt attracted many Bright Young Things (and perhaps some of Lord Moyne's political friends) because of its close proximity to Goodwood and unspoilt Climping beach. When the natural transition to luxurious hotel took place in 1948, the appeal of Baillifscourt remained as popular as ever. Now the four posters, open log fires, purpose-built spa, two tennis courts, croquet lawn and beautiful views across the countryside draw in a new generation of BYTs seeking good hospitality and great food. Menus at Tapestry Restaurant are eclectic, and in summer you can eat out in the rose-clad courtyard or walled garden.

PRICE FROM:
£259

FEATURES:
Beach access; Family friendly; Helipad; Restaurant; Spa

ACTIVITIES:
Cycling; Tennis; Walking

NEARBY:
Arundel Castle; Goodwood Racecourse and estate; Chichester Festival Theatre; Beach access to Climping beach; Golf

GETTING THERE:
A24; A23; A27

+44 (0)1903 723511 ☎
condenastjohansens.com/bailiffscourt 🌐
Climping, Arundel, West Sussex BN17 5RW, England 🏠

Ockenden Manor Hotel & Spa

Enchanting West Sussex Elizabethan manor house

Brimming with tales of yore and packed with personality, Ockenden Manor Hotel & Spa snuggles within acres of private gardens and parkland in the pretty Tudor village of Cuckfield. An Elizabethan manor house, Ockenden's history has been traced back as far as 1520. Initially a family home, then a Jewish boys' school and residence for Canadian troops during WWII, Ockenden's life as a hotel began in the late 1940s. Ideally positioned for exploring Sussex and Kent (the chalky hills of the South Downs, Cuckmere Valley, Brighton and Lewes), the manor looks out to far-reaching West Sussex countryside, and from the minute you step through its doors you're swept away by warm hospitality and culinary delights. The 28 distinctive bedrooms and suites have fascinating quirks and nooks and crannies at every turn. Climb the private staircase to Elizabeth, indulge in a Victorian-style bath in Hugh or enjoy the huge four-poster bed in Charles. No visit to Ockenden is complete without sampling the creative Michelin Starred cuisine of Head Chef Stephen Crane. Choose from fixed price menus or the seven-course Tasting Menu in this utterly romantic restaurant looking out to sweeping vistas of the garden and beyond. Must do: pampering at Ockenden's ultra-modern, luxury spa set within the walled gardens with indoor/outdoor pool and rooms filled with natural light.

Park House

Soaking up the natural beauty in South Downs' countryside

Get the camera charged and paint brushes at the ready. Park House's scenic setting in private acres of South Downs National Park (an official Area of Outstanding Natural Beauty) is one that you'll want to capture. The archetypal English countryside scene, Park House is in the quaint village of Bepton, a short drive from the historic market town of Midhurst. A family-run hotel with a welcoming atmosphere and home-from-home quality, Park House is as warm as it is stylish with a designer finesse to the interiors whose classic country chic style has been given a contemporary interpretation that brings everything up-to-date and on-trend. Guest rooms are located in the main hotel or there are three cottages nestled in the grounds. Most main hotel rooms look out to the pretty rose garden and grounds, which include grass tennis courts, croquet and bowls lawns, a six-hole golf course and summer outdoor pool. Three more private cottages (available for exclusive use) are well-equipped sanctuaries great for long-term stays, groups of friends, families or romantic sojourns. The Bay Tree Cottage has its very own kitchen although the seasonal, locally sourced dishes at the restaurant are irresistible and promise English classics. Two bonus features: the PH$_2$O Spa, a state-of-the-art therapeutic facility, and the restored barn available for parties/business events.

PRICE FROM:
£140

FEATURES:
Gym; Pool; Restaurant; Spa

ACTIVITIES:
Fishing; Golf; Horse riding

NEARBY:
West Dean Gardens; Petworth House; Goodwood Racecourse and estate; Cowdray ruins

GETTING THERE:
A3; London Gatwick Airport; London Heathrow Airport

Dogs X

+44 (0)1730 819 020 ☎
condenastjohansens.com/parkhousehotel 🌐
Bepton, Near Midhurst, West Sussex GU29 0JB, England 🏠

The Spread Eagle Hotel & Spa

A charming step back in time in the market town of Midhurst

PRICE FROM:
£190

FEATURES:
Family friendly; Pet friendly; Pool; Restaurant; Spa

ACTIVITIES:
Cycling; Shooting; Walking

NEARBY:
Petworth House; Cowdray Park; Goodwood Racecourse and estate; Chichester Cathedral; West Dean Gardens

GETTING THERE:
Just off A272/A286; M25 jct 9; London Gatwick Airport

Rich in charm and period features, The Spread Eagle Hotel & Spa in Midhurst is one of England's oldest coaching inns. Dating from 1430, age-old oak beams, original open fireplaces and stained-glass windows generate an atmosphere of centuries past while modern comforts such as pampering spa services and gourmet meals bring it right up-to-date. Perhaps The Spread Eagle's most unexpected card is its Scandinavian-inspired luxury spa. Wonderfully contemporary with an impressive vaulted glass ceiling and plenty of wet areas; it also has a fitness suite. Back within the 15th-century walls of The Spread Eagle, pre-dinner cocktails are provided by the new Gin Bar stocked with more than 30 varieties from local Sussex suppliers and the restaurant's Head Chef Richard Cave-Toye whips up modern classic dishes using seasonal flavours. As you would expect, the bedrooms are peppered with antiques and some have four-poster beds. The White Room has a secret passage and is said to have been used by smugglers to evade the king's men. Queen Elizabeth I reputedly stayed in the Queen's Suite in 1591. With easy access to Sussex and the South Downs, this is a great base for exploring the area with one of The Spread Eagle's cream teas waiting for you on your return - children's high teas too. Note to dog owners: well-behaved four-legged friends are most welcome.

☎ +44 (0)1730 816911
🌐 condenastjohansens.com/spreadeaglemidhurst
🏠 South Street, Midhurst, West Sussex GU29 9NH, England

Alexander House Hotel and Utopia Spa

Stately manor house-cum-countryside spa hideaway

Alexander House Hotel and Utopia Spa, West Sussex, strikes that fine balance between contemporary comfort and historic charm. Cosy during every season with summer courtyard sunshine and wintry fireside lounging, Alexander House is conveniently located for Gatwick Airport and central London. It's the perfect last-minute getaway. Check into your elegantly designed room (tip: choose one of the designer Cedar Lodge Suites), don a soft towelling robe and prepare to spend most of your stay loafing about. However, the irrationally beautiful views of the 120 acres of countryside outside your window might just tempt you to temporarily leave your suite's comfort. And the Grecian-styled Utopia Spa is always on call to rid you of those niggling knots. Everything is comfortable and familiar at Alexander House but there's nothing standard about it. This principle is also true for the elegant, classic dishes served in the two restaurants and private dining rooms. Do not leave without trying Alexander's afternoon tea of clotted cream scones and sandwiches served with smiles. And burn off these well-worth-it calories with a garden stroll followed by a tipple from the 1608 Champagne Bar's menu (take your time, the list includes more than 175 Champagnes, wines and cocktails). Bonus: the fully-serviced two-bedroom Gatehouse is ideal for groups, families and wedding parties.

PRICE FROM:
£125

FEATURES:
Gym; Pool; Restaurant; Spa; Wheelchair access

ACTIVITIES:
Cycling; Tennis; Walking

NEARBY:
Wakehurst Place; Sussex Polo Club; Ashdown Forest; Bluebell Railway; Glyndebourne

GETTING THERE:
East Grinstead Railway Station; Helipad on-site; London Gatwick Airport

+44 (0)1342 714914 ☎
condenastjohansens.com/alexanderhouse 🌐
East Street, Turner's Hill, West Sussex RH10 4QD, England 🏠

Gravetye Manor

Elizabethan manor house enveloped by Sussex woodland

PRICE FROM:
£260

FEATURES:
Michelin Starred restaurant

ACTIVITIES:
Golf; Horse riding; Walking

NEARBY:
Royal Ashdown Golf Course; Wakehurst Place; Hever Castle;
Standen (National Trust)

GETTING THERE:
M25 jct 6; East Grinstead Railway Station; London Gatwick
Airport

☎ +44 (0)1342 810567
🌐 condenastjohansens.com/gravetyemanor
🏠 Vowels Lane, Near West Hoathly, West Sussex RH19 4LJ,
England

In the quaint English village of West Hoathly on Vowels Lane, Gravetye Manor conjures a barrage of "ooo"s. Originally built for a bride as the great beginning for her happy ever after, this grand house was subsequently the late William Robinson's (father of the English flower garden) home for more than 50 years. It then evolved into the archetypal English country estate it is today, set in 1,000 acres of Sussex countryside. Outside, Robinson's world-famous horticultural work draws attention to exquisite blooms, colours and textures. Inside, wood panelling, roaring fires, leather Chesterfields and fine works of art set the scene to create an utterly relaxing atmosphere. Book a garden view room and wake up feeling fresh as a daisy. Spend days with walks along the lawns and to the kitchen garden. Or simply while away the time by reading beside the fire followed by afternoon tea in the Sitting Room. But if all this kicking back has you itching for some excitement, speak to the Gravetye staff to take part in deer stalking or riding the Bluebell Railway. They can also arrange tickets to nearby Glyndebourne music events. However, if you do nothing else, reserve a table at Gravetye's Michelin Starred restaurant. Head Chef George Blogg offers a variety of menus (Sunday lunch, a tasting menu, Garden Menu, à la carte, fixed price) that all take advantage of the on-site kitchen garden ingredients.

The Castle Inn

Medieval timepiece in the heart of the Cotswolds

Castle Combe is the Cotswold village that time forgot. It's a perfectly preserved 15th-century piece of history in Wiltshire's north-west corner often referred to as the "prettiest village in England". There's not one street light, overhead cable or TV aerial in sight, just rows of yellow Cotswold stone houses along narrow roads leading to a medieval church and 14th-century market cross. If it all looks a little familiar it's possibly because Hollywood has immortalised the village most recently in Steven Speilberg's War Horse, and perhaps most famously as Puddleby-on-the-Marsh in the 1967 adaptation of Dr Doolittle. Facing the market cross is The Castle Inn whose origins trace as far back as the 12th century. However, there's nothing antiquated about its standard of service or facilities despite its respectful preservation of unique historic character and features that remain true to its setting. In fact, The Castle Inn has a surprisingly contemporary flair with 11 bedrooms dressed in sumptuous fabrics alongside swish bathrooms. No English inn is complete without a cosy bar with open fire and The Castle Inn doesn't disappoint. Dishing up traditional favourites and an à la carte menu for dinner, there's also the private Oak Room and relaxed, alfresco Terrace Patio when the weather permits.

PRICE FROM:
£125

FEATURES:
Family friendly; Restaurant

ACTIVITIES:
Fishing; Golf; Walking

NEARBY:
Bath; Lacock; Cotswold villages; Bradford-on-Avon

GETTING THERE:
M4 jct 17; Chippenham Railway Station; Bristol Airport

+44 (0)1249 783030 ☎
condenastjohansens.com/castleinn 🌐
Castle Combe, Wiltshire SN14 7HN, England 🏠

Lucknam Park Hotel & Spa

Spectacular Palladian mansion in picturesque, private Wiltshire estate

PRICE FROM:
£290

FEATURES:
Gym; Michelin Starred restaurant; Pet friendly; Pool; Spa

ACTIVITIES:
Horse riding; Tennis; Walking

NEARBY:
Bath; Lacock; The Cotswolds; Longleat; Stonehenge

GETTING THERE:
A420; M4 jct 18; Bristol Airport

Lucknam Park Hotel & Spa, Wiltshire, is an authority on the high life; a Palladian mansion in hundreds of private green acres, a short drive from historic Bath. Beyond the imposing exterior resides a collection of suites and bedrooms dressed in fine fabrics with antiques reflecting each room's personality; bathrooms are a flawless sweep of marble. Book in advance to guarantee a table at Restaurant Hywel Jones whose Michelin Starred dishes are a celebration of organic ingredients, local produce and garden-grown herbs that result in eyes-closed appreciation (now open for dinner Tuesday to Sunday in addition to Sunday lunch). Or there's the relaxed Brasserie - next to the spa so you can easily enjoy the facilities of one then the other - complete with open kitchen, wood-fired oven, lounge area, bar and restaurant serving all day. But who can resist traditional afternoon tea of home-made scones, clotted cream, cakes and tea in the Drawing Room or wood-panelled Library? If feeling a little guilty after all this indulgence, head to The Spa at Lucknam Park for a health kick (with the Well Being at Lucknam Park Spa promising instant results), the Equestrian Centre, tennis courts or football pitch. Foodie bonus: Lucknam's Cookery School hosts courses led by Head Chef Ben Taylor. A Master Class with Michelin Starred Chef Hywel Jones is also available. Even the children can join in during the school holidays.

☎ +44 (0)1225 742777
🌐 condenastjohansens.com/lucknampark
🏠 Colerne, Chippenham (Near Bath), Wiltshire SN14 8AZ, England

Dormy House

Setting new heights of hospitality in Worcestershire

Broadway in Worcestershire is a charming slice of yore known as the "jewel of the Cotswolds." Lined with red chestnut trees and 16th-century Cotswold limestone buildings, the nickname is well deserved. Numerous artistic talents including Elgar, J M Barrie and William Morris chose Broadway as their home (clearly no lack of inspiration here) and it's now a hub for the art, antique and outdoor loving enthusiast. Standing high on Willersey Hill, the 17th-century farmhouse that's now the utterly chic and charming Dormy House is a showcase of talent from leading designers, landscapers, spa innovators and an ambitious chef. It's a hotel that feels like a home offering exceptional services such as ethical, prize-winning spa treatments, a new kind of casual fine-dining experience, afternoon teas with a modern twist and tasting menus to dream over. The Main House rooms and private Rose Cottage with hot tub uphold Dormy's traditional essence, while The Emily Wing rooms are a vision of the 1950s. When it comes to food, Dormy House has always been a forerunner and now, Head Chef Ryan Swift is dishing up classic flavours with an exciting punch in The Garden Room (alfresco in summer) and in the casual Potting Shed. Don't miss: Dormy's House Spa with 16-metre infinity pool, Champagne nail parlour, six treatment rooms, more than 50 treatments, mud room and two gyms.

PRICE FROM:
£250

FEATURES:
Family friendly; Helipad; Restaurant; Spa; Wheelchair access

ACTIVITIES:
Shopping; Sightseeing; Walking

NEARBY:
The Cotswolds; Cheltenham; Stratford-upon-Avon; Hidcote Manor; Kiftsgate Gardens

GETTING THERE:
A44; M40 jct 8/15; Birmingham International Airport

+44 (0)1386 852711 ☎
condenastjohansens.com/dormyhouse 🌐
Willersey Hill, Broadway, Worcestershire WR12 7LF, England 🏠

UK/Scotland

Please go to condenastjohansens.com/scotland

The spectacular surrounds of Airds Hotel & Restaurant, page 241

Douneside House

Warm Scottish Highlands country home hotel

The self-made MacRobert family's turn-of-the-century country estate has lost none of its character and homely warmth over the decades. The 17-acre setting of perfectly manicured gardens also remain intact just as Lady MacRobert would have wished and the swoonworthy Scottish Highlands views to the Grampian Mountains continue to force jaws to the floor. Inside, Douneside House's main hotel bedrooms (classic-contemporary style, antique furnishings, original artwork) are 14 of the 30 rooms on offer. Alternative accommodations are located within the adjacent Casa Memoria comprising four apartments, in addition to four cottages with private gardens. Remember to reserve your table at Douneside's Restaurant (popular with locals and foodies in-the-know) whose Tasting Menu and table d'hôte menu contain produce grown on the estate and meat from premier butchers. But if the occasion calls for some privacy, meals may be taken in the Douneside library, which is where Chef also serves his speciality afternoon tea. A brand new fixture to Douneside is the Health Club complete with indoor pool, a high-tech gym and scheduled yoga and Pilates classes. Dates to note: Douneside exclusively hosts military personnel from mid-July to end of August and the Christmas period.

PRICE FROM:
£140

FEATURES:
Family friendly; Gym; Pool; Restaurant

ACTIVITIES:
Fishing; Golf; Tennis

NEARBY:
Tarland Golf Club; Castle Trail including Crathes, Drum, Craigievar and Castle Fraser; Balmoral Castle; Whisky Trail; Cairngorms National Park

GETTING THERE:
A90; A96; Aberdeen Airport

+44 (0)13398 81230 ☎
condenastjohansens.com/dounesidehouse 🌐
Tarland, Aberdeenshire AB34 4UL, Scotland 🏠

Airds Hotel & Restaurant

Loch-side romance on the west coast of Scotland

PRICE FROM:
£147.50 (per person, DBB, based on double occupancy)

FEATURES:
Family friendly; Helipad; Pet friendly; Restaurant

ACTIVITIES:
Cycling; Horse riding; Walking

NEARBY:
Isle of Lismore; Oban; Glencoe; Ben Nevis; Isle of Mull

GETTING THERE:
Oban Railway Station; Glasgow International Airport;
Edinburgh International Airport

Whatever you do, bring your camera on a visit to Airds Hotel & Restaurant, Argyll. For the scenery surrounding this understated treasure with gourmet restaurant is an image you'll want to capture and take home with you. Like the otherwordly scenery that fades in and out on your computer's screensaver, here it is in reality, in the stunning hamlet of Port Appin beside Loch Linnhe on the west coast of Scotland, near Oban. Airds began its life as an 18th-century ferry inn before establishing itself as a noteworthy romantic hotel whose relaxed yet professional staff raises the level of charm and welcoming atmosphere to an exceptional level. (The owners are previous guests who couldn't resist its allure). The eight bedrooms, three suites and two-bedroom self-catering cottage within the grounds, all offer sophisticated, homely rooms that further enhance the intimate warmth and atmosphere of tranquillity. Some have awe-inspiring views across Loch Linnhe with the Morvern mountains behind. Renowned as one of the finest in Scotland, the restaurant sources only the best local ingredients, including world-class fish and seafood to produce award-winning cuisine.

☎ +44 (0)1631 730236
🌐 condenastjohansens.com/airdshotel
🏠 Port Appin, Appin, Argyll PA38 4DF, Scotland

Inverlochy Castle

Fairy-tale castle romance in the foothills of Ben Nevis

After a week of sketching and painting at Lord Abinger's Inverlochy Castle in 1873, Queen Victoria wrote, "I never saw a lovelier or more romantic spot." Built 10 years prior to her visit, not far from its original 13th-century fort namesake, (the first) Lord Abinger could not have picked a more scenic location within the foothills of Ben Nevis in the Western Highlands. Today, the mighty castle is one of Scotland's finest hotels managed with passion and professionalism by Jane Watson. Jane and her staff make every effort to put each guest completely at ease in this most grandiose of settings whose imposing reception room displays Venetian crystal chandeliers and a Michelangelo-style ceiling, and leads to three elaborately decorated dining rooms. In contrast, whilst being spacious and in-keeping with the essence of the Castle, Inverlochy's rooms and suites unveil a fresh, modern take on the traditional floral and tartan-clad theme alongside incredibly stylish bathrooms that keep matters very 21st century. Maintaining high standards in the kitchen, Chef Andy Turnbull's modern British cuisine uses local game, hand-picked wild mushrooms and scallops from the Isle of Skye. Worth noting: Inverlochy Castle Management International (ICMI) manages the property.

PRICE FROM:
£335

FEATURES:
Family friendly; Helipad; Pet friendly; Restaurant

ACTIVITIES:
Fishing; Golf; Walking

NEARBY:
Ben Nevis; Glencoe; Glenfinnan; Loch Ness; The Jacobite steam train - aka Hogwarts Express

GETTING THERE:
On the A82; Fort William Railway Station; Inverness Airport

+44 (0)1397 702177 ☎
condenastjohansens.com/inverlochy 🌐
Torlundy, Fort William PH33 6SN, Highland, Scotland 🏰

Rocpool Reserve Hotel & Chez Roux

Inverness retreat leading the way in interior design and cuisine

PRICE FROM:
£195

FEATURES:
Pet friendly; Restaurant; Wheelchair access

ACTIVITIES:
Fishing; Golf; Sightseeing

NEARBY:
Inverness High Street; Castle Stuart Golf Course; Loch Ness; Caledonian Canal; Culloden Battlefield

GETTING THERE:
Inverness Railway Station; Inverness Airport

☎ +44 (0)1463 240089
🌐 condenastjohansens.com/rocpool
🏠 Culduthel Road, Inverness IV2 4AG, Highland, Scotland

In the UK's northernmost city of Inverness, the 11-room boutique Rocpool Reserve Hotel & Chez Roux is making waves in the hospitality scene. Just a quick dash from the High Street and Inverness Castle, this city centre retreat looks out to the River Ness. Designer rooms exemplify classic elegance and contemporary grace while the superb staff demonstrates first-class service and phenomenal attention to detail. The seriously stylish bedrooms come in four categories (Hip, Chic, Decadent and Extra Decadent) but all have emperor-size beds and fixtures such as plasma TVs, DVD players and luxuries that include Egyptian linens and Italian ceramics in the bathrooms. Two have hot tubs on private terraces. Unwinding at r Bar at Reserve is made exceptionally easy during cocktail hour before dining in the triumphant Chez Roux. Facing the river, menus (choose from à la carte or a set menu) showcase local Scottish produce blended with classic French country cuisine, all overseen by multi award-winning Chef Albert Roux OBE, KFO, head of the famous cooking dynasty behind such establishments as Le Gavroche, that was the first ever restaurant in the UK to be awarded 3 Michelin Stars. Worthy note: Rocpool Reserve and Chez Roux is managed by Inverlochy Castle Management International (ICMI).

Inver Lodge Hotel and Chez Roux

A handsome, charming and tasteful Highland belter

An inspired location for a special hotel, Inver Lodge Hotel and Chez Roux in the Scottish Highlands has it all. Remote enough to feel out-of-the-way yet accessible to Inverness (two hours by car, and what a drive!), Inver Lodge has more than a dram or two of Scottish charm plus a world-class restaurant. Utterly serene, this hilltop retreat looks down to the sleepy fishing village of Lochinver, across the waters of Loch Inver and over to the Western Isles. You'll be grabbing your hiking boots before you know it and wading on in the nearby river and/or loch for a spot of trout or salmon fishing. Inside, it's all about muted colours and clean lines with a splash of elegant tartan. Bedrooms are oversized so the whole family are comfortable here (superior rooms come with even more space). However, when the views are this spectacular and the log fires are roaring, romance is always in the air. Before relishing the hearty country cooking at the exquisite Chez Roux restaurant – overseen by Chef Albert Roux OBE, KFO – time spent in the foyer lounge sets you up for the gourmet delights ahead. Worth noting: highly respected Inverlochy Castle Management International (ICMI) runs Inver Lodge.

PRICE FROM:
£250

FEATURES:
Family friendly; Helipad; Lake views; Pet friendly; Restaurant

ACTIVITIES:
Fishing; Shooting; Walking

NEARBY:
Bird-watching; Rugged Sutherland coastline; Assynt Hills; Ardveck Castle; The Bone Caves of Allt-nan-uamh

GETTING THERE:
Inverness Railway Station; Lairg Railway Station; Inverness Airport

+44 (0)1571 844496 ☎
condenastjohansens.com/inverlodge 🌐
Lochinver, Sutherland IV27 4LU, Highland, Scotland 🏠

Crossbasket Castle

Reinvented, regenerated and resplendent castle-hotel just outside Glasgow

PRICE FROM:
£250

FEATURES:
Family friendly; Restaurant; Wheelchair access

ACTIVITIES:
Golf; Horse riding; Walking

NEARBY:
Strathaven Golf Club; Chatelherault Country Park; The Falls of Clyde; Busby Riding Centre

GETTING THERE:
Blantyre Railway Station; Glasgow Airport; Edinburgh Airport

Masterfully restored to its former glory, the 600-year-old Crossbasket Castle was rescued from ruin in 2011 and opened as a five-star hotel in 2016. The oldest part of the castle dates back to the 16th century - the Lindsay Tower - located high on a hill above the River Calder. And today, this is the ultimate bridal suite spanning four floors reached via a sweeping spiral stone staircase. All this majesty is situated in the hamlet of Blantyre (birthplace of explorer David Livingstone), on the outskirts of Glasgow. Conveniently accessed from the city, Crossbasket Castle is a tranquil, luxurious getaway with nine palatial bedrooms, each unique in character and named after a former owner of the castle. It's also an idyllic exclusive-use venue with stunning new Grand Ballroom seating up to 250 guests for corporate gatherings and special occasions. Furthermore, the fine-dining restaurant is overseen by renowned Chef Albert Roux (OBE, KFO) and Michel Roux Jr to offer an indulgent gourmet experience for all the senses. Bonus fact: Inverlochy Castle Management International (ICMI) manages the smooth running of the exceptional service.

☎ +44 (0)1698 829461
🌐 condenastjohansens.com/crossbasket
🏠 Crossbasket Estate, Stoneymeadow Road, High Blantyre, Near Glasgow, South Lanarkshire G72 9UE, Scotland

Greywalls and Chez Roux

Elegant Edwardian retreat on the edge of Muirfield Championship Golf Course

Minutes from the world-famous Muirfield Championship Golf Course (15-time host of The British Open) and an impressive 10 golf courses within a five-mile radius, Greywalls is a golfer's dream. However, it would be unfair to confine this delightful retreat to a single glory. A handsome 1901 Edwardian country house designed by Sir Edwin Lutyens, Greywalls and Chez Roux in East Lothian is seductively charming. Bedrooms are full of Edwardian character with modern luxuries (dados and padded headboards meet plush pillows and en-suite bathrooms), all with superb views of the verdant Scottish countryside. There's excellent cuisine to be had at Chez Roux under the direction of Chef Albert Roux OBE, KFO, head of the Roux cooking dynasty, not to mention boundless opportunities to ease away any stresses with pleasant strolls in the acres of walled gardens encompassing a putting green, croquet lawn, tennis courts, herbaceous borders, beehives and chicken coops. Visits to the Whisky Room will relax you to your toes. Greywalls is also a fabulous venue for large parties, well catered for in the Colonel's House, a self-catering lodge perfect for a family holiday or golfing group. For fact fans: Greywalls and Chez Roux is managed by Inverlochy Castle Management International (ICMI).

PRICE FROM:
£255

FEATURES:
Helipad; Pet friendly; Restaurant

ACTIVITIES:
Sightseeing; Tennis; Walking

NEARBY:
Edinburgh; Muirfield Championship Golf Course; Beaches; Tantallon Castle; Glenkinchie Distillery

GETTING THERE:
A1; Edinburgh International Airport

+44 (0)1620 842 144 ☎
condenastjohansens.com/greywalls 🌐
Muirfield, Gullane, East Lothian EH31 2EG, Scotland 🏠

Cromlix and Chez Roux

Picturesque Perthshire's Victorian grande dame

PRICE FROM:
£220

FEATURES:
Family friendly; Pet friendly; Restaurant

ACTIVITIES:
Fishing; Tennis; Walking

NEARBY:
Dunblane; Stirling; The Trossachs

GETTING THERE:
Edinburgh International Airport; Glasgow International Airport

Proving that he's just as savvy off the tennis court as he is on it, 2016 Wimbledon Champion Andy Murray is owner of Cromlix and Chez Roux, Perthshire. Located a short drive from Gleneagles (host of the Ryder Cup, September 2014), Cromlix opened in the spring of 2014 following a hotly anticipated and revitalising overhaul. Directed by the professional team at Inverlochy Castle Management International, ICMI, (Inverlochy Castle and Rocpool Reserve are just two of nine first-class properties in their dependable hands), a modern injection into this Victorian mansion is just what the doctor ordered. Cromlix comprises 10 bedrooms, five suites, a one-bedroom gate lodge, a billiards room, bar, lounge, drawing room and restaurant, as well as meeting facilities at an executive level for day and 24-hour delegate rates. Plus, there are approximately 34 acres of parkland surrounding the estate complete with four lochs and two mineral springs. But the ace that's going to secure its success? The gourmet restaurant with open kitchen located in a glass conservatory overseen by Chef Albert Roux OBE, KFO. Its convenient location for Stirling, Edinburgh and Glasgow, in addition to nearby attractions such as Stirling Castle, Wallace Monument and Bannockburn certainly seal the deal.

☎ +44 (0)1786 822125
🌐 condenastjohansens.com/cromlix
🏠 Kinbuck, By Dunblane, Near Stirling FK15 9JT, Perth & Kinross, Scotland

UK/Wales

Please go to condenastjohansens.com/wales

The rural splendour of The Bell At Skenfrith, page 250

The Falcondale Hotel & Restaurant

A touch of Italian flair in South West Wales

PRICE FROM:
£100

FEATURES:
Pet friendly; Restaurant

ACTIVITIES:
Cycling; Sightseeing; Walking

NEARBY:
Llanerchaeron (National Trust); Dolaucothi gold mines (National Trust); Cardigan Bay and Cambrian mountains; National Botanic Garden of Wales

GETTING THERE:
M4; Carmarthen/Aberystwyth Railway Stations; Cardiff Airport

☎ +44 (0)1570 422910
🌐 condenastjohansens.com/falcondale
🏠 Falcondale Drive, Lampeter, Ceredigion SA48 7RX, Wales

By far the nicest bolthole in Teifi Valley, The Falcondale Hotel & Restaurant near Lampeter is what every British country house hotel should strive to be. Comfortable, relaxed and peaceful with roaring log fires, cosy rooms, good food and an ever-ready warm welcome, what sets The Falcondale apart is its huge heart. Not to mention those sweeping Valley views! Set in acres of lush green gardens of its own, this charming Victorian Italianate villa is the ideal starting point for a romp or cycle around the surrounding Cambrian mountains and nearby Brecon Beacons. You're also close to the coast and Irish Sea, National Trust cliff walks and dolphin watching from Cardigan Bay. Windswept or suntanned, you'll return ravenous and Falcondale will be prepared. Recipient of not one but 2 AA Rosettes, the menu is a locally-sourced feast featuring treats such as Golden Cenarth cheese, Welsh mountain lamb and Burry Port mussels. However, The Falcondale's wine list spans the world of more than 100 bins from South Australia to Bourdeaux, France. Guest rooms vary in size and range from standard doubles to "Best" rooms, with romantic four posters and Teifi Valley viewing rooms in between. This is somewhere to bring your loved-one, a pack of cards and the dog who will be spoilt rotten with a special blanket, bowl and biscuits.

The Bell At Skenfrith

Cosy out-of-the-way Monmouthshire inn with big appeal

Built shortly after the Norman Conquest in 1066, the Grade II listed Skenfrith Castle is the village's most famous attraction. However, the 17th-century coaching inn, The Bell At Skenfrith, is a hot contender. Just outside the village, beside the River Monnow where the rolling green hills go on for as far as the eye can see, this inn is an acclaimed 11-room countryside pocket of peace. In Wales' south-east corner, The Bell is practically on the England/Wales border, popular with locals and country-crossing travellers alike. One of the main reasons for this (apart from the romantic scenery, fantastic walking trails, warm hospitality and old world charm) is The Bell's restaurant and accompanying, great value for money wine and Champagne list. Dishes are simple, farm fresh and unpretentious. Many of the ingredients on the numerous menus - à la carte, daily specials, set lunch menu, picnic menu, children's menu and flexible Sunday lunches (from 12pm to 8pm) - hail from The Bell's large kitchen garden with natural spring. And now the newly-opened Dog and Boot Bar brings another reason for locals and visitors to stay that bit longer. Full of character, the guest rooms and suites vary in shape and size with quirky elements such as sloping walls, in-room bathtubs and lofts with bathrooms.

PRICE FROM:
£130

FEATURES:
Family friendly; Pet friendly; Restaurant

ACTIVITIES:
Fishing; Golf; Horse riding

NEARBY:
Llanthony Priory, Abergavenny; Tintern Abbey; Monmouth; Ross-on-Wye

GETTING THERE:
Off the B4521; A466; M4 jct 24

+44 (0)1600 750235 ☎
condenastjohansens.com/bellskenfrith 🌐
Skenfrith, Monmouthshire NP7 8UH, Wales 🏠

Hammet House

An on-trend revelation tucked away in Pembrokeshire countryside

PRICE FROM:
£120

FEATURES:
Family friendly; Restaurant

ACTIVITIES:
Sightseeing; Walking

NEARBY:
Llechryd village; Cilgerran Castle; Narberth; Cardigan; Poppit Sands beach

GETTING THERE:
A484; M4; Clunderwen Railway Station

☎ +44 (0)1239 682382
🌐 condenastjohansens.com/hammethouse
🏠 Llechryd, Cardigan, Pembrokeshire SA43 2QA, Wales

Judge this book by its cover and you're in for a surprise. Beyond the croquet lawn and behind that ivy covered, very symmetrical (very Jane Austen) Georgian façade is an artistic expression of pared back, avant-garde interior design. Not a floral curtain or swirly patterned carpet in sight! This is the brainchild of owners/managers Owen and Philippa Gale who purchased Hammet House in 2011. The transformation into the 15-room boutique hotel it is today has been a passion project. And as they raise their family here, this is now a home that welcomes everyone (including children) seeking bucolic serenity. Directly on the Pembrokeshire/Ceredigion border with the banks of the River Teifi within the hotel grounds, the Pembrokeshire National Park is a five-minute drive and Cardigan - where dolphin watching boat trips leave - is a mere 10 minutes by car. But many locals and guests visit Hammet House for its fine-dining, modern British restaurant, which presents a superb seven-course tasting menu (book in advance) and organic wine list. The full and Champagne afternoon tea also draws a steady crowd to Hammet's Library Bar, Drawing Room, Den and croquet lawn. Please note: room categories vary from Tiny to Outstanding so please enquire about room dimensions and amenities when booking. All rooms can be exclusively hired for weddings and parties.

Llangoed Hall

A celebration of Welsh countryside and Edwardian architecture

Left for ruin in the 1980s, the saviour of centuries-old Llangoed Hall in Wye Valley's designated Area of Outstanding Natural Beauty was Sir Bernard Ashley. Armed with an artistic flair, dogged determination, his children's professional expertise and the memory of late wife and business partner (Laura Ashley of chic country-style fame), the resurrection of Llangoed Hall took three years. Architect Sir Bertram Clough Williams-Ellis's 1912 redesign had been preserved. 26 years on and Llangoed is under new ownership determined to continue the rural home ambience Sir Bernard created. Although sensitive to Llangoed's Jacobean legacy (specifically the south wing's arched porch), the Hall is a mass of Edwardian style exhibiting many of the era's artistic greats. Antiques and artworks fashioned by Walter Sickert, Augustus John and Rex Whistler adorn the interiors. It's all a very British affair. In fact, only products with The Royal Warrant Holders Association stamp will do. Timeless and elegant, the formal Dining Room is a testament to local Welsh produce (black beef and Radnorshire lamb) seasoned to perfection with herbs from Llangoed's gardens.

PRICE FROM:
£125

FEATURES:
Helipad; Pet friendly; Restaurant

ACTIVITIES:
Fishing; Sightseeing; Walking

NEARBY:
Brecon Beacons National Park; Black mountains; Hay-on-Wye specialist book shops; Hereford Cathedral; Tretower Court

GETTING THERE:
A470; M4 jct 24; Cardiff Airport

+44 (0)1874 754525 ☎
condenastjohansens.com/llangoedhall 🌐
Llyswen, Brecon, Powys LD3 0YP, Wales 🏠

THE MINI LIST
The Americas, Caribbean & Pacific

CANADA - BRITISH COLUMBIA (BANFF)

Siwash Lake Wilderness Resort

Box 39, 70 Mile House, British Columbia
V0K 2K0, Canada

Tel: +1 250 395 6541

condenastjohansens.com/siwashlakewildernessresort

CANADA - BRITISH COLUMBIA (PORT MCNEILL)

Nimmo Bay Wilderness Resort

1978 Broughton Boulevard, Port McNeill,
British Columbia V0N 2R0, Canada

Tel: +1 800 837 4354

condenastjohansens.com/nimmobay

CANADA - BRITISH COLUMBIA (SONORA ISLAND)

Sonora Resort

Sonora Island, British Columbia, Canada

Tel: +1 604 233 0460

condenastjohansens.com/sonoraresort

CANADA - BRITISH COLUMBIA (TOFINO)

Wickaninnish Inn

Osprey Lane at Chesterman Beach, Tofino,
British Columbia V0R 2Z0, Canada

Tel: +1 250 725 3100

condenastjohansens.com/wickaninnish

CANADA - BRITISH COLUMBIA (VANCOUVER)

OPUS Vancouver

322 Davie Street, Vancouver, British Columbia
V6B 5Z6, Canada

Tel: +1 604 642 6787

condenastjohansens.com/opushotel

CANADA - BRITISH COLUMBIA (VANCOUVER)

Wedgewood Hotel & Spa

845 Hornby Street, Vancouver, British
Columbia V6Z 1V1, Canada

Tel: +1 604 689 7777

condenastjohansens.com/wedgewoodbc

CANADA - BRITISH COLUMBIA (VERNON)

Sparkling Hill Resort

888 Sparkling Place, Vernon, British Columbia
V1H 2K7, Canada

Tel: +1 250 275 1556

condenastjohansens.com/sparklinghill

CANADA - BRITISH COLUMBIA (VICTORIA)

The Magnolia Hotel & Spa

623 Courtney Street, Victoria, British
Columbia V8W 1B8, Canada

Tel: +1 250 381 0999

condenastjohansens.com/magnoliahotel

CANADA - BRITISH COLUMBIA (WHISTLER)

Nita Lake Lodge

2131 Lake Placid Road, Whistler, British
Columbia V0N 1B2, Canada

Tel: +1 888 755 6482

condenastjohansens.com/nitalakelodge

CANADA - NOVA SCOTIA (EAST KEMPTVILLE)

Trout Point Lodge of Nova Scotia

189 Trout Point Road, Off the East Branch
Road and Highway 203, East Kemptville,
Nova Scotia B5A 5X9, Canada

Tel: +1 902 761 2142

condenastjohansens.com/troutpoint

CANADA - NOVA SCOTIA (WALLACE)

Fox Harb'r Resort

1337 Fox Harb'r Road, Wallace, Cumberland
County, Nova Scotia B0K 1Y0, Canada

Tel: +1 866 956 8217

condenastjohansens.com/foxharbr

CANADA - QUÉBEC (MONT-TREMBLANT)

Hôtel Quintessence

3004 chemin de la chapelle, Mont-Tremblant,
Québec J8E 1E1, Canada

Tel: +1 866 425 3400

condenastjohansens.com/quintessence

MÉXICO - JALISCO (COSTALEGRE - PUERTO VALLARTA)

Las Alamandas Resort

Carretera Federal 200, Km 82, Costalegre,
Jalisco 48850, México

Tel: +52 322 285 5500

condenastjohansens.com/alamandas

MÉXICO - MORELOS (TEPOZTLÁN)

Casa Fernanda

Niño Artillero 20, Barrio de San José,
Tepoztlán, Morelos 62520, México

Tel: +52 139 395 0522

condenastjohansens.com/casafernanda

MÉXICO - MORELOS (TEPOZTLÁN)

Hostal de La Luz

Carretera Federal Tepoztlán, Amatlán Km 4,
Tepoztlán, Morelos 62524, México

Tel: +1 739 393 3076

condenastjohansens.com/hostaldelaluz

MÉXICO - QUINTANA ROO (PLAYA DEL CARMEN)

Le Rêve Hotel & Spa

Playa Xcalacoco Fraccion 2A, Playa del
Carmen, Quintana Roo 77710, México

Tel: +55 984 1095660

condenastjohansens.com/hotellereve

Properties listed can be found in our 2017 The Americas, Caribbean & Pacific Guide and online at condenastjohansens.com

Top image: Sophia Hotel, Colombia

THE MINI LIST
The Americas, Caribbean & Pacific

MÉXICO - QUINTANA ROO (TULUM)

Ana y Jose Charming Hotel & Spa

Carretera Tulum, Boca Paila km 7, Tulum, Quintana Roo 77780, México

Tel: +52 984 871 1300

condenastjohansens.com/anayjose

MÉXICO - QUINTANA ROO (TULUM)

Coral Tulum Hotel Boutique

Carretera Federal Tulum, Boca Paila, Km 6, Zona Hotelera, 77766 Tulum, Quintana Roo, México

Tel: +52 998 880 6022

condenastjohansens.com/coraltulum

MÉXICO - YUCATÁN (MÉRIDA)

Casa Azul

Calle 60, 343 por 35 y 37, Mérida, Yucatán 97000, México

Tel: +52 999 925 50 16

condenastjohansens.com/casaazul

MÉXICO - YUCATÁN (MÉRIDA)

Hacienda Xcanatún - Casa de Piedra

Calle 20 S/N, Comisaría Xcanatún, Km 12 Carretera Mérida - Progreso, Mérida, Yucatán 97302, México

Tel: +52 999 930 2140

condenastjohansens.com/xcanatun

USA - ARIZONA (PARADISE VALLEY)

The Hermosa Inn

5532 North Palo Cristi Road, Paradise Valley, Arizona 85253, USA

Tel: +1 602 955 8614

condenastjohansens.com/hermosa

USA - CALIFORNIA (CALISTOGA)

The Chanric Inn

1805 Foothill Boulevard, Calistoga, California 94515, USA

Tel: +1 707 942 4535

condenastjohansens.com/chanricinn

USA - CALIFORNIA (HEALDSBURG)

Hotel Les Mars

27 North Street, Healdsburg, California 95448, USA

Tel: +1 707 433 4211

condenastjohansens.com/lesmarshotel

USA - CALIFORNIA (MENDOCINO)

The Stanford Inn By The Sea

Coast Highway One & Comptche-Ukiah Road, Mendocino, California 95460, USA

Tel: +1 707 937 5615

condenastjohansens.com/stanfordinn

USA - CALIFORNIA (PISMO BEACH)

Dolphin Bay Resort & Spa

2727 Shell Beach Road, Pismo Beach, California 93449, USA

Tel: +1 800 516 0112

condenastjohansens.com/thedolphinbay

USA - DELAWARE (WILMINGTON)

Inn at Montchanin Village & Spa

Route 100 & Kirk Road, Montchanin, Wilmington, Delaware 19710, USA

Tel: +1 302 888 2133

condenastjohansens.com/montchanin

USA - FLORIDA (AMELIA ISLAND)

Elizabeth Pointe Lodge

98 South Fletcher Avenue, Amelia Island, Florida 32034, USA

Tel: +1 888 757 1910

condenastjohansens.com/elizabethpointelodge

USA - FLORIDA (APALACHICOLA)

Coombs Inn & Suites

80 Sixth Street, Corner of Avenue E & 6th Street, Apalachicola, Florida 32320, USA

Tel: +1 850 653 9199

condenastjohansens.com/coombshouse

USA - FLORIDA (DESTIN)

Henderson Park Inn

2700 Scenic Highway 98, Destin, Florida 32541, USA

Tel: +1 866 398 4432

condenastjohansens.com/henderson

USA - FLORIDA (FISHER ISLAND)

Fisher Island Club Hotel

One Fisher Island Drive, Fisher Island, Florida 33109, USA

Tel: +1 305 535 6000

condenastjohansens.com/fisherisland

USA - FLORIDA (FORT LAUDERDALE)

The Pillars Hotel

111 North Birch Road, Fort Lauderdale, Florida 33304, USA

Tel: +1 954 467 9639

condenastjohansens.com/pillarshotel

USA - FLORIDA (MIAMI BEACH)

The Betsy - South Beach

1440 Ocean Drive, Miami Beach, Florida 33139, USA

Tel: +1 305 531 6100

condenastjohansens.com/thebetsyhotel

USA - GEORGIA (CUMBERLAND ISLAND)

Greyfield Inn

Cumberland Island, Georgia, USA

Tel: +1 904 261 6408

condenastjohansens.com/greyfieldinn

USA - MASSACHUSETTS (BOSTON)

Boston Harbor Hotel

70 Rowes Wharf, Boston, Massachusetts 02110, USA

Tel: +1 617 439 7000

condenastjohansens.com/bhh

USA - MASSACHUSETTS (LENOX)

Blantyre

16 Blantyre Road, PO Box 995, Lenox, Massachusetts 01240, USA

Tel: +1 413 637 3556

condenastjohansens.com/blantyre

USA - NEW YORK (VERONA)

The Lodge at Turning Stone

5218 Patrick Road, Verona, New York 13478, USA

Tel: +1 315 361 8525

condenastjohansens.com/turningstone

Properties listed can be found in our 2017 The Americas, Caribbean & Pacific Guide and online at condenastjohansens.com

THE MINI LIST
The Americas, Caribbean & Pacific

USA - NEW YORK/LONG ISLAND (EAST HAMPTON)

The 1770 House

143 Main Street, East Hampton, New York 11937, USA

Tel: +1 631 324 1770

condenastjohansens.com/1770house

USA - NEW YORK/LONG ISLAND (EAST HAMPTON)

The Baker House 1650

181 Main Street, East Hampton, New York 11937, USA

Tel: +1 631 324 4081

condenastjohansens.com/bakerhouse

USA - NORTH CAROLINA (CARY)

The Mayton Inn

301 South Academy Street, Cary, North Carolina 27511, USA

Tel: +1 919 670 5000

condenastjohansens.com/maytoninn

USA - SOUTH CAROLINA (CHARLESTON)

The Restoration

75 Wentworth Street, Charleston, South Carolina 29401, USA

Tel: +1 843 518 5100

condenastjohansens.com/restoration

USA - SOUTH CAROLINA (HILTON HEAD ISLAND)

The Inn & Club at Harbour Town

7 Lighthouse Lane, Hilton Head Island, South Carolina 29928, USA

Tel: +1 843 785 3333

condenastjohansens.com/innandclubharbourtown

USA - TEXAS (DALLAS)

The Joule

1530 Main Street, Dallas, Texas 75201, USA

Tel: +1 214 748 1300

condenastjohansens.com/thejoule

USA - UTAH (MOAB)

Sorrel River Ranch Resort & Spa

Mile 17 Highway 128, Moab, Utah 84532, USA

Tel: +1 435 259 4642

condenastjohansens.com/sorrelriver

USA - VIRGINIA (MIDDLEBURG)

Goodstone Inn & Restaurant

36205 Snake Hill Road, Middleburg, Virginia 20117, USA

Tel: +1 540 687 3333

condenastjohansens.com/goodstoneinn

BELIZE - AMBERGRIS CAYE (CAYO ESPANTO)

Cayo Espanto a private island

Ambergris Caye, Cayo Espanto, Belize

Tel: +910 323 8355

condenastjohansens.com/cayoespanto

BELIZE - AMBERGRIS CAYE (SAN PEDRO)

The Phoenix Resort

San Pedro, Ambergris Caye, Belize

Tel: +501 226 2083

condenastjohansens.com/thephoenixbelize

BELIZE - AMBERGRIS CAYE (SAN PEDRO)

Victoria House

San Pedro, Ambergris Caye, Belize

Tel: +501 226 2067

condenastjohansens.com/victoriahouse

BELIZE - AMBERGRIS CAYE (NEAR SAN PEDRO)

El Secreto

11 miles north of San Pedro, Ambergris Caye, Belize

Tel: +501 236 5111

condenastjohansens.com/elsecreto

BELIZE - AMBERGRIS CAYE (NEAR SAN PEDRO)

Las Terrazas Resort & Residences

3.5 miles north of San Pedro, Ambergris Caye, Belize

Tel: +1 713 780 1233

condenastjohansens.com/lasterrazas

BELIZE - AMBERGRIS CAYE (NEAR SAN PEDRO)

Matachica Resort & Spa

5 miles north of San Pedro, Ambergris Caye, Belize

Tel: +501 226 5010/1

condenastjohansens.com/matachica

BELIZE - CAYO DISTRICT (MOUNTAIN PINE RIDGE)

Gaïa Riverlodge

Mountain Pine Ridge, Cayo, Belize

Tel: +501 834 4005

condenastjohansens.com/gaiariverlodge

BELIZE - TOLEDO DISTRICT (PUNTA GORDA)

Belcampo Lodge Belize

Wilson Road, Punta Gorda, Toledo District, Belize

Tel: +501 722 0050

condenastjohansens.com/belcampo

COSTA RICA - PUNTARENAS PROVINCE (MAL PAÍS)

Casa Chameleon

Nicoya Peninsula, Mal País, Puntarenas Province, Costa Rica

Tel: +506 2288 2879

condenastjohansens.com/casachameleon

COSTA RICA - PUNTARENAS PROVINCE (MANUEL ANTONIO)

Gaia Hotel & Reserve

Km 2.7 Ctra Quepos, Manuel Antonio, Puntarenas Province, Costa Rica

Tel: +506 2777 9797

condenastjohansens.com/gaiahr

COSTA RICA - SAN JOSÉ PROVINCE (SANTA ANA)

Hotel Alta Las Palomas

Alto de las Palomas, Old Road Escazu, Santa Ana, San José Province, Costa Rica

Tel: +506 2282 4160

condenastjohansens.com/altahotel

EL SALVADOR - SAN MIGUEL DEPARTMENT (SAN MIGUEL)

Las Flores Resort

Playa Las Flores, El Cuco Street, Chirilagua, San Miguel Department, El Salvador

Tel: +503 7861 4097

condenastjohansens.com/lasfloresresort

Properties listed can be found in our 2017 The Americas, Caribbean & Pacific Guide and online at condenastjohansens.com

255

THE MINI LIST
The Americas, Caribbean & Pacific

GUATEMALA - SACATEPÉQUEZ DEPARTMENT (ANTIGUA GUATEMALA)

El Convento Boutique Hotel

2a Avenue Norte 11, Antigua Guatemala, Sacatepéquez Department, Guatemala

Tel: +502 7720 7272

condenastjohansens.com/elconventoantigua

ARGENTINA - BUENOS AIRES (SAN ISIDRO)

Hotel Del Casco

Avenida del Libertador 16,170, B1642CKV, San Isidro, Buenos Aires, Argentina

Tel: +54 11 4732 3993/3553

condenastjohansens.com/hoteldelcasco

BRAZIL - ALAGOAS (MARAGOGI)

Pousada Camurim Grande

Rodovia Al 101 Norte, Km 124, Maragogi, Alagoas, Brazil

Tel: +55 82 3296 2044

condenastjohansens.com/camurimgrande

BRAZIL - ALAGOAS (PORTO DE PEDRAS)

Pousada Patacho

Praia do Patacho s/n, Porto de Pedras, Alagoas 57945-000, Brazil

Tel: +55 82 3298 1253

condenastjohansens.com/pousadapatacho

BRAZIL - BAHIA (ARRAIAL D'AJUDA)

Hotel Maitei

Estrada do Mucugê 475, Arraial D'Ajuda, Porto Seguro, Bahia 45816-000, Brazil

Tel: +55 73 3575 3877/3799

condenastjohansens.com/maitei

BRAZIL - BAHIA (ITACARÉ)

Txai Itacaré

Rod Ilhéus-Itacaré km 48, Itacaré, Bahia 45530-000, Brazil

Tel: +55 11 3040 5010

condenastjohansens.com/txairesort

BRAZIL - BAHIA (MARAÚ)

Casa dos Arandis

Península de Maraú, Bahia 45520-000, Brazil

Tel: +55 73 41020799

condenastjohansens.com/casadosarandis

BRAZIL - BAHIA (TRANCOSO)

Estrela D'Água

Estrada Arraial d'Ajuda/Trancoso, 1011, Trancoso, Porto Seguro, Bahia 45818-000, Brazil

Tel: +55 73 3668 1030

condenastjohansens.com/estreladagua

BRAZIL - CEARÁ (AQUIRAZ)

Carmel Charme Resort

Rua Barro Preto, S/N, Barro Preto, Aquiraz, Ceará 61700-000, Brazil

Tel: +55 85 3266 6100

condenastjohansens.com/carmelcharme

BRAZIL - CEARÁ (CRUZ)

Rancho do Peixe

Rua da Praia, s/n Cruz, Ceará 62595-000, Brazil

Tel: +55 88 3660 3118

condenastjohansens.com/ranchodopeixe

BRAZIL - CEARÁ (JERICOACOARA)

The Chili Beach Hotel

Rua da Igreja, 62, 598-000 Jericoacoara, Ceará, Brazil

Tel: +55 88 99909 9135

condenastjohansens.com/chilibeach

BRAZIL - CEARÁ (JERICOACOARA)

Essenza Hotel

Av Beira Mar, sn, 62598-000 Jericoacoara, Ceará, Brazil

Tel: +55 88 99989 0040

condenastjohansens.com/essenzahotel

BRAZIL - CEARÁ (JERICOACOARA)

Vila Kalango

Rua das Dunas 30, Jericoacoara, Ceará 62598-000, Brazil

Tel: +55 88 99961 9364

condenastjohansens.com/vilakalango

BRAZIL - GOIÁS (PIRENÓPOLIS)

Casarão Villa do Império

Rua Direita número 79, Centro Histórico, Pirenópolis, Goiás 72980-000, Brazil

Tel: +55 62 3331 2662/1966

condenastjohansens.com/casaraovilladoimperio

BRAZIL - MATO GROSSO (ALTA FLORESTA)

Cristalino Lodge

Av Perimetral Oeste 2001, Alta Floresta, Mato Grosso 78580-000, Brazil

Tel: +55 11 3071 0104

condenastjohansens.com/cristalinolodge

BRAZIL - MINAS GERAIS (LIMA DUARTE)

Reserva do Ibitipoca

Fazenda do Engenho, s/n Conceição do Ibitipoca, Lima Duarte, Minas Gerais 36140-000, Brazil

Tel: +55 32 3281 8144

condenastjohansens.com/reservadoibitipoca

BRAZIL - MINAS GERAIS (SERRA DO CIPÓ)

Capim do Mato Pousada & Spa

Serra do Cipó, Alameda Rubens Ferreira Belisário, Minas Gerais, 35830-000, Brazil

Tel: +55 31 3718 7480

condenastjohansens.com/capimdomato

BRAZIL - PARANÁ (LAPA)

Lapinha Spa

Estrada da Lapa, Rio Negro, Km 16, Lapa, Paraná 83750-000, Brazil

Tel: +55 41 3622 1044

condenastjohansens.com/lapinha

BRAZIL - PERNAMBUCO (PORTO DE GALINHAS)

Nannai Resort & Spa

Rodovia PE-09, acesso à Muro Alto, Km 3, Ipojuca, Pernambuco 55590-000, Brazil

Tel: +55 81 3552 0100

condenastjohansens.com/nannaibeach

BRAZIL - RIO DE JANEIRO (BÚZIOS)

Casas Brancas Boutique Hotel & Spa

Alto do Humaitá 10, Armação dos Búzios, Rio de Janeiro 28950-000, Brazil

Tel: +55 22 2623 1458

condenastjohansens.com/casasbrancas

Properties listed can be found in our 2017 The Americas, Caribbean & Pacific Guide and online at condenastjohansens.com

256

BRAZIL - RIO DE JANEIRO (PARATY)

Pousada Literária

Rua Tenente, Francisco Antônio, 362, Paraty, 23970-000 Rio de Janeiro, Brazil

Tel: +55 24 3371 1460

condenastjohansens.com/pousadaliteraria

BRAZIL - RIO GRANDE DO SUL (GRAMADO)

La Hacienda Inn and Restaurant

Estrada da Serra Grande 4200, Gramado, Rio Grande do Sul 95670-000, Brazil

Tel: +55 54 3295 3025/88

condenastjohansens.com/lahacienda

BRAZIL - SÃO PAULO (AMPARO)

Lake Villas Charm Hotel & Spa

Amparo, Circuito das Águas, São Paulo 13900-970, Brazil

Tel: +55 19 2512 1773

condenastjohansens.com/lakevillas

BRAZIL - SÃO PAULO (SÃO PAULO)

Hotel Unique

Avenida Brigadeiro Luis Antonio, 4700 São Paulo, São Paulo 01402-002, Brazil

Tel: +55 11 3055 4710/00

condenastjohansens.com/hotelunique

BRAZIL - SÃO PAULO (SERRA DA CANTAREIRA)

Unique Garden Hotel & Spa

Estrada Laramara, 3500, Mairiporã, São Paulo 07600-970, Brazil

Tel: +55 11 4486 8700

condenastjohansens.com/uniquegarden

COLOMBIA - BOLÍVAR DEPARTMENT (CARTAGENA DE INDIAS)

Bastión Luxury Hotel

Calle del Sargento Mayor No 6 - 87, 34646 Cartagena de Indias, Bolívar Department, Colombia

Tel: +575 642 4100

condenastjohansens.com/bastionluxury

COLOMBIA - BOLÍVAR DEPARTMENT (CARTAGENA DE INDIAS)

Bóvedas de Santa Clara Hotel Boutique

Calle del Torno No 39-114, Barrio San Diego, Cartagena de Indias, Bolívar Department, Colombia

Tel: +57 5 650 44 65

condenastjohansens.com/bovedasdesantaclara

COLOMBIA - BOLÍVAR DEPARTMENT (CARTAGENA DE INDIAS)

Casa Pestagua

Calle Santo Domingo No 33-63, Cartagena de Indias, Bolívar Department, Colombia

Tel: +57 5 664 9510/6286

condenastjohansens.com/casapestagua

COLOMBIA - BOLÍVAR DEPARTMENT (CARTAGENA DE INDIAS)

Hotel Boutique LM

Centro Calle de la Mantilla No 3-56, Cartagena de Indias, Bolívar Department, Colombia

Tel: +57 5 664 9100

condenastjohansens.com/hotellm

COLOMBIA - BOLÍVAR DEPARTMENT (CARTAGENA DE INDIAS)

Hotel Boutique Santo Toribio

Calle Segunda De Badillo Nº 36 - 87, San Diego - Cartagena, Bolívar Department, Colombia

Tel: +57 3 178 936464

condenastjohansens.com/santotoribio

COLOMBIA - BOLÍVAR DEPARTMENT (CARTAGENA DE INDIAS)

Hotel Quadrifolio

Calle del Cuartel (Cra 5) No 36-118, Centro Amurallado, Cartagena de Indias, Bolívar Department, Colombia

Tel: +57 5 664 6053

condenastjohansens.com/hotelquadrifolio

COLOMBIA - BOLÍVAR DEPARTMENT (CARTAGENA DE INDIAS)

Hotel San Pedro de Majagua

Isla Grande, Islas del Rosario, Cartagena de Indias, Bolívar Department, Colombia

Tel: +57 5 6930987

condenastjohansens.com/hotelmajagua

COLOMBIA - BOLÍVAR DEPARTMENT (CARTAGENA DE INDIAS)

Sophia Hotel

Calle 32, 4-45 Plaza de la Aduana, Cartagena de Indias, Bolívar Department, Colombia

Tel: +575 651 7007

condenastjohansens.com/sophiahotel

COLOMBIA - BOLÍVAR DEPARTMENT (CARTAGENA DE INDIAS)

Tcherassi Hotel + Spa

Calle Sargento Mayor 6-21, Cartagena de Indias, Bolívar Department, Colombia

Tel: +57 5 664 4445

condenastjohansens.com/tcherassihotels

COLOMBIA - CUNDINAMARCA DEPARTMENT (APULO)

Entremonte Wellness Hotel & Spa

Km 5, Vereda Guacamayas, Apulo, Cundinamarca Department, Colombia

Tel: +57 320 3324541

condenastjohansens.com/entremonte

COLOMBIA - CUNDINAMARCA DEPARTMENT (BOGOTÁ)

93 Luxury Suites and Residences

Carrera 13A No 93 - 51, Bogotá, Cundinamarca Department, Colombia

Tel: +571 745 4430

condenastjohansens.com/93luxurysuites

COLOMBIA - CUNDINAMARCA DEPARTMENT (BOGOTÁ)

ESTELAR Parque de la 93

Calle 93 No 11 - 19, Bogotá, Cundinamarca Department, Colombia

Tel: +571 511 1555

condenastjohansens.com/estelar

COLOMBIA - MAGDALENA DEPARTMENT (SANTA MARTA)

Hotel Boutique Don Pepe

Calle 16 # 1C - 92, Santa Marta, Magdalena Department, Colombia

Tel: +57 5 4210215

condenastjohansens.com/donpepe

COLOMBIA - MAGDALENA DEPARTMENT (SANTA MARTA)

Merecumbe Hotel

Km 48, Via Santa Marta - Riohacha, Santa Marta, Magdalena Department, Colombia

Tel: +57 310 725 4704

condenastjohansens.com/merecumbehotel

COLOMBIA - SAN ANDRÉS Y PROVIDENCIA DEPARTMENT (ISLA DE PROVIDENCIA)

Deep Blue

Maracaibo Bay, Isla de Providencia, San Andrés y Providencia Department, Colombia

Tel: +57 315 324 8443

condenastjohansens.com/deepblue

Properties listed can be found in our 2017 The Americas, Caribbean & Pacific Guide and online at condenastjohansens.com

257

THE MINI LIST
The Americas, Caribbean & Pacific

COLOMBIA - VALLE DEL CAUCA DEPARTMENT (SANTIAGO DE CALI)

AcquaSanta Lofts Hotel

Carrera 106A, 18-51 Santiago de Cali, Valle del Cauca Department, Colombia

Tel: +57 310 6045718

condenastjohansens.com/acquasanta

ECUADOR - AZUAY PROVINCE (CUENCA)

Mansión Alcázar Boutique Hotel

Calle Bolívar 12-55 Y Tarqui, Cuenca, Azuay Province, Ecuador

Tel: +593 72823 918

condenastjohansens.com/mansionalcazar

ECUADOR - IMBABURA PROVINCE (COTACACHI)

La Mirage Garden Hotel & Spa

Calle 10 de Agosto, EC 100350 Cotacachi, Imbabura Province, Ecuador

Tel: +593 6 291 5237

condenastjohansens.com/mirage

ECUADOR - PICHINCHA PROVINCE (QUITO)

Boutique Hotel Mansión del Ángel

Calle Los Ríos N13-134 y Pasaje Ascencio Gándara, Quito, Pichincha Province, Ecuador

Tel: +593 2 2557721

condenastjohansens.com/mansiondelangel

ECUADOR - PICHINCHA PROVINCE (QUITO)

Hotel Plaza Grande

Calle García Moreno, N5-16 y Chile, Quito, Pichincha Province, Ecuador

Tel: +593 2 2510 777

condenastjohansens.com/plazagrandequito

PERÚ - CUSCO PROVINCE (CUSCO)

El Mercado

Calle 7 Cuartones 306, Cusco, Cusco Province, Perú

Tel: +5184 582640

condenastjohansens.com/elmercado

PERÚ - LIMA PROVINCE (IQUITOS)

Delfin Amazon Cruises

Pacaya Samiria National Reserve, Lima Province, Perú

Tel: +511 719 0998

condenastjohansens.com/delfinamazoncruises

PERÚ - LIMA PROVINCE (LIMA)

Swissôtel Lima

Av Santo Toribio 173-Vía Central 150, Centro Empresarial Real - San Isidro, Lima Province, Perú

Tel: +511 421 4400

condenastjohansens.com/swissotellima

CARIBBEAN - ANGUILLA (WEST END)

Sheriva Luxury Villas & Suites

Maundays Bay Road, West End AI-2640, Anguilla

Tel: +1 264 498 9898

condenastjohansens.com/sheriva

CARIBBEAN - BAHAMAS (GREAT ABACO)

The Abaco Club on Winding Bay

Cherokee Road on Winding Bay, Marsh Harbour, Abaco Islands, Great Abaco, The Bahamas

Tel: +1 242 225 7033

condenastjohansens.com/abacoclub

CARIBBEAN - BAHAMAS (SOUTH ANDROS)

Tiamo Resort&Spa

Drigg's Hill, South Andros Island, The Bahamas

Tel: +1 786 374 2442

condenastjohansens.com/tiamoresort

CARIBBEAN - BARBADOS (CHRIST CHURCH)

Little Arches Boutique Hotel

Enterprise Beach Road, Christ Church, Barbados

Tel: +1 246 420 4689

condenastjohansens.com/littlearches

CARIBBEAN - BARBUDA (CODRINGTON)

Barbuda Belle

Cedar Tree Point, Codrington, Barbuda

Tel: +1 268 783 4779

condenastjohansens.com/barbudabelle

CARIBBEAN - BRITISH VIRGIN ISLANDS (PETER ISLAND)

Peter Island Resort & Spa

Peter Island, British Virgin Islands

Tel: +616 458 6767

condenastjohansens.com/peterislandresort

CARIBBEAN - BRITISH VIRGIN ISLANDS (TORTOLA)

Tingalayo BVI

Romney Park, Tortola, British Virgin Islands

Tel: +1 284 499 2535

condenastjohansens.com/tingalayo

CARIBBEAN - BRITISH VIRGIN ISLANDS (VIRGIN GORDA)

Katitche Point Greathouse

Virgin Gorda, VG 1550, British Virgin Islands

Tel: +49 761 552930

condenastjohansens.com/katitchepoint

CARIBBEAN - BRITISH VIRGIN ISLANDS (VIRGIN GORDA)

Red Rock Villa and Spa

Virgin Gorda, VG 1550, British Virgin Islands

Tel: +1 284 340 3000

condenastjohansens.com/redrockvilla

CARIBBEAN - CUBA (CAYO SANTA MARÍA)

Meliá Buenavista All Inclusive, The Level & Spa

Punta Madruguilla, Oeste Cayo Santa María, Caibarién, Villa Clara, Cuba

Tel: +53 24 204 55 77 ext 1442

condenastjohansens.com/meliabuenavista

CARIBBEAN - CUBA (PLAYA ESMERALDA)

Royal Service Paradisus Río de Oro

Playa Esmeralda, Carretera Guardalavaca, Holguín, Rafael Freyre, Cuba

Tel: +53 24 430 090

condenastjohansens.com/royalserviceriodeoro

CARIBBEAN - CUBA (VARADERO)

Family Concierge at Paradisus Varadero

Punta Francés, Varadero, Matanzas 42200, Cuba

Tel: +53 45 668 700 ext 6526

condenastjohansens.com/familyparadisusvaradero

Properties listed can be found in our 2017 The Americas, Caribbean & Pacific Guide and online at condenastjohansens.com

258

CARIBBEAN - CUBA (VARADERO)

Royal Service Paradisus Princesa del Mar

Autopista Sur, Carretera Las Morlas, Km 19 ½, Varadero, Matanzas, Cuba

Tel: +53 45 667 200 ext 150

condenastjohansens.com/royalserviceprincesa

CARIBBEAN - CUBA (VARADERO)

Royal Service Paradisus Varadero

Punta Francés, Varadero, Matanzas 42200, Cuba

Tel: +53 45 668 700

condenastjohansens.com/paradisusvaradero

CARIBBEAN - DOMINICA (PORTSMOUTH)

Secret Bay

Ross Blvd, Portsmouth, Saint John Parish, Dominica

Tel: +1 767 445 4444

condenastjohansens.com/secretbay

CARIBBEAN - DOMINICA (ROSALIE)

Rosalie Bay Resort

Rosalie, Dominica

Tel: +1 767 446 1010

condenastjohansens.com/rosaliebay

CARIBBEAN - DOMINICAN REPUBLIC (LA ROMANA)

Casa de Campo Resort & Villas

La Romana, Dominican Republic

Tel: +1 809 523 3333

condenastjohansens.com/casadecampo

CARIBBEAN - DOMINICAN REPUBLIC (PUNTA CANA)

Eden Roc at Cap Cana

Cap Cana, Juanillo, Punta Cana, Provincia La Altagracia 23000, Dominican Republic

Tel: +1 809 469 7469

condenastjohansens.com/edenroc

CARIBBEAN - DOMINICAN REPUBLIC (PUNTA CANA)

Tortuga Bay, Puntacana Resort & Club

Punta Cana, Dominican Republic

Tel: +1 809 959 8229

condenastjohansens.com/puntacana

CARIBBEAN - GRENADA (ST GEORGE'S)

Calabash Luxury Boutique Hotel & Spa

L'anse Aux Epines Beach, St George's, Grenada

Tel: +1 473 444 4334

condenastjohansens.com/calabashhotel

CARIBBEAN - GRENADA (ST GEORGE'S)

Spice Island Beach Resort

Grand Anse Beach, St George's, Grenada

Tel: +1 473 444 4258/4423

condenastjohansens.com/spiceisland

CARIBBEAN - ST KITTS AND NEVIS (CHARLESTON)

Paradise Beach Nevis

Paradise Estates, St Thomas' Parish, Nevis, St Kitts and Nevis

Tel: +1 869 469 7900

condenastjohansens.com/paradisebeachnevis

CARIBBEAN - ST LUCIA (ANSE COCHON)

Ti Kaye Resort & Spa

Anse Cochon, St Lucia

Tel: +1 758 456 8103

condenastjohansens.com/tikaye

CARIBBEAN - ST LUCIA (GROS ISLET)

The Landings St. Lucia

Pigeon Island Causeway, Rodney Bay, Gros Islet, St Lucia

Tel: +1 758 458 7300

condenastjohansens.com/landingsstlucia

CARIBBEAN - ST LUCIA (MARIGOT BAY)

Capella Marigot Bay Resort and Marina

Marigot Bay, Castries, St Lucia

Tel: +1 758 458 5300

condenastjohansens.com/capellamarigot

CARIBBEAN - ST LUCIA (SOUFRIÈRE)

Anse Chastanet

Soufrière, St Lucia

Tel: +1 758 459 7000/6100

condenastjohansens.com/ansechastanet

CARIBBEAN - TURKS AND CAICOS ISLANDS (PINE CAY)

The Meridian Club, Turks and Caicos

Pine Cay, Turks and Caicos Islands

Tel: +1 888 286 7993

condenastjohansens.com/meridianclub

CARIBBEAN - TURKS AND CAICOS ISLANDS (PROVIDENCIALES)

Grace Bay Club

Grace Bay Circle Road, Grace Bay, Providenciales, Turks and Caicos Islands

Tel: +1 649 946 5050

condenastjohansens.com/gracebayclub

CARIBBEAN - TURKS AND CAICOS ISLANDS (PROVIDENCIALES)

The Palms Turks and Caicos

16 Princess Drive, Grace Bay Beach, Providenciales, Turks and Caicos Islands

Tel: +1 649 946 8666

condenastjohansens.com/palmstc

CARIBBEAN - TURKS AND CAICOS ISLANDS (PROVIDENCIALES)

Windsong Resort Turks & Caicos

Stubbs Road, Providenciales, Turks and Caicos Islands

Tel: +1 649 333 7700

condenastjohansens.com/windsongresort

PACIFIC - FIJI ISLANDS (TAVEUNI)

Qamea Resort & Spa

PA Matei, Qamea Island, Fiji Islands

Tel: +64 9 360 0858

condenastjohansens.com/qamea

Properties listed can be found in our 2017 The Americas, Caribbean & Pacific Guide and online at condenastjohansens.com

259

DAYS OUT

CHANNEL ISLANDS

Guernsey

Sausmarez Manor - Sausmarez Road, St Martin, Guernsey GY4 6SG.
+44 (0)1481 235571

FRANCE

Loire Valley

Château de Chenonceau - 37150 Chenonceaux, Loire Valley 37150.
+33 2 4723 4406

IRELAND

County Cork

Blarney Castle & Gardens - Blarney, County Cork. +353 21 438 5252
Titanic Experience Cobh - White Star Line Building, 20 Casement Square,
Cobh, County Cork. +353 21 481 4412

County Galway

Kylemore Abbey & Victorian Walled Gardens - Kylemore, Connemara, County
Galway. +353 95 52001

County Kildare

The Irish National Stud & Gardens - The Irish National Stud, Tully, Kildare
Town, County Kildare, R51 DD56. +353 45 521617

County Wicklow

Russborough House & Parklands - Blessington, County Wicklow.
+353 45 865239

SPAIN

Barcelona

Torres Vineyard (Bodegas Torres) - Finca el Maset, s/n, Pacs del Penedès,
Villafranca del Penedès, Barcelona 08796. +34 93 8177400

Madrid

Corral de la Morería - (Spanish Tablao Flamenco) - Moreria Street 17, Madrid
28005. +34 91365 8446

Mallorca

Katmandú Park - Avenida Pedro Vaquer Ramis 9, Calvia, Mallorca 07181.
+34 91 134 660

Tarragona

PortAventura World - Avenida Alcalde Pere Molas, Km 2, Vila-Seca, Tarragona
43480. +34 902 202 220

Tenerife

Loro Parque - Avenida Loro Parque, Puerta de la Cruz, Tenerife 38400.
+34 922 373 841
Siam Park - Avenida Siam Park s/n Adeje, Costa Adeje, Tenerife.
+34 922 373 841

UK/ENGLAND

Bedfordshire

Queen Anne's Summerhouse - Shuttleworth Estate, Old Warden, Bedfordshire
SG18 9EP. +44 (0)1628 825925

Buckinghamshire

Nether Winchendon House - Near Aylesbury, Buckinghamshire HP18 0DY.
+44 (0)1844 290101
The Roald Dahl Museum and Story Centre - 81-83 High Street, Great
Missenden, Buckinghamshire HP16 0AL. +44 (0)1494 892192

Cheshire

Rode Hall - Church Lane, Scholar Green, Cheshire ST7 3QP.
+44 (0)1270 882961
Tabley House Collection - Tabley Lane, Knutsford, Cheshire WA16 0HB.
+44 (0)1565 750 151

Cornwall

Burncoose Nurseries and Garden - Gwennap, Redruth, Cornwall TR16 6BJ.
+44 (0)1209 861112
Caerhays Castle and Gardens - Estate Office, Gorran, St Austell, Cornwall
PL26 6LY. +44 (0)1872 501310
Pencarrow House and Gardens - Washway, Bodmin, Cornwall PL30 3AG.
+44 (0)1208 841369
Prideaux Place - Padstow, Cornwall PL28 8RP. +44 (0)1841 532411
Trebah Garden - Mawnan Smith, Falmouth, Cornwall TR11 5JZ.
+44 (0)1326 252200

Cumbria

Ravenglass & Eskdale Railway - The Ravenglass and Eskdale Railway,
Ravenglass, Cumbria CA18 1SW. +44 (0)1229 717 171
Ullswater 'Steamers' - The Pier House, Glenridding, Cumbria CA11 0US.
+44 (0)17684 82229

Derbyshire

Melbourne Hall & Gardens - Melbourne, Derbyshire DE73 8EN.
+44 (0)1332 862502

Devon

Bowringsleigh - Bowringsleigh, Kingsbridge, Devon TQ7 3LL.
+44 (0)1548 852014
Downes - Crediton, Devon EX17 3PL. +44 (0)1363 775142

Image: Torres Vineyard (Bodegas Torres), Spain

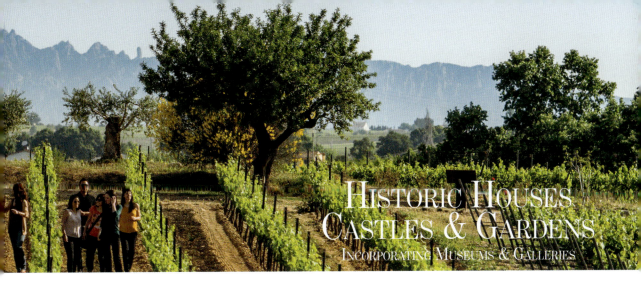

River Cottage Cookery Courses - River Cottage HQ, Trinity Hill Road, Axminster, Devon EX13 8TB. +44 (0)1297 630300

Dorset

Clavell Tower - Kimmeridge, Near Wareham, Dorset. +44 (0)1628 825925
Moignes Court - Owermoigne, Dorchester, Dorset DT2 8HY. +44 (0)1305 853300

Essex

Ingatestone Hall - Hall Lane, Ingatestone, Essex CM4 9NR. +44 (0)1277 353010

Gloucestershire

Hardwicke Court Estate - Near Gloucester, Gloucestershire GL2 4RS. +44 (0)1453 834 777
Sezincote House & Garden - Near Moreton-in-Marsh, Gloucestershire GL56 9AW. +44 (0)1386 700444

Hampshire

Avington Park - Winchester, Hampshire SO21 1DB. +44 (0)1962 779260
Greywell Hill House - Greywell, Hook, Hampshire RG29 1DG. +44 (0)1256 703565
Stansted Park - Rowlands Castle, Hampshire PO9 6DX. +44 (0)23 9241 2265

Herefordshire

Chase Distillery - Rosemaund Farm, Hereford, Herefordshire HR1 3PG. +44 (0)1432 820 455

Hertfordshire

Hatfield House - Hatfield, Hertfordshire AL9 5NQ. +44 (0)1707 287010

Kent

Belmont House and Gardens - Belmont Park, Throwley, Near Faversham, Kent ME13 0HH. +44 (0)1795 890202
The Grange - Ramsgate, Kent CT11 9NY. +44 (0)1628 825925
Hever Castle and Gardens - Near Edenbridge, Kent TN8 7NG. +44 (0)1732 861710
Leeds Castle and Gardens - Maidstone, Kent ME17 1PL. +44 (0)1622 765400
The New College of Cobham - Cobhambury Road, Cobham, Near Gravesend, Kent DA12 3BG. +44 (0)1474 812503

London

Afternoon Tea at the National Theatre - National Theatre, Upper Ground, South Bank, London SE1 9PX. +44 (0)20 7452 3010
Chelsea Physic Garden - 66 Royal Hospital Road, Chelsea, London SW3 4HS. +44 (0)20 7352 5646
Dulwich Picture Gallery - Gallery Road, London SE21 7AD. +44 (0)20 8693 5254

Leighton House Museum - 12 Holland Park Road, London W14 8LZ. +44 (0)20 7602 3316
Syon Park - Syon Park, Brentford, London TW8 8JF. +44 (0)20 8560 0882
The Wimbledon Lawn Tennis Museum & Tour - The All UK/England Lawn Tennis Club, Church Road, Wimbledon, London SW19 5AE. +44 (0)20 8944 1066

Manchester

Elizabeth Gaskell's House - 84 Plymouth Grove, Manchester M13 9LW. +44 (0)161 273 2215

Merseyside

Meols Hall, Churchtown - Southport, Merseyside PR9 7LZ. +44 (0)1704 228326

West Midlands

The Birmingham Botanical Gardens & Glasshouses - Westbourne Road, Edgbaston, Birmingham, West Midlands B15 3TR. +44 (0)121 454 1860

Norfolk

South Elmham Hall - Hall Lane, St Cross, Harleston, Norfolk IP20 OPY. +44 (0)1986 782526

Northumberland

Bamburgh Castle - Bamburgh, Northumberland ME69 7DF. +44 (0)1668 214208
Chipchase Castle & Gardens - Wark on Tyne, Hexham, Northumberland NE48 3NT. +44 (0)1434 230203

Oxfordshire

Burford Garden Company - Shilton Road, Burford, Oxfordshire OX18 4PA. +44 (0)1993 823117
Buscot Park - Faringdon, Oxfordshire SN7 8BU. +44 (0)1367 240786
Hook Norton Brewery Tours and Visitor Centre - Brewery Lane, Hook Norton Near Banbury, Oxfordshire OX15 5NY. +44 (0)1608 730384
Punting at Cherwell Boathouse - Cherwell Boathouse, Bardwell Road, Oxford, Oxfordshire OX2 6ST. +44 (0)1865 515978
Stonor Park - Near Henley-on-Thames, Oxfordshire RG9 6HF. +44 (0)1491 638587

Shropshire

Hodnet Hall Gardens - Hodnet, Market Drayton, Shropshire TF9 3NN. +44 (0)1630 685786
Ludlow Castle - Castle Square, Ludlow, Shropshire SY8 1AY. +44 (0)1584 874465

Somerset

Orchard Wyndham - Williton, Taunton, Somerset TA4 4HH. +44 (0)1984 632309

INDEX

Days Out incorporating Historic Houses, Castles & Gardens, Museums & Galleries

Image: Trebah Garden, UK/England

INDEX BY COUNTRY

INDEX
by Country

Hillside Beach Club, Turkey, page 148

INDEX
by Country

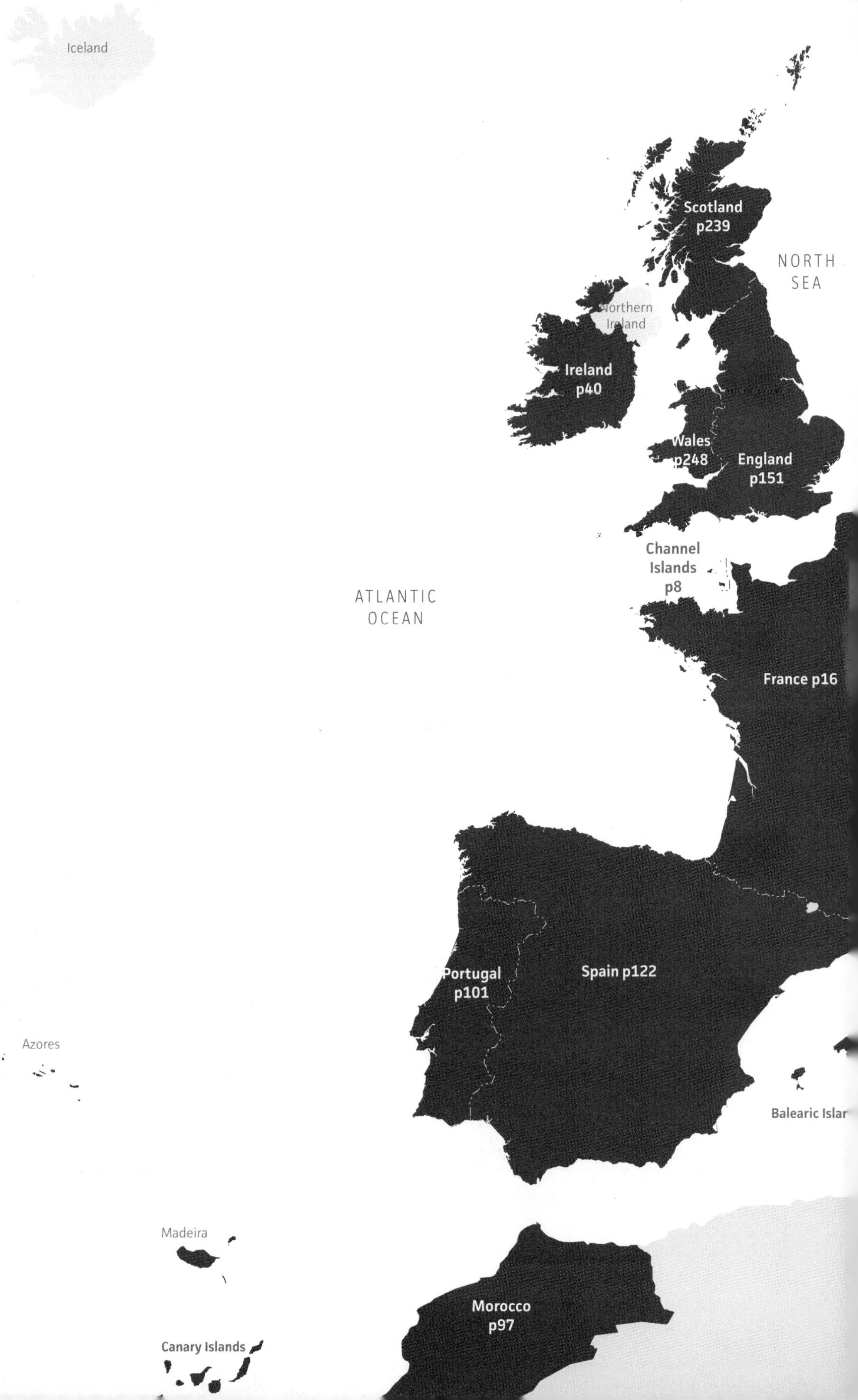

Iceland

Scotland
p239

NORTH
SEA

Northern
Ireland

Ireland
p40

Wales
p248

England
p151

Channel
Islands
p8

ATLANTIC
OCEAN

France p16

Portugal
p101

Spain p122

Azores

Balearic Islar

Madeira

Morocco
p97

Canary Islands

Norway

Sweden

Russia

Denmark

Latvia

Lithuania

Belarus

The
Netherlands

Poland

Ukraine

**Germany
p30**

elgium

Czech Republic

Slovakia

Moldova

**Austria
p6**

**Hungary
p38**

Romania

**Switzerland
p139**

Slovenia

BLACK
SEA

Croatia p12

Italy p44

Bosnia and
Herzegovina

Serbia

Bulgaria

**Montenegro
p95**

Macedonia
(FYROM)

Turkey p142

Corsica

Albania

Sardinia

Greece p32

MEDITERRANEAN SEA

Cyprus

Malta p93

INDEX BY HOTEL ORGANISATION

 Châteaux & Hôtels Collection

 Great Hotels of the World

Leading Hotels of the World

 Pride of Britain Hotels

 Relais & Châteaux

 Small Luxury Hotels of the World

DESIGN HOTELS Design Hotels

Preferred Preferred Hotels & Resorts

Image: Dormy House, UK/England, page 238